WAR ON CHRISTMAS

WRITTEN AND DRAWN BY
MIKE NORTON

COLORED BY
ALLEN PASSALAQUA

LETTERED BY
CRANK!

IMAGE COMICS, INC. • Robert Kirkman: Chief Operating Officer • Erik Larsen: Chief Financial Officer • Todd McFarlane: President • Marc Silvestri: Chief Executive Officer • Jim Valentino: Vice President • Eric Stephenson: Publisher / Chief Creative Officer • Jeff Boison: Director of Publishing Planning & Book Trade Sales • Chris Ross: Director of Digital Services • Jeff Stang: Director of Direct Market Sales • Kat Salazar: Director of PR & Marketing • Drew Gill: Cover Editor • Heather Doornink: Production Director • Nicole Lapalme: Controller • IMAGECOMICS.COM

• Deanna Phelps: Production Artist for BATTLEPUG •

BATTLEPUG, VOL. 1: WAR ON CHRISTMAS. First printing. February 2020. Published by Image Comics, Inc. Office of publication: 2701 NW Vaughn St., Suite 780, Portland, OR 97210. Copyright © 2020 Mike Norton. All rights reserved. Contains material originally published in single magazine form as BATTLEPUG #1-5. "Battlepug," its logos, and the likenesses of all characters herein are trademarks of Mike Norton, unless otherwise noted. "Image" and the Image Comics logos are registered trademarks of Image Comics, Inc. No part of this publication may be reproduced or transmitted, in any form or by any means (except for short excerpts for journalistic or review purposes), without the express written permission of Mike Norton, or Image Comics, Inc. All names, characters, events, and locales in this publication are entirely fictional. Any resemblance to actual persons (living or dead), events, or places, without satirical intent, is coincidental. Printed in the USA. For information regarding the CPSIA on this printed material call: 203-595-3636. For international rights, contact: foreignlicensing@imagecomics.com. ISBN: 978-1-5343-1502-0.

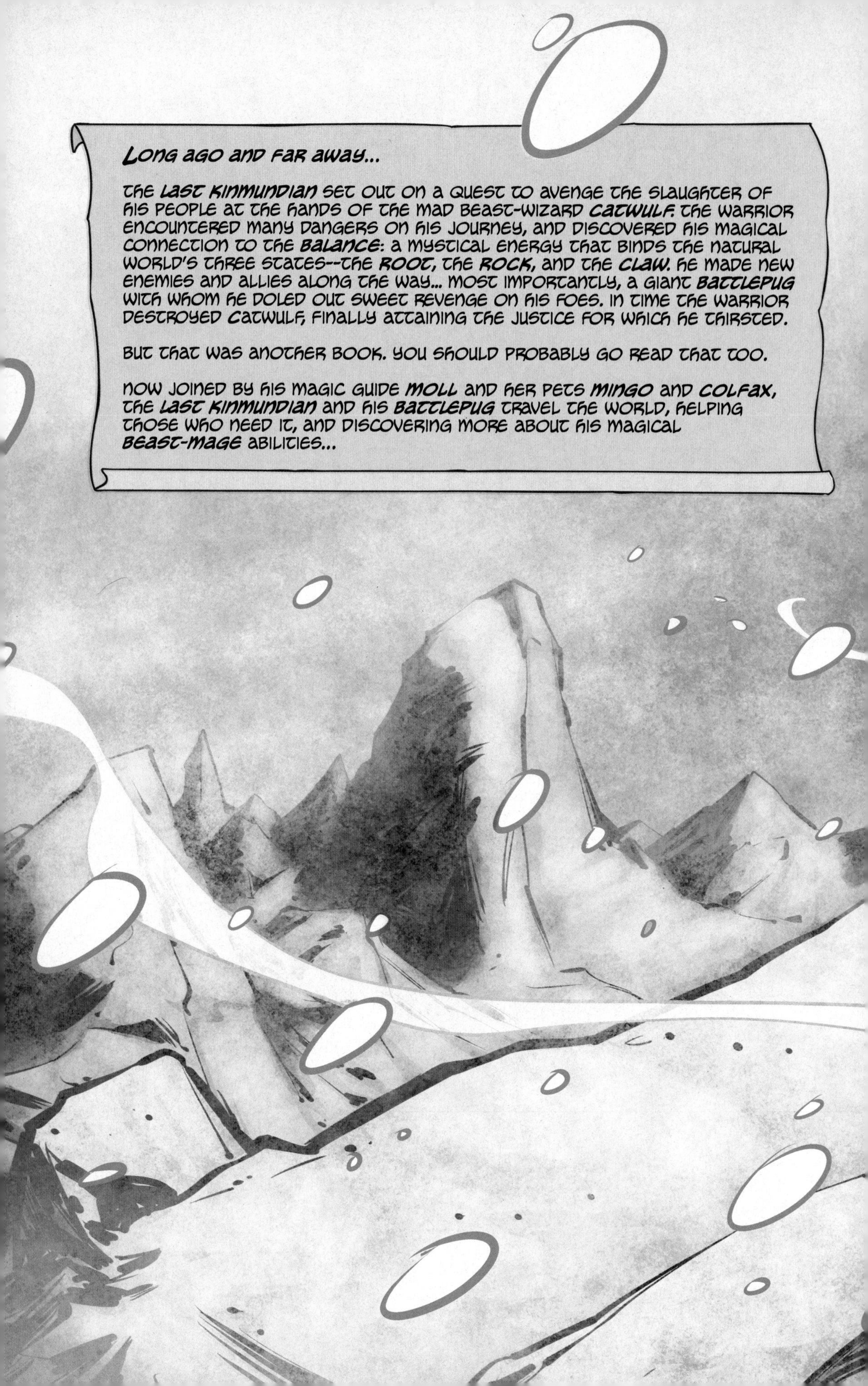
LONG AGO AND FAR AWAY...
THE LAST KINMUNDIAN SET OUT ON A QUEST TO AVENGE THE SLAUGHTER OF HIS PEOPLE AT THE HANDS OF THE MAD BEAST-WIZARD CATWULF. THE WARRIOR ENCOUNTERED MANY DANGERS ON HIS JOURNEY, AND DISCOVERED HIS MAGICAL CONNECTION TO THE BALANCE: A MYSTICAL ENERGY THAT BINDS THE NATURAL WORLD'S THREE STATES--THE ROOT, THE ROCK, AND THE CLAW. HE MADE NEW ENEMIES AND ALLIES ALONG THE WAY... MOST IMPORTANTLY, A GIANT BATTLEPUG WITH WHOM HE DOLED OUT SWEET REVENGE ON HIS FOES. IN TIME THE WARRIOR DESTROYED CATWULF, FINALLY ATTAINING THE JUSTICE FOR WHICH HE THIRSTED.
BUT THAT WAS ANOTHER BOOK. YOU SHOULD PROBABLY GO READ THAT TOO.
NOW JOINED BY HIS MAGIC GUIDE MOLL AND HER PETS MINGO AND COLFAX, THE LAST KINMUNDIAN AND HIS BATTLEPUG TRAVEL THE WORLD, HELPING THOSE WHO NEED IT, AND DISCOVERING MORE ABOUT HIS MAGICAL BEAST-MAGE ABILITIES...

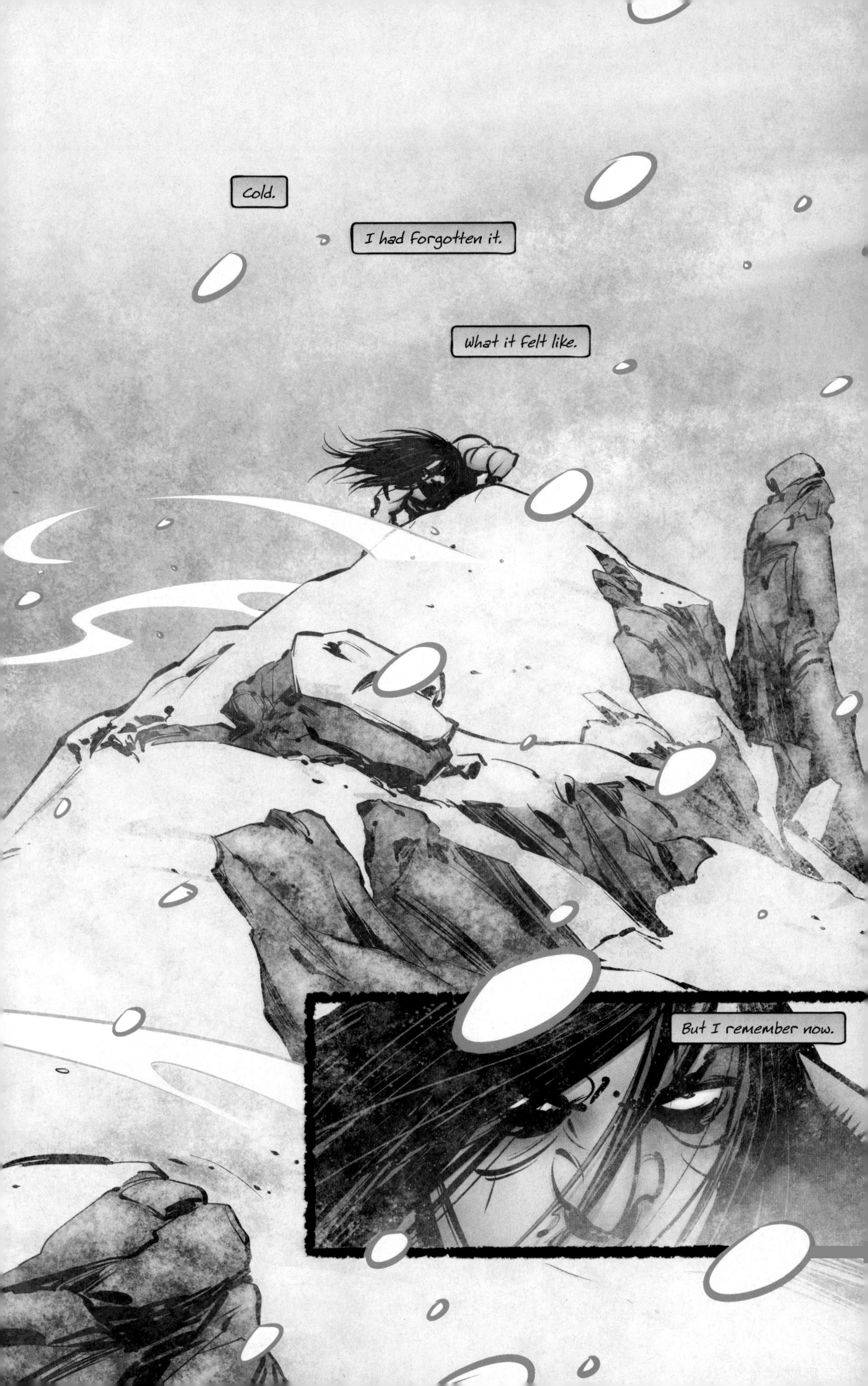
Cold.
I had forgotten it.
What it felt like.
But I remember now.

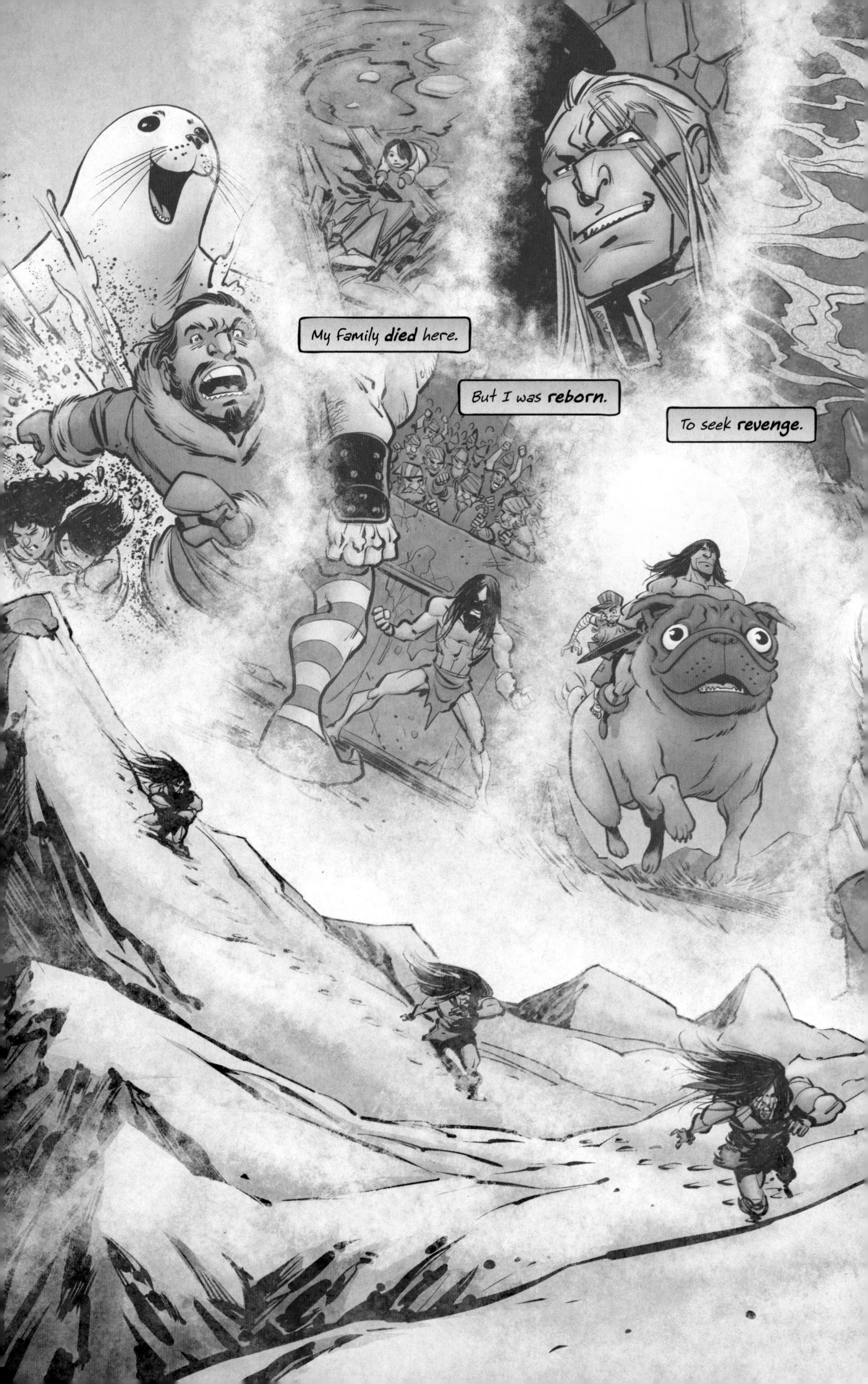
My family died here.
But I was reborn.
To seek revenge.

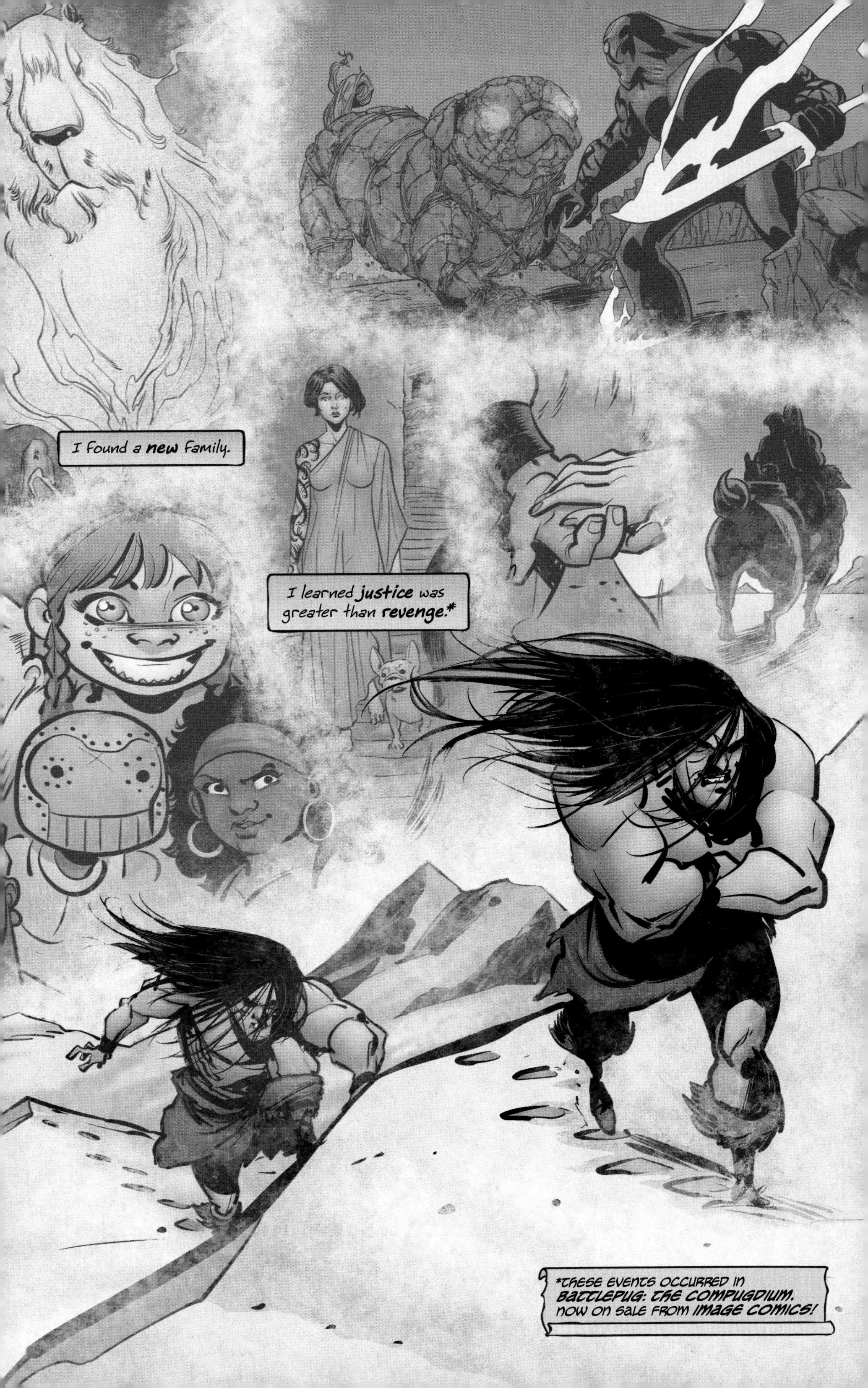
I found a **new** family.
I learned **justice** was greater than **revenge.***
*THESE EVENTS OCCURRED IN BATTLEPUG: THE COMPUGDIUM. NOW ON SALE FROM IMAGE COMICS!

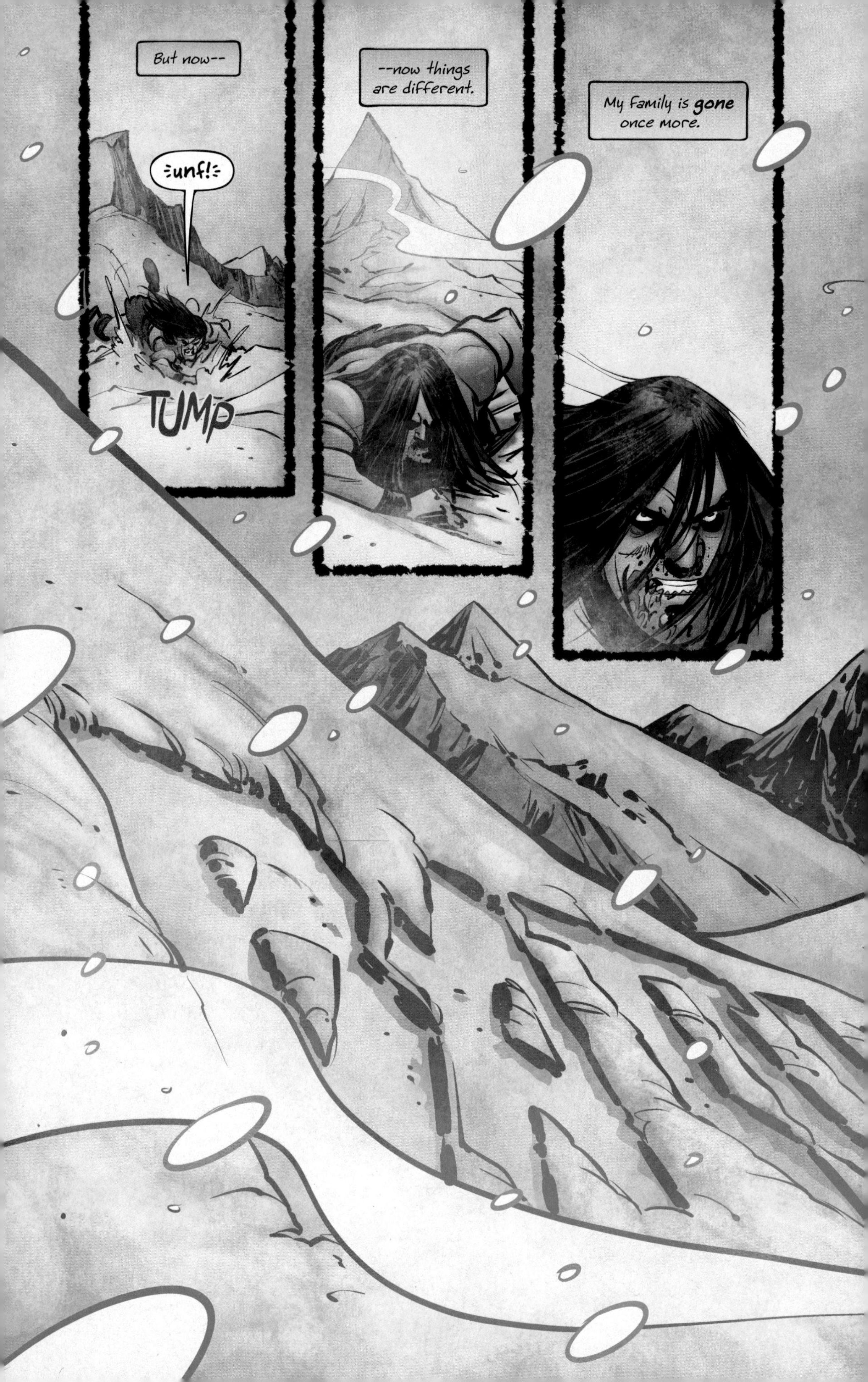
But now--
=unf!=
TUMP
--now things are different.
My family is **gone** once more.

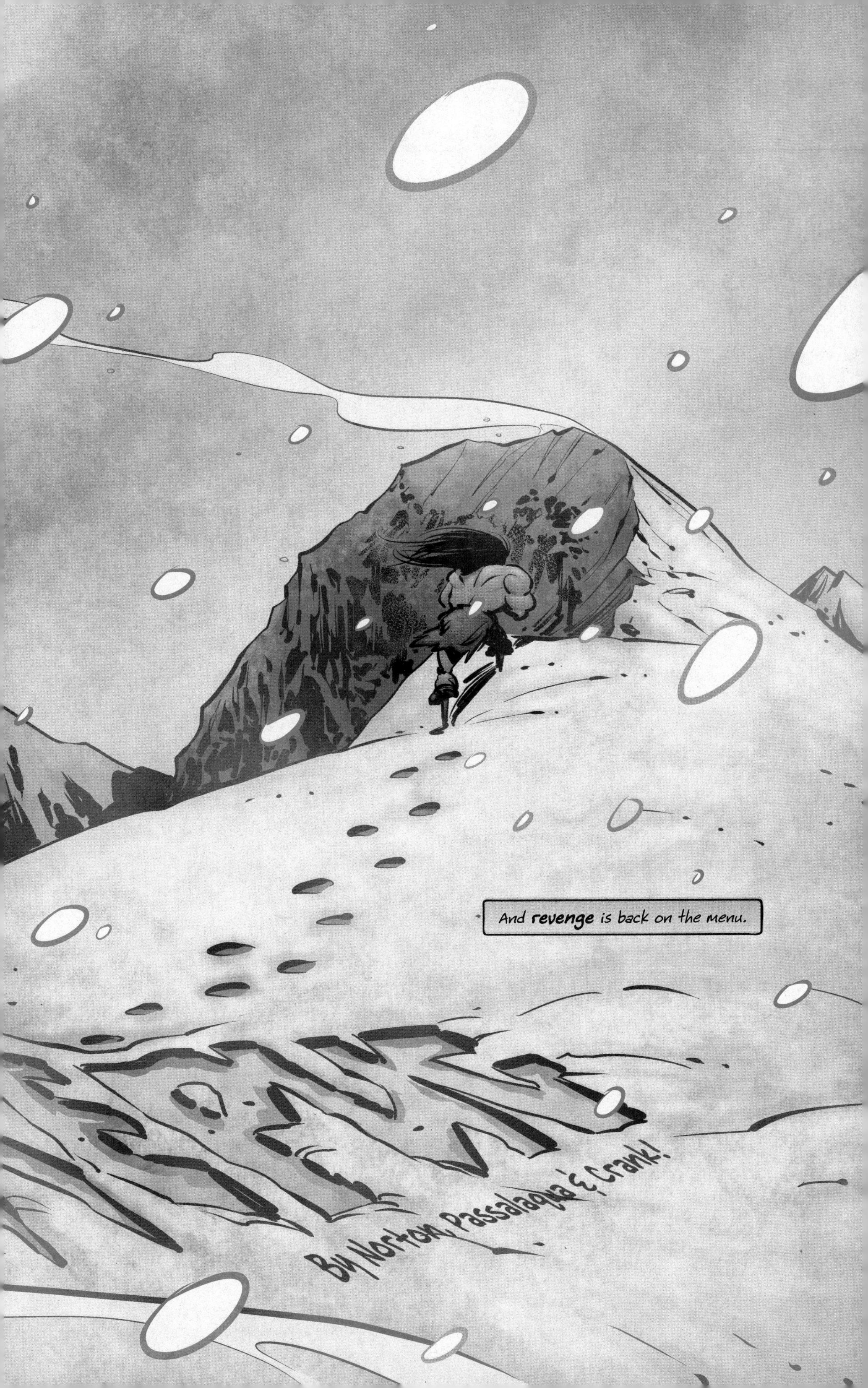
And revenge is back on the menu.
By Norton, Passalaqua & Crank!

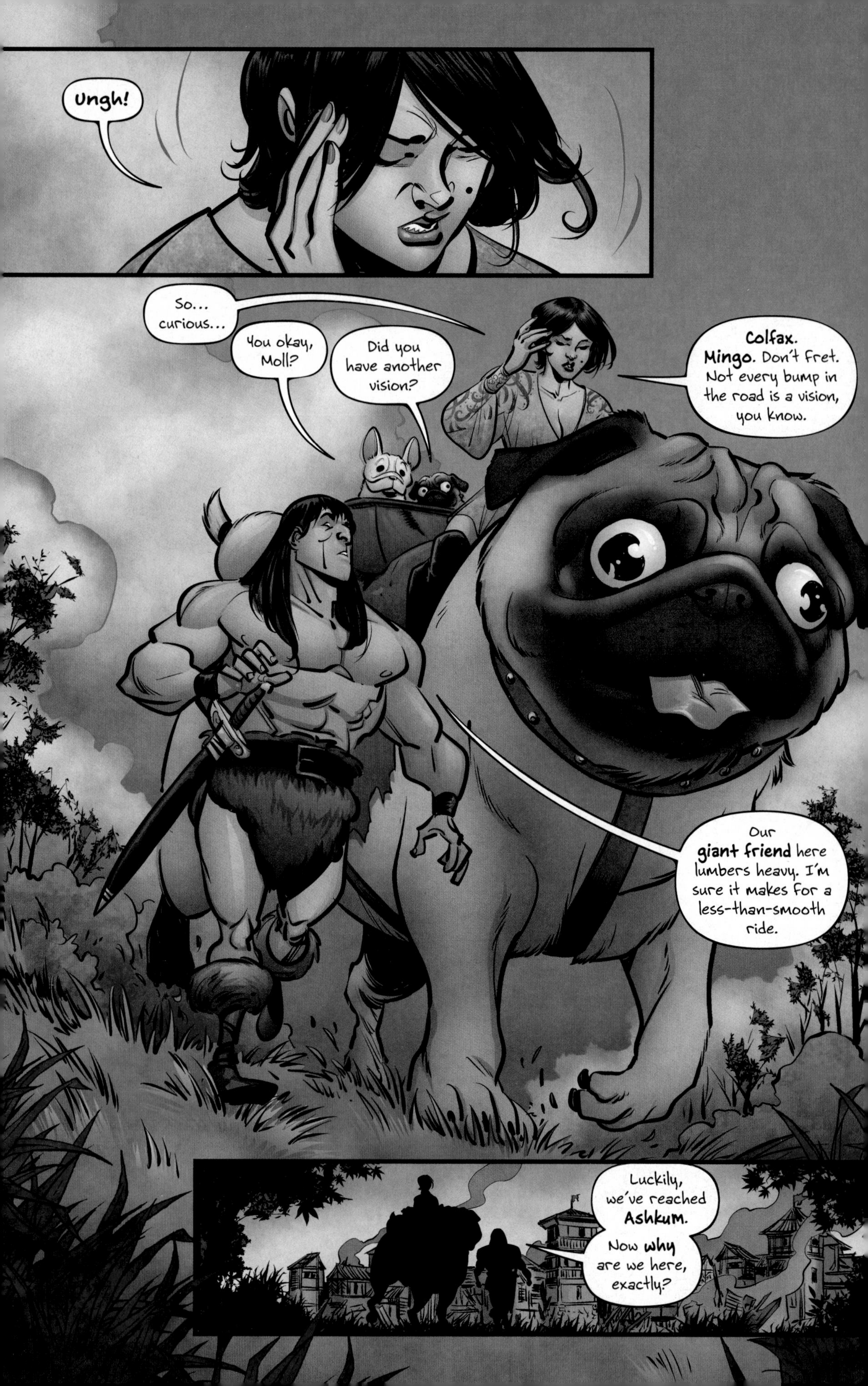
Ungh!
So... curious...
You okay, Moll?
Did you have another vision?
Colfax. Mingo. Don't fret. Not every bump in the road is a vision, you know.
Our giant friend here lumbers heavy. I'm sure it makes for a less-than-smooth ride.
Luckily, we've reached Ashkum.
Now why are we here, exactly?

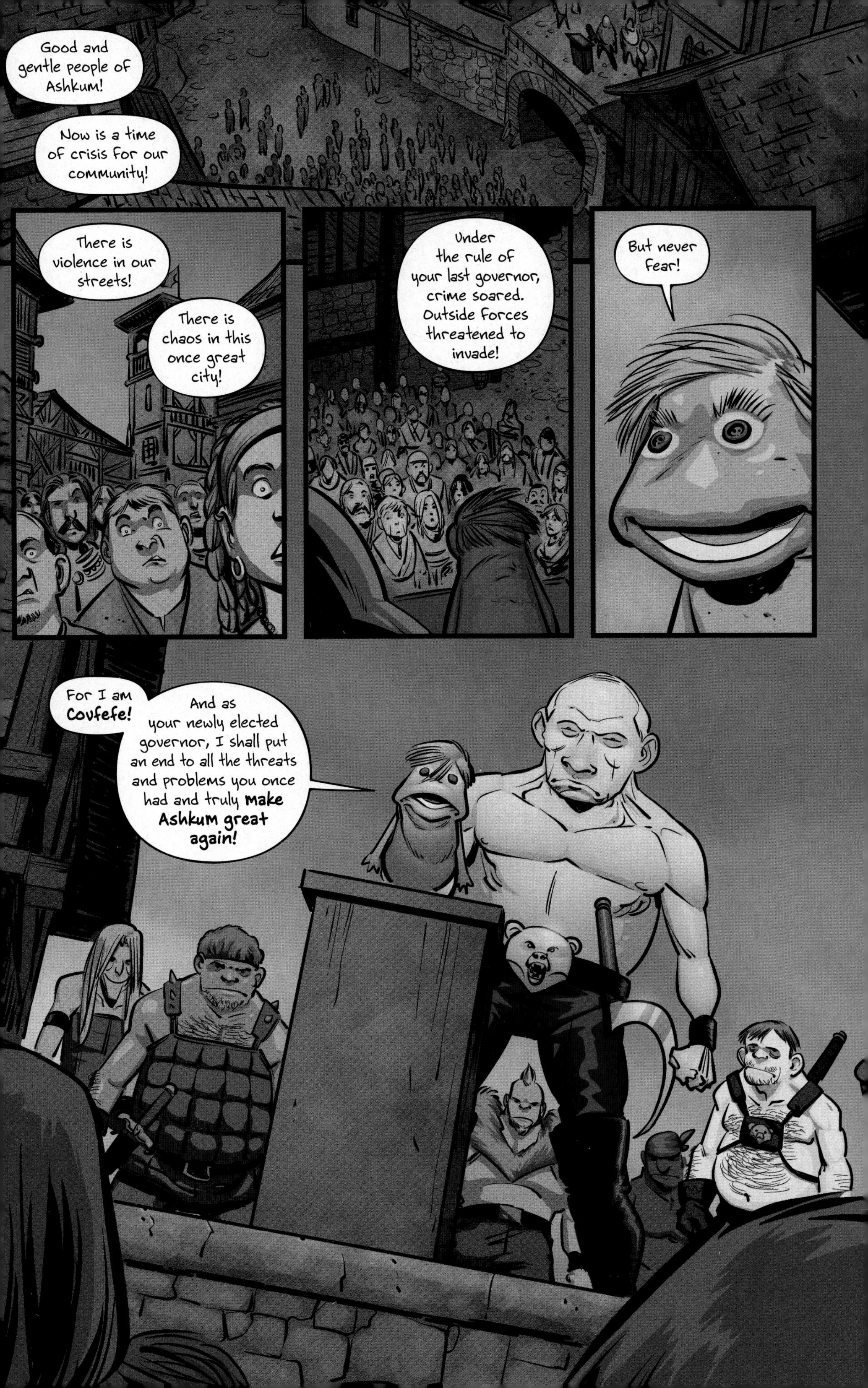
Good and gentle people of Ashkum!
Now is a time of crisis for our community!
There is violence in our streets!
There is chaos in this once great city!
Under the rule of your last governor, crime soared. Outside forces threatened to invade!
But never fear!
For I am **Covfefe!**
And as your newly elected governor, I shall put an end to all the threats and problems you once had and truly **make Ashkum great again!**

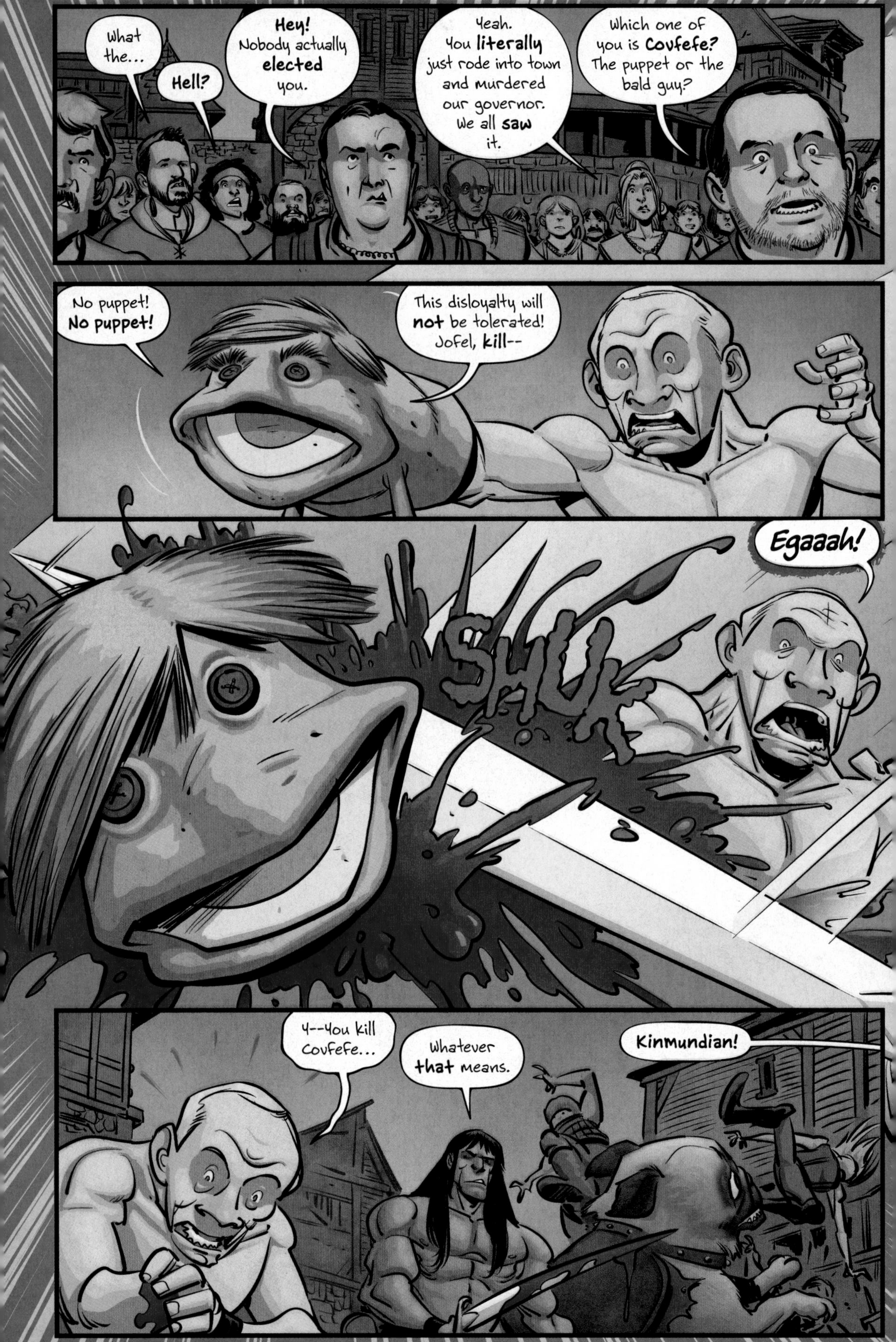
What the...
Hell?
Hey! Nobody actually elected you.
Yeah. You literally just rode into town and murdered our governor. We all saw it.
Which one of you is Covfefe? The puppet or the bald guy?
No puppet! No puppet!
This disloyalty will not be tolerated! Jofel, kill--
Egaaah!
SHUK
Y--You kill Covfefe...
Whatever that means.
Kinmundian!

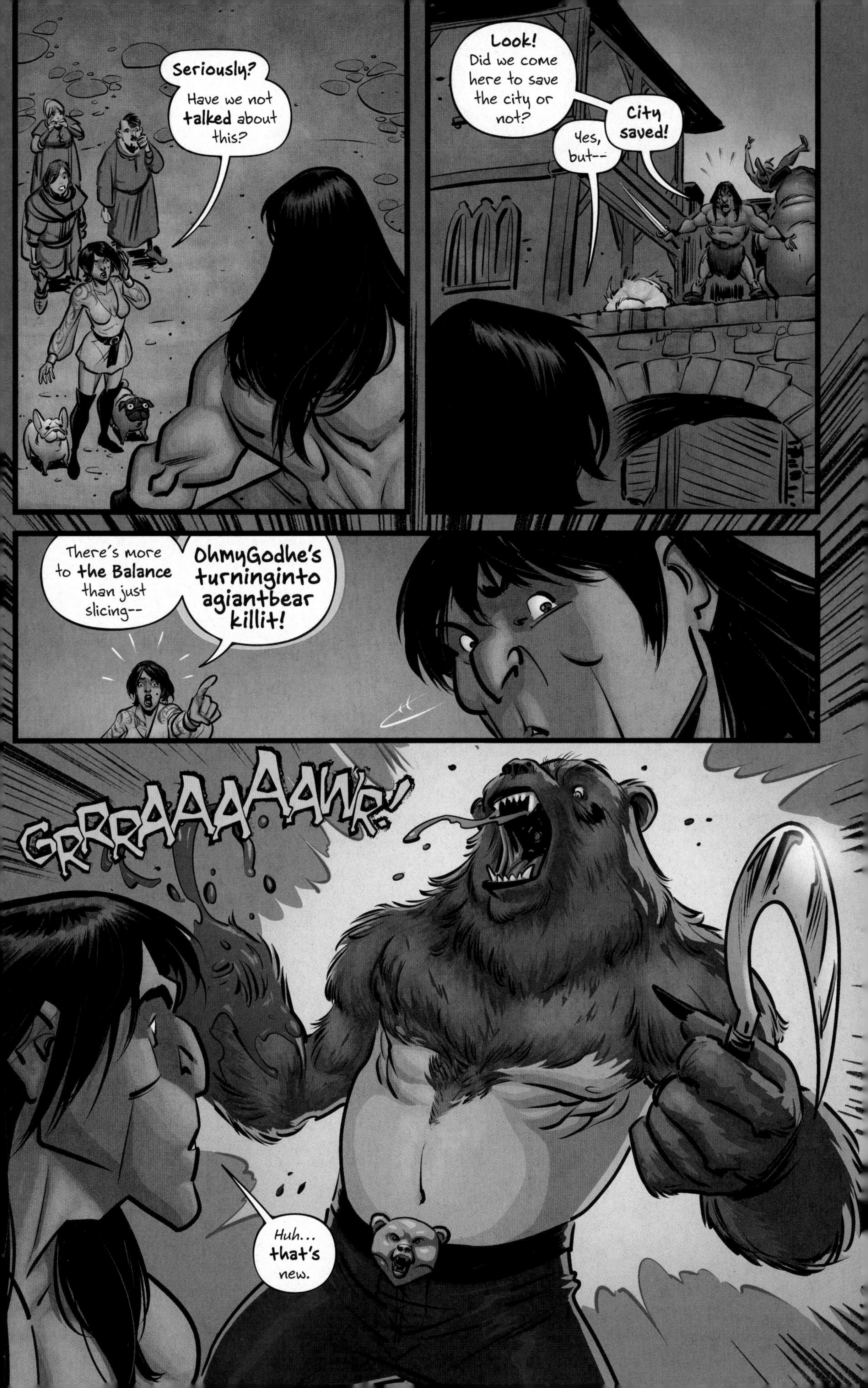
Seriously? Have we not talked about this?
Look! Did we come here to save the city or not?
Yes, but--
City saved!
There's more to the Balance than just slicing--
OhmyGodhe's turninginto agiantbear killit!
GRRRAAAAAAWR!
Huh... that's new.

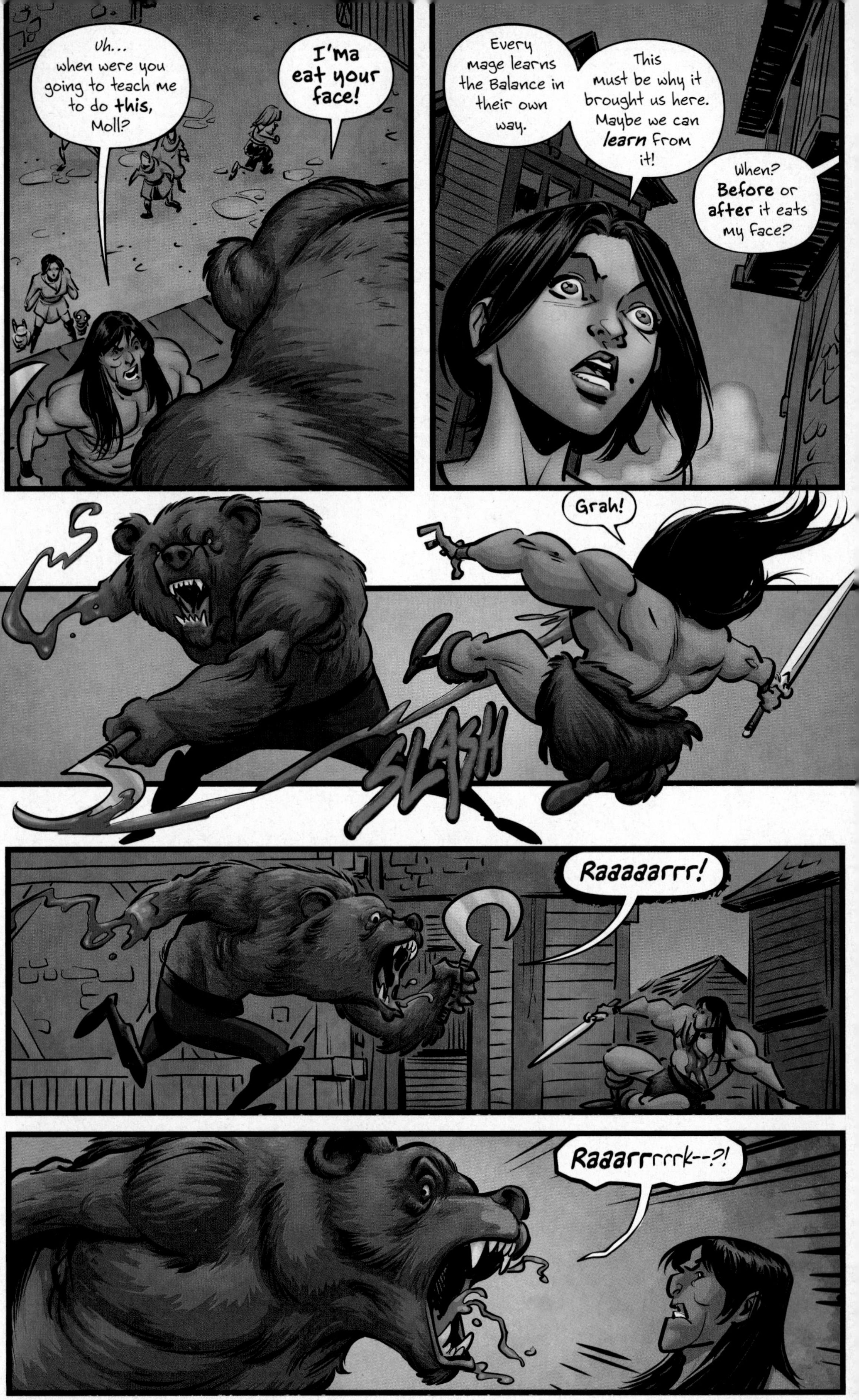
Uh... when were you going to teach me to do this, Moll?
I'ma eat your face!
Every mage learns the Balance in their own way.
This must be why it brought us here. Maybe we can learn from it!
When? Before or after it eats my face?
Grah!
SLASH
Raaaaarrr!
Raaarrrrrk--?!

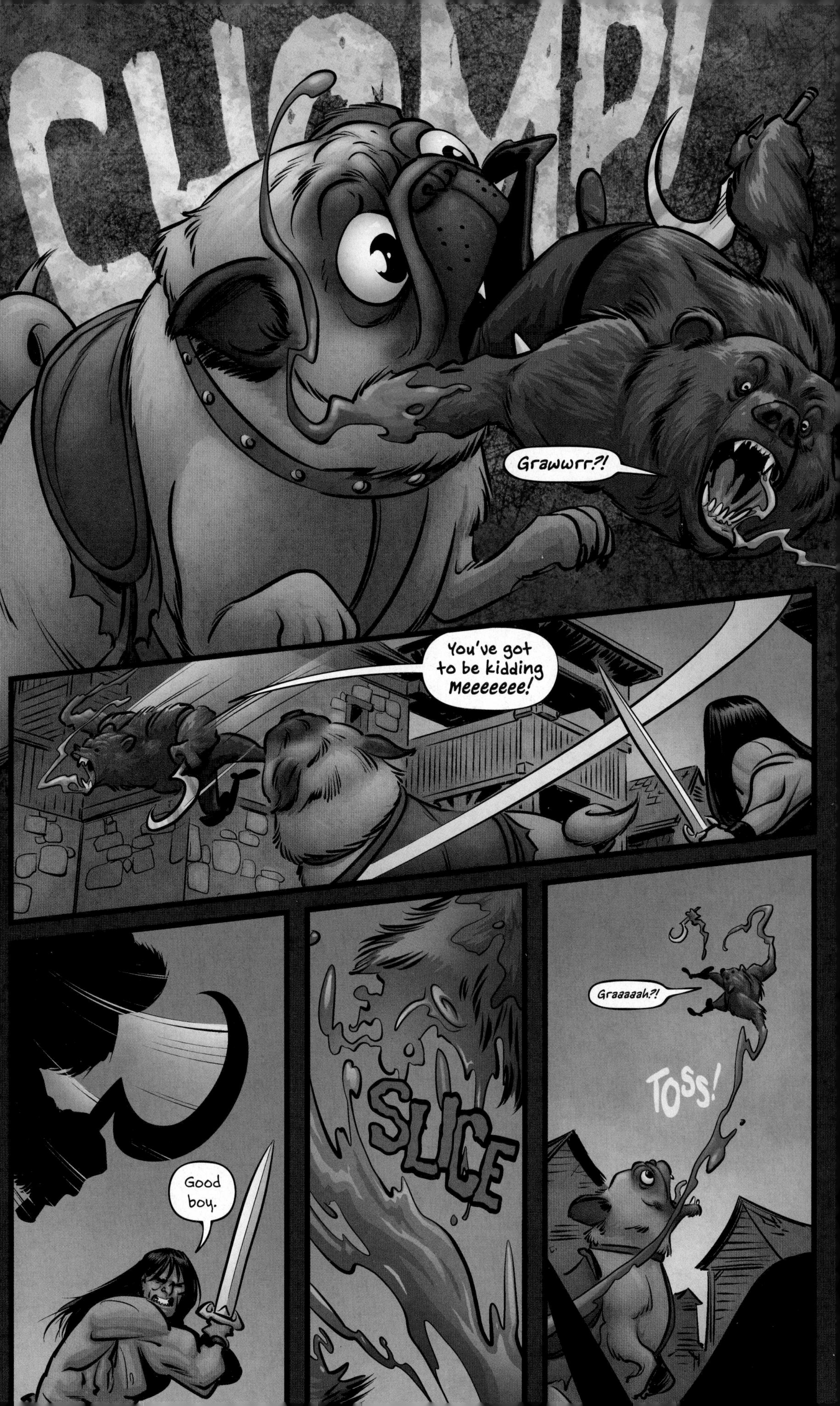
CHOMP!
Grawwrr?!
You've got to be kidding Meeeeeee!
Good boy.
SLICE
Graaaaah?!
TOSS!

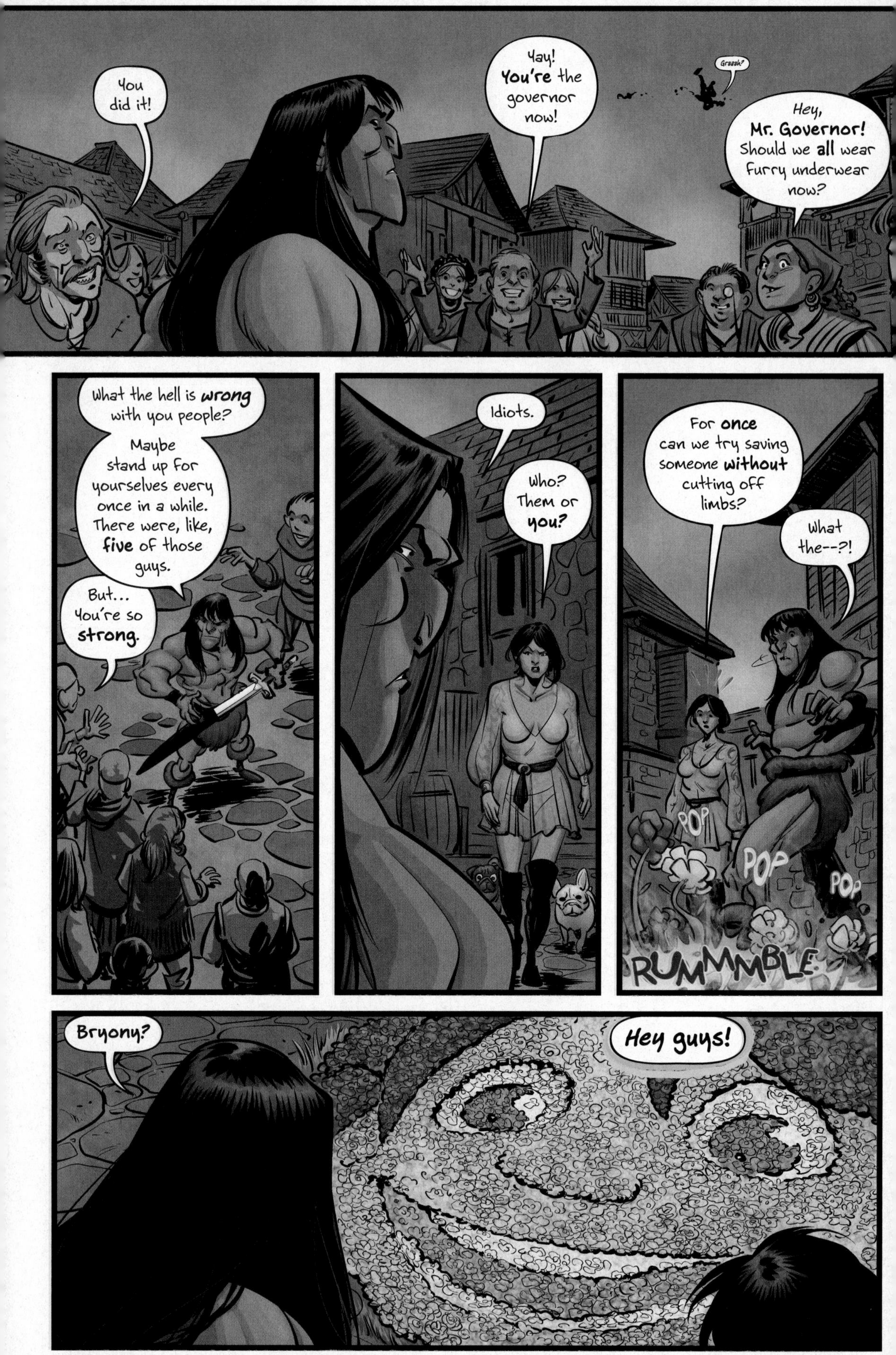
You did it!
Yay! You're the governor now!
Graaak?
Hey, Mr. Governor! Should we all wear furry underwear now?
What the hell is wrong with you people?
Maybe stand up for yourselves every once in a while. There were, like, five of those guys.
But... You're so strong.
Idiots.
Who? Them or you?
For once can we try saving someone without cutting off limbs?
What the--?!
POP
POP
POP
RUMMMBLE
Bryony?
Hey guys!

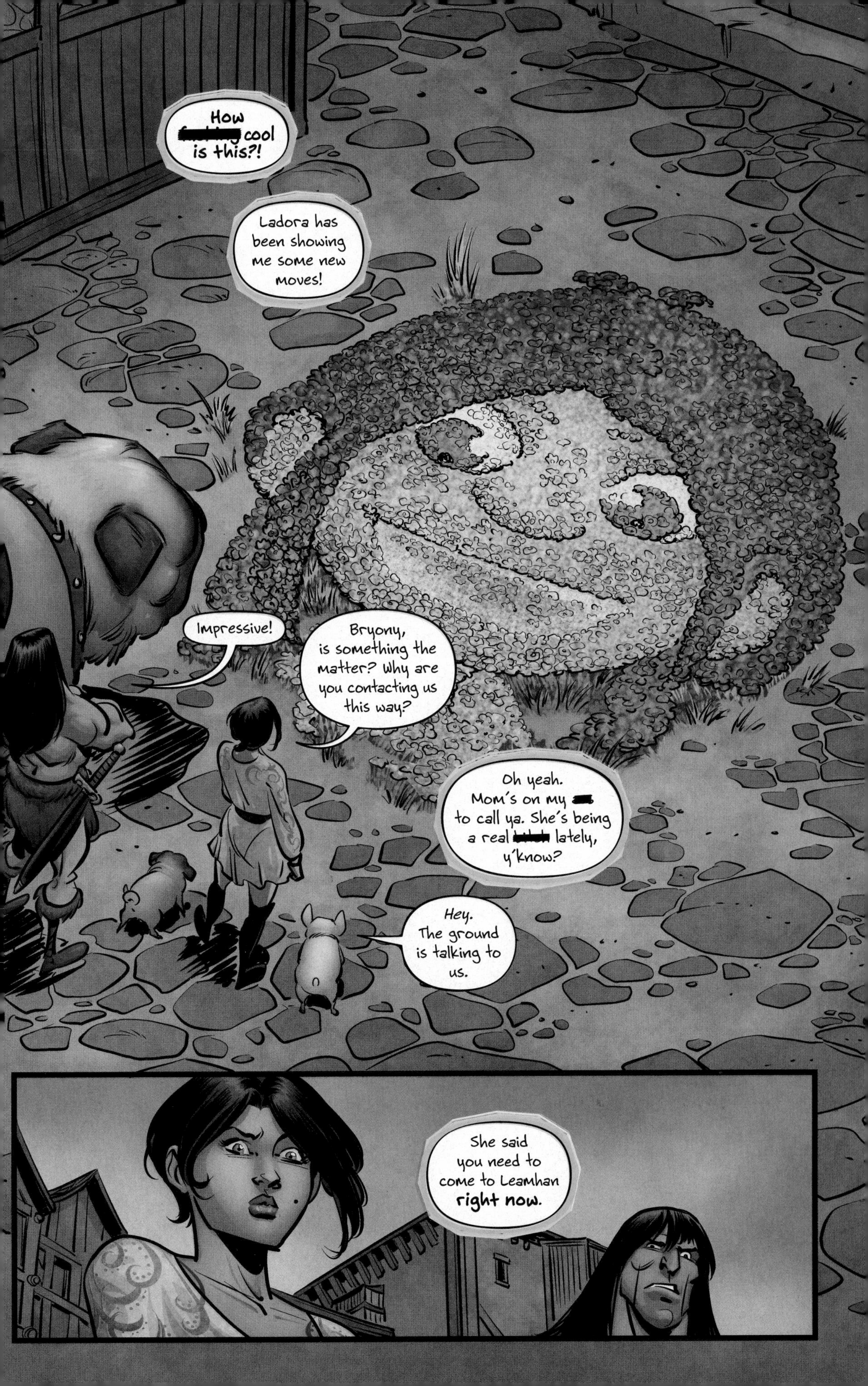
How [redacted] cool is this?!
Ladora has been showing me some new moves!
Impressive!
Bryony, is something the matter? Why are you contacting us this way?
Oh yeah. Mom's on my [redacted] to call ya. She's being a real [redacted] lately, y'know?
Hey. The ground is talking to us.
She said you need to come to Leamhan **right now.**

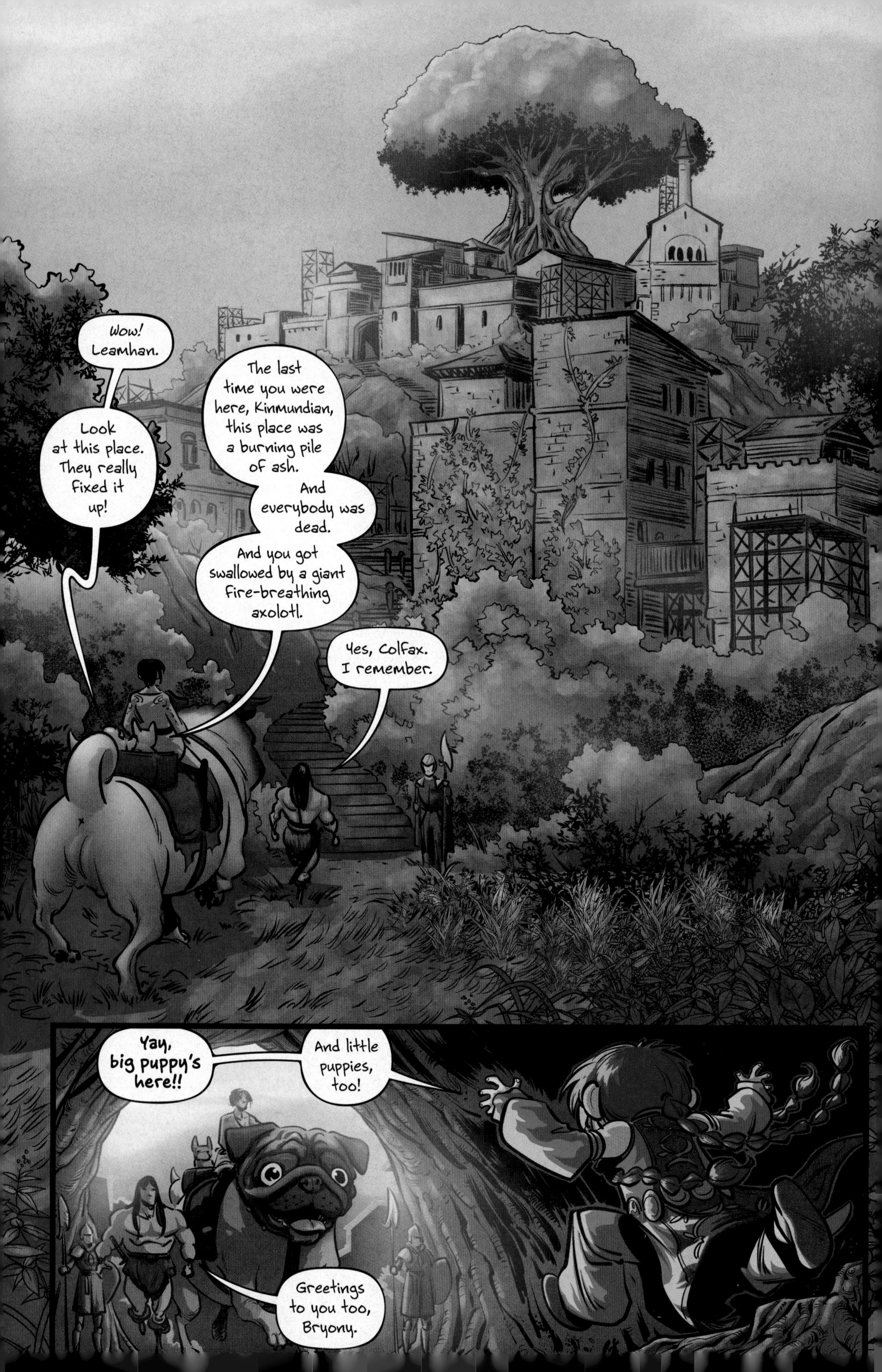
Wow! Leamhan.
Look at this place. They really fixed it up!
The last time you were here, Kinmundian, this place was a burning pile of ash.
And everybody was dead.
And you got swallowed by a giant fire-breathing axolotl.
Yes, Colfax. I remember.
Yay, big puppy's here!!
And little puppies, too!
Greetings to you too, Bryony.

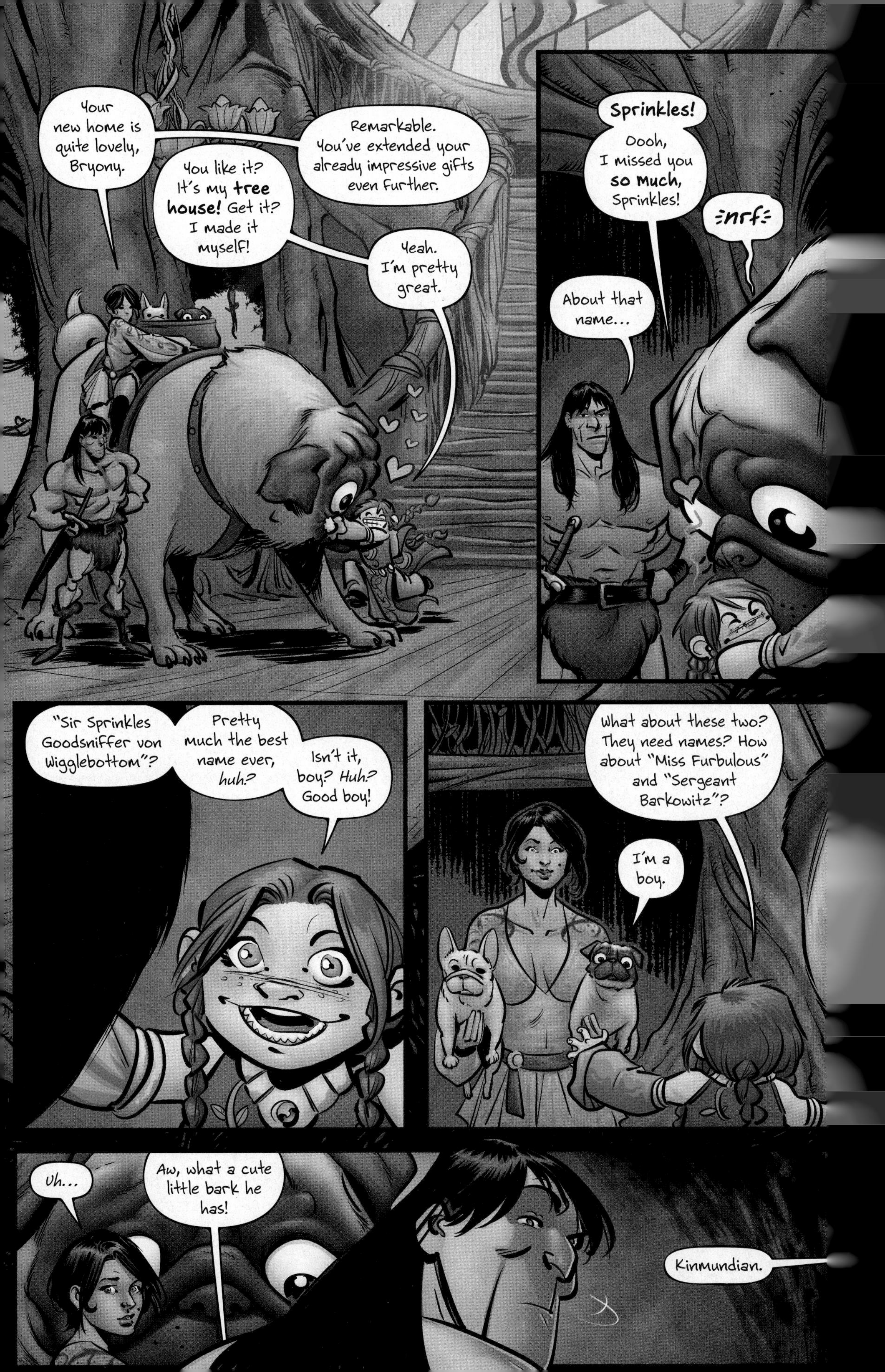
Your new home is quite lovely, Bryony.
Remarkable. You've extended your already impressive gifts even further.
You like it? It's my **tree house!** Get it? I made it myself!
Yeah. I'm pretty great.
Sprinkles!
Oooh, I missed you **so much,** Sprinkles!
nrf
About that name...
"Sir Sprinkles Goodsniffer von Wigglebottom"?
Pretty much the best name ever, *huh?*
Isn't it, boy? Huh? Good boy!
What about these two? They need names? How about "Miss Furbulous" and "Sergeant Barkowitz"?
I'm a boy.
Uh...
Aw, what a cute little bark he has!
Kinmundian.

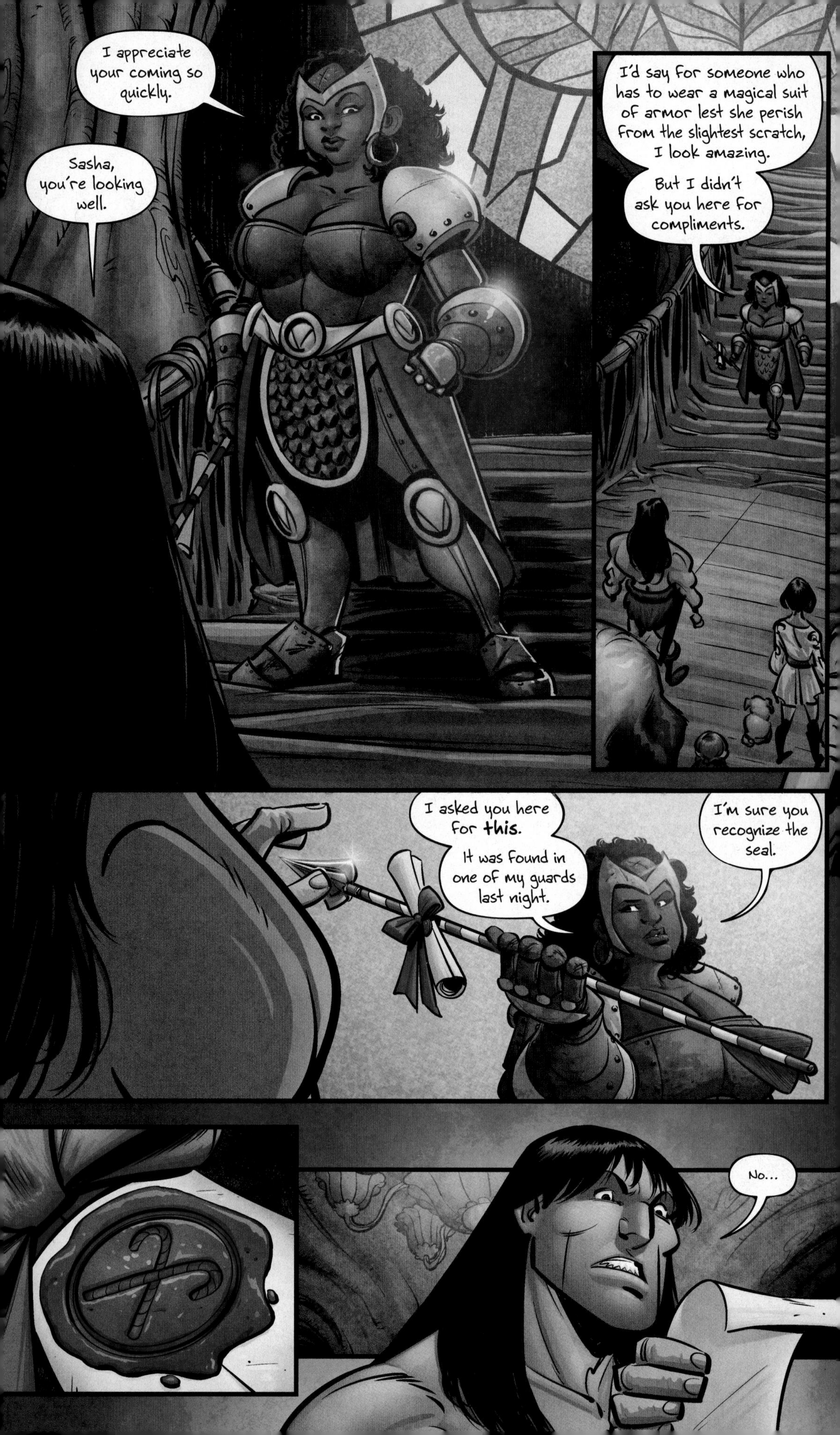

Sasha, you're looking well.
I appreciate your coming so quickly.
I'd say for someone who has to wear a magical suit of armor lest she perish from the slightest scratch, I look amazing.
But I didn't ask you here for compliments.
I asked you here for **this**.
It was found in one of my guards last night.
I'm sure you recognize the seal.
No...

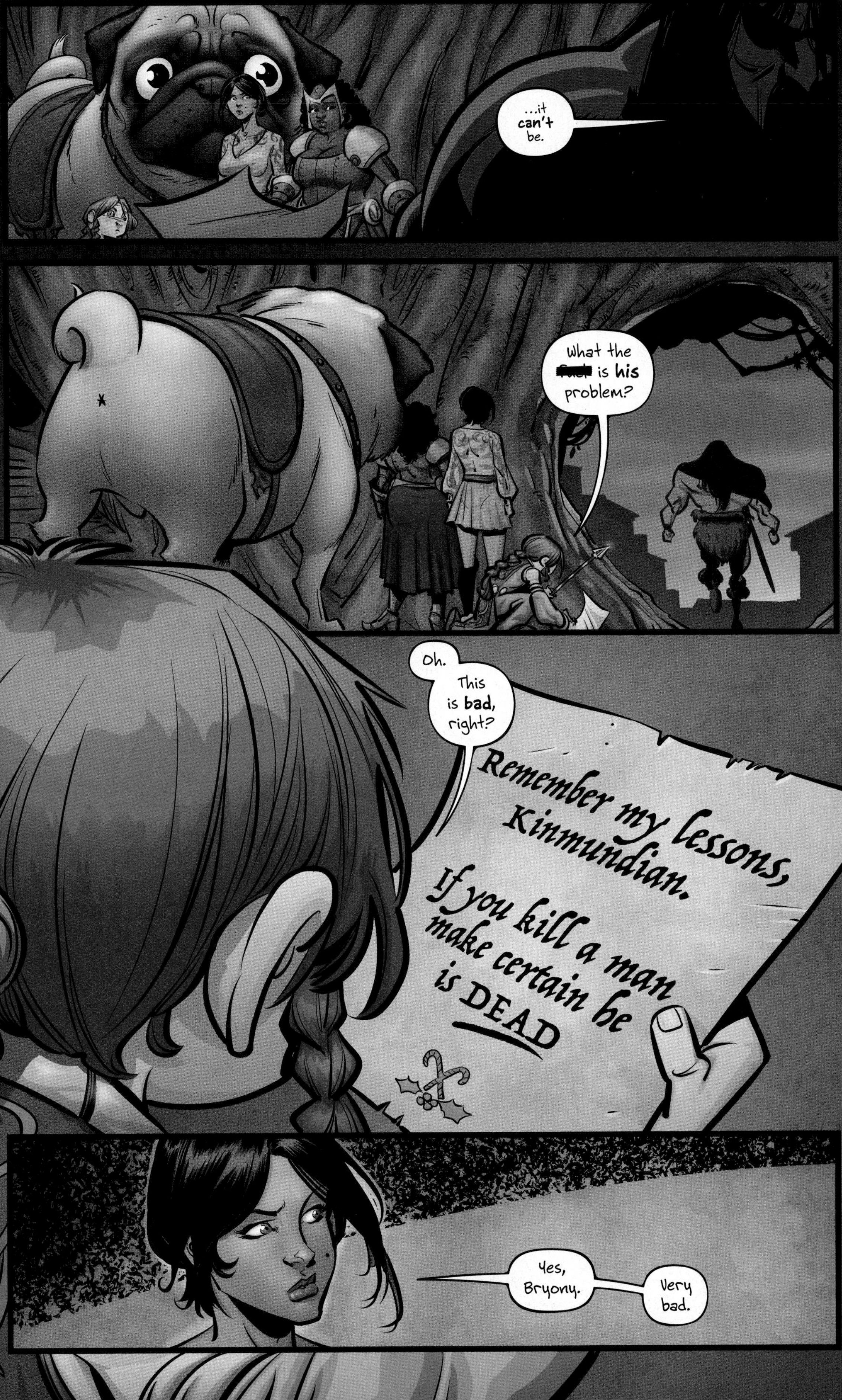
...it can't be.
What the [redacted] is his problem?
Oh.
This is bad, right?
Remember my lessons, Kinmundian.
If you kill a man make certain he is DEAD
Yes, Bryony.
Very bad.

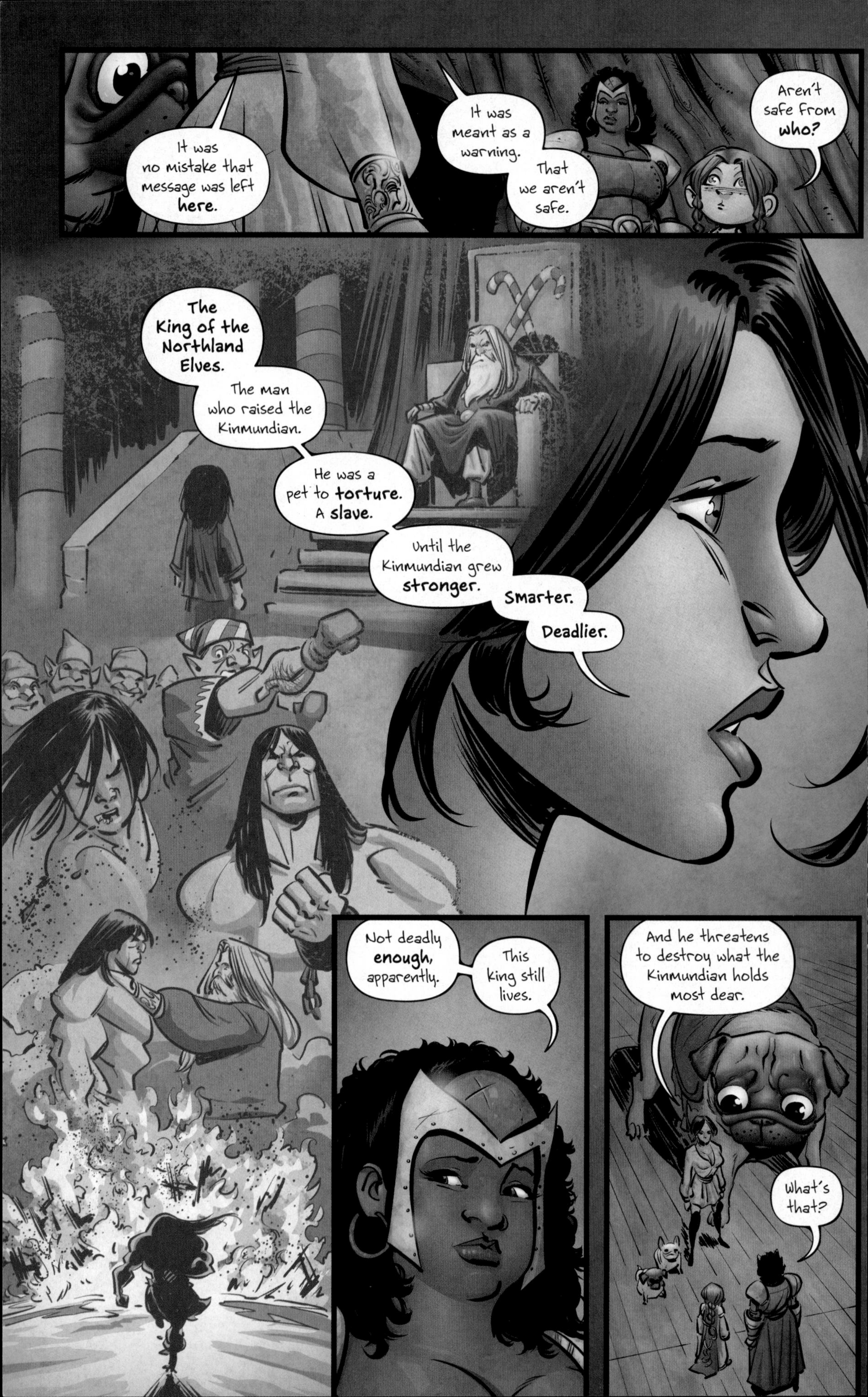
It was no mistake that message was left here.
It was meant as a warning.
That we aren't safe.
Aren't safe from who?
The King of the Northland Elves.
The man who raised the Kinmundian.
He was a pet to torture. A slave.
Until the Kinmundian grew stronger.
Smarter.
Deadlier.
Not deadly enough, apparently.
This king still lives.
And he threatens to destroy what the Kinmundian holds most dear.
What's that?

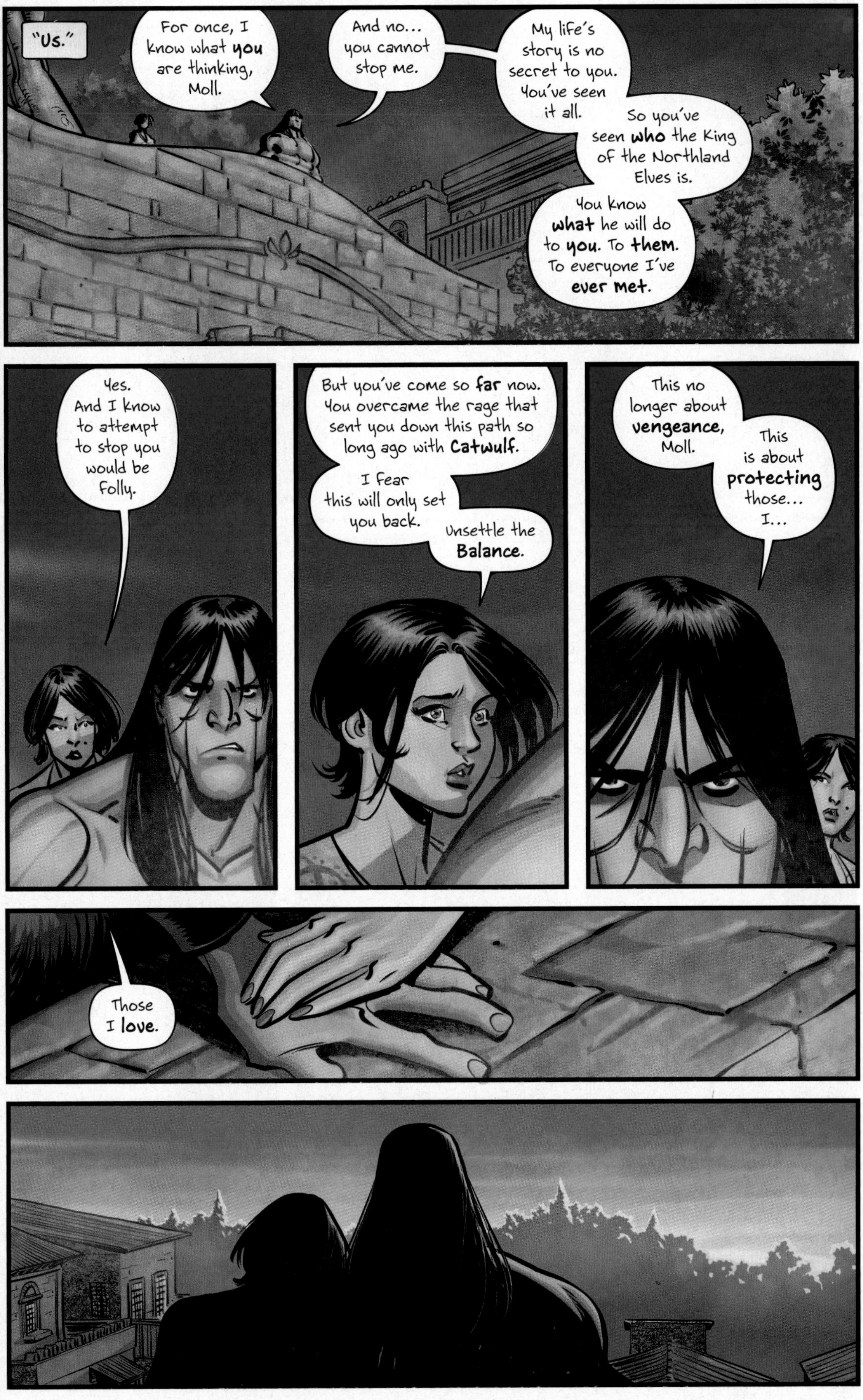
"Us."
For once, I know what you are thinking, Moll.
And no... you cannot stop me.
My life's story is no secret to you. You've seen it all.
So you've seen who the King of the Northland Elves is.
You know what he will do to you. To them. To everyone I've ever met.
Yes. And I know to attempt to stop you would be folly.
But you've come so far now. You overcame the rage that sent you down this path so long ago with Catwulf.
I fear this will only set you back.
Unsettle the Balance.
This no longer about vengeance, Moll.
This is about protecting those... I...
Those I love.

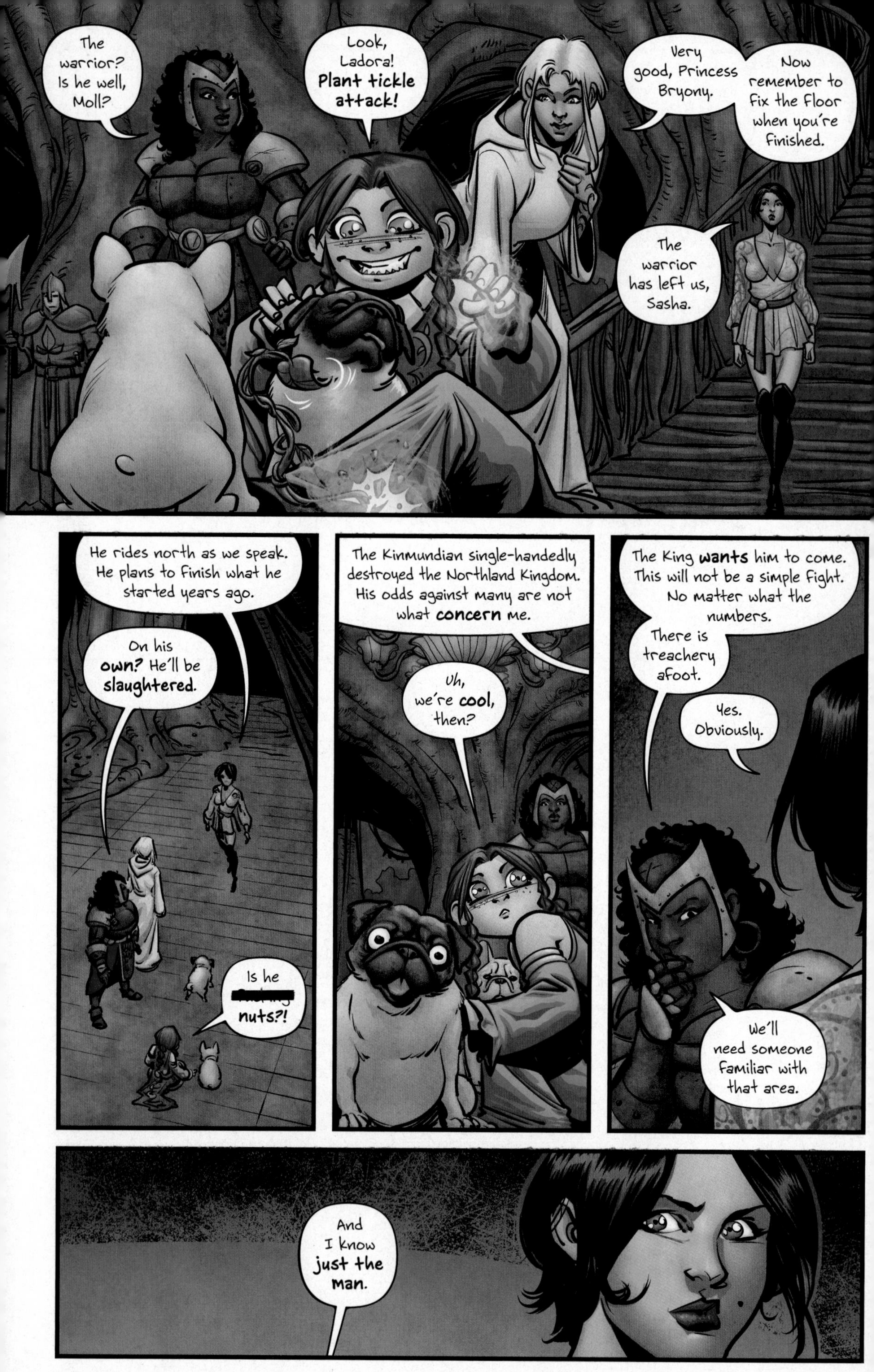
The warrior? Is he well, Moll?
Look, Ladora! **Plant tickle attack!**
Very good, Princess Bryony.
Now remember to fix the floor when you're finished.
The warrior has left us, Sasha.
He rides north as we speak. He plans to finish what he started years ago.
On his **own?** He'll be **slaughtered.**
Is he [redacted] **nuts?!**
The Kinmundian single-handedly destroyed the Northland Kingdom. His odds against many are not what **concern** me.
Uh, we're **cool,** then?
The King **wants** him to come. This will not be a simple fight. No matter what the numbers.
There is treachery afoot.
Yes. Obviously.
We'll need someone familiar with that area.
And I know **just the man.**

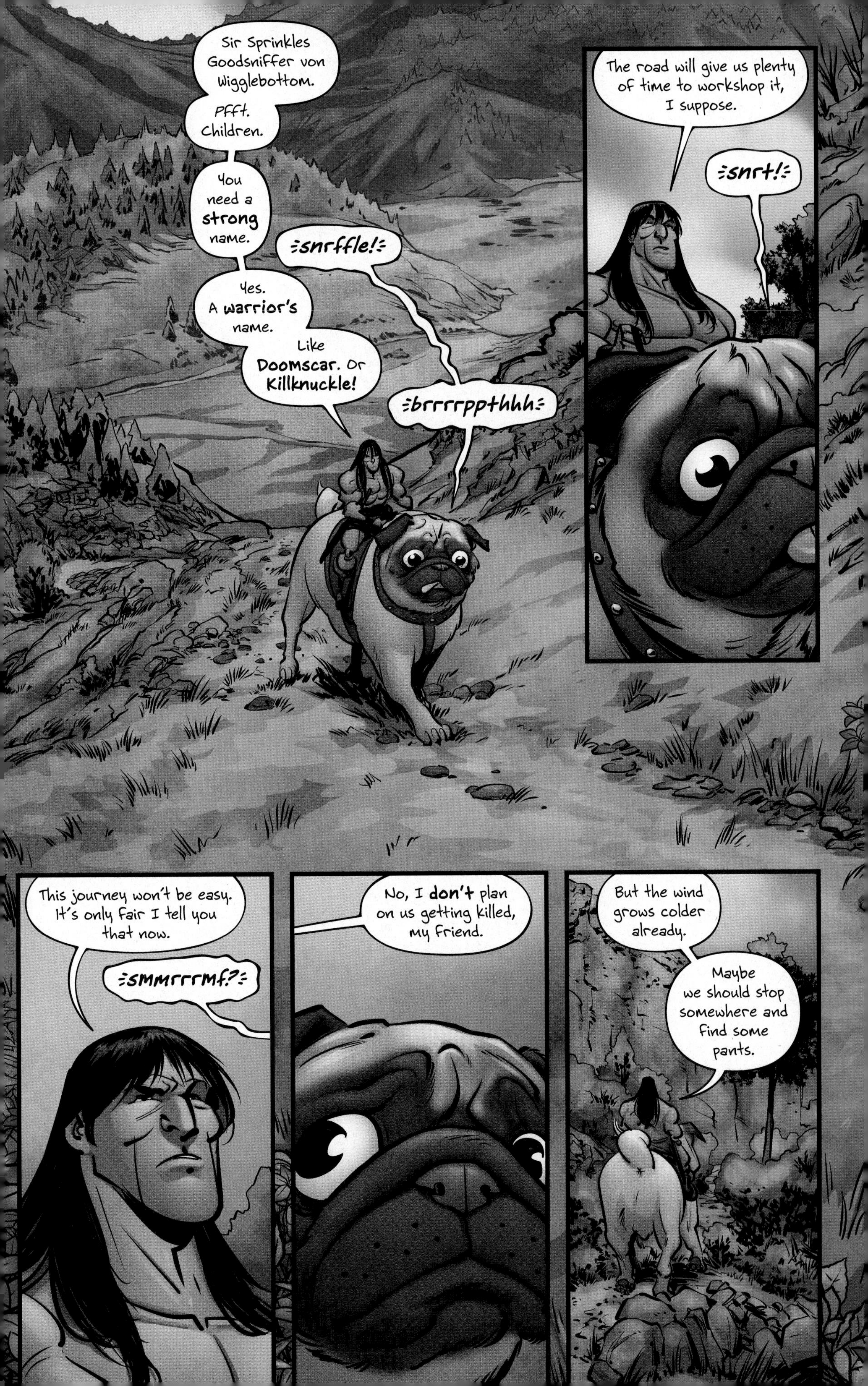
Sir Sprinkles Goodsniffer von Wigglebottom.
Pfft. Children.
You need a **strong** name.
=snrffle!=
Yes. A **warrior's** name.
Like **Doomscar.** Or **Killknuckle!**
=brrrrppthhh=
The road will give us plenty of time to workshop it, I suppose.
=snrt!=
This journey won't be easy. It's only fair I tell you that now.
=smmrrrmf?=
No, I **don't** plan on us getting killed, my friend.
But the wind grows colder already.
Maybe we should stop somewhere and find some pants.

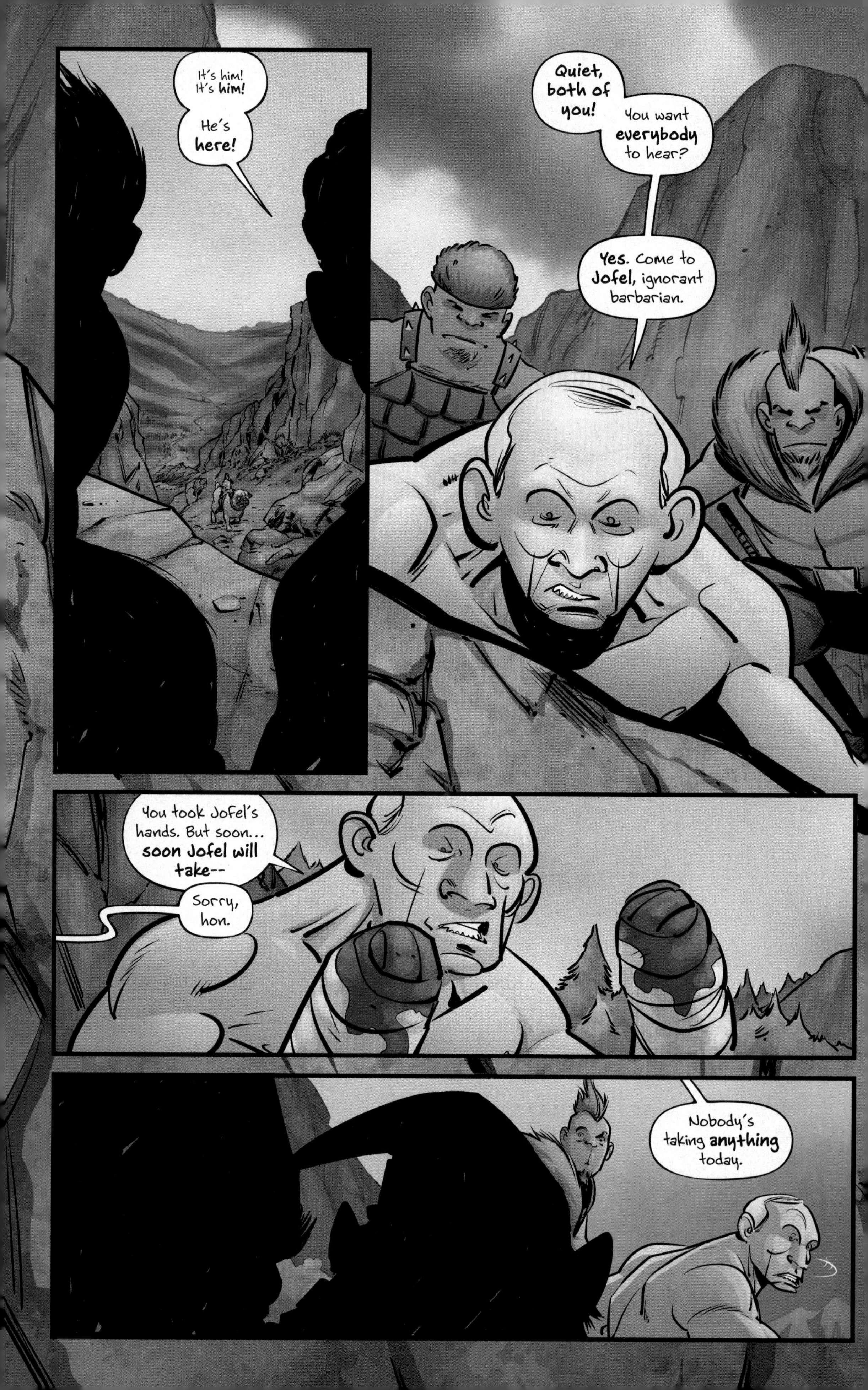
It's him! It's him!
He's here!
Quiet, both of you!
You want everybody to hear?
Yes. Come to Jofel, ignorant barbarian.
You took Jofel's hands. But soon... soon Jofel will take--
Sorry, hon.
Nobody's taking anything today.

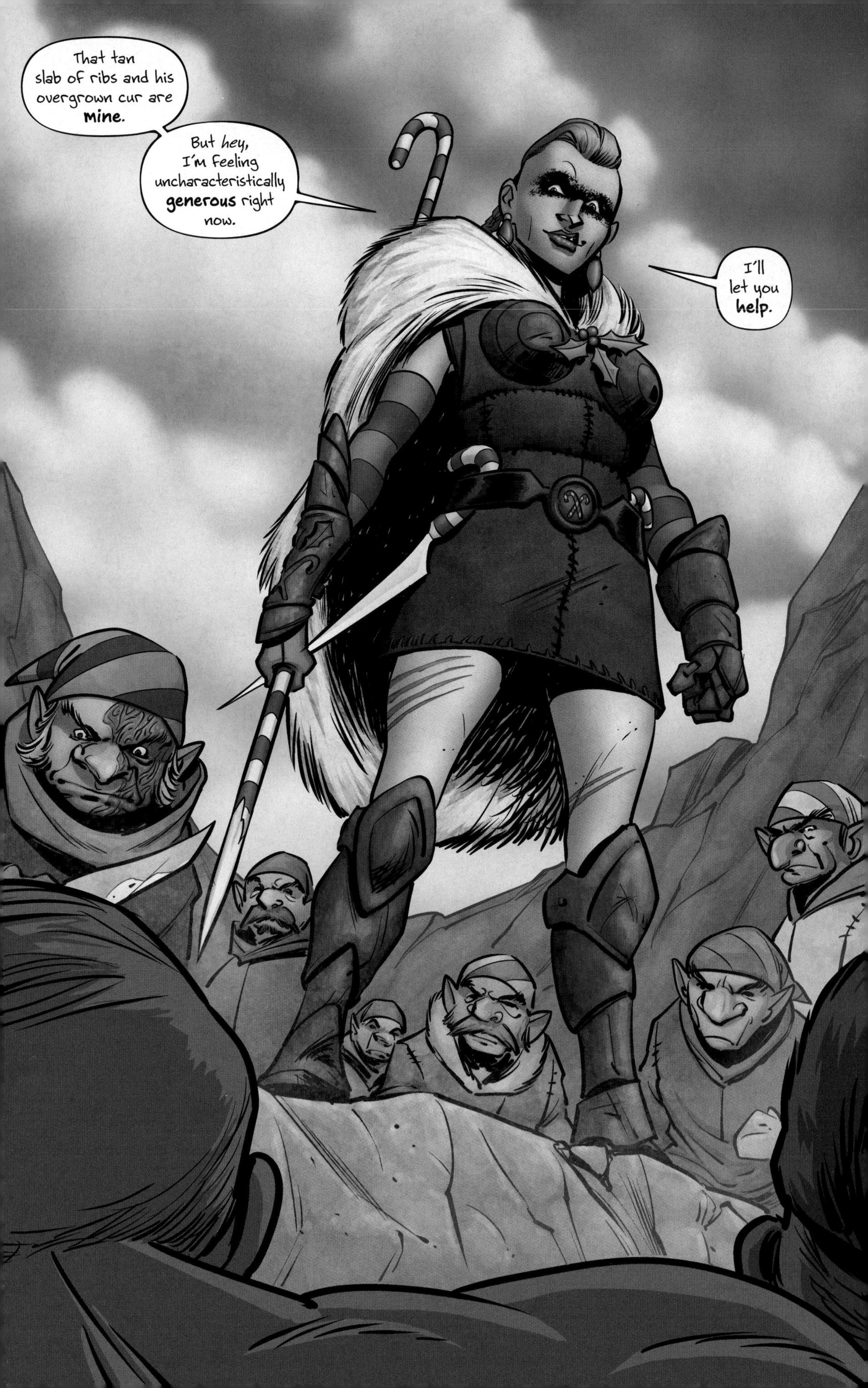
That tan slab of ribs and his overgrown cur are **mine**.
But hey, I'm feeling uncharacteristically **generous** right now.
I'll let you **help**.

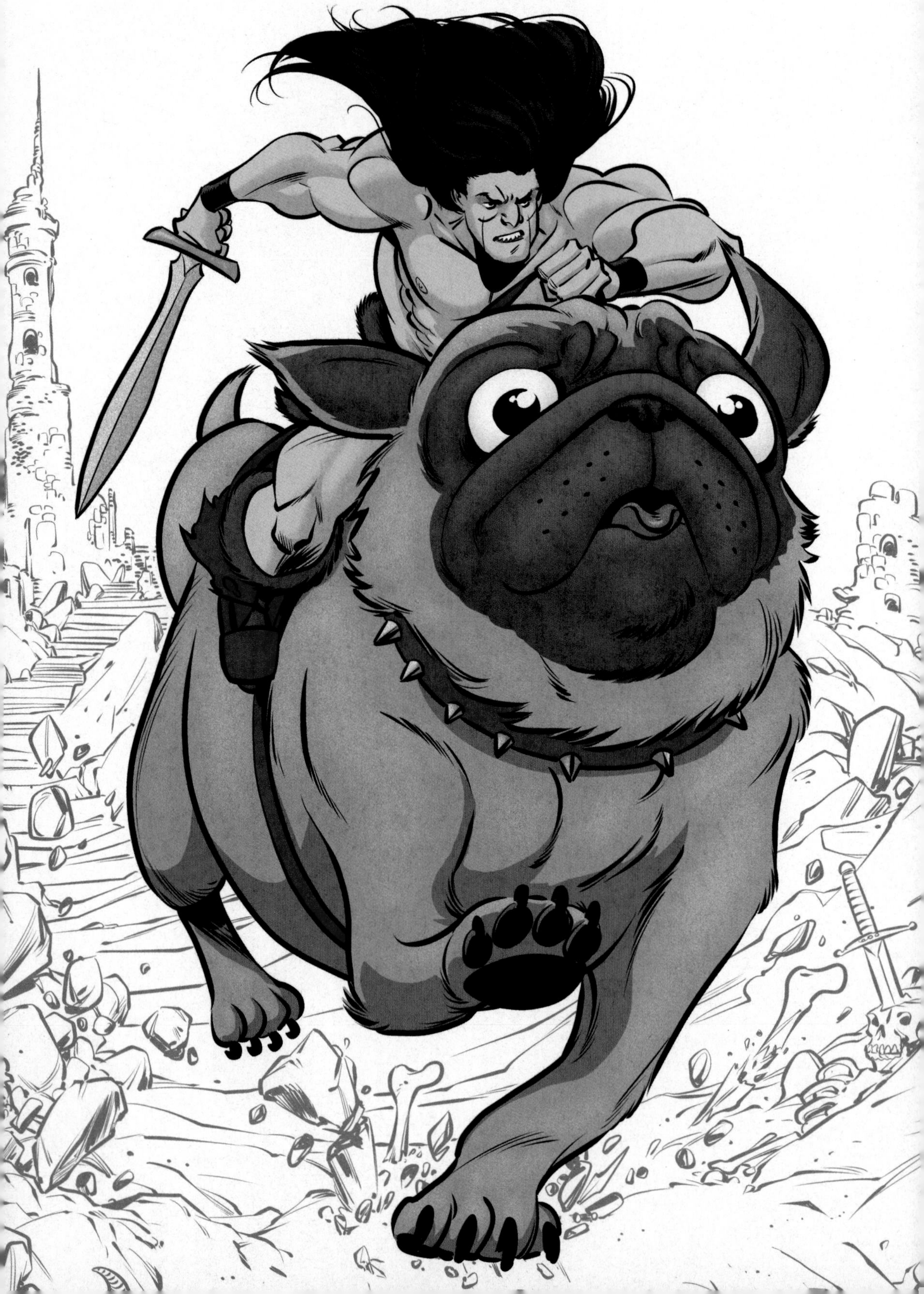

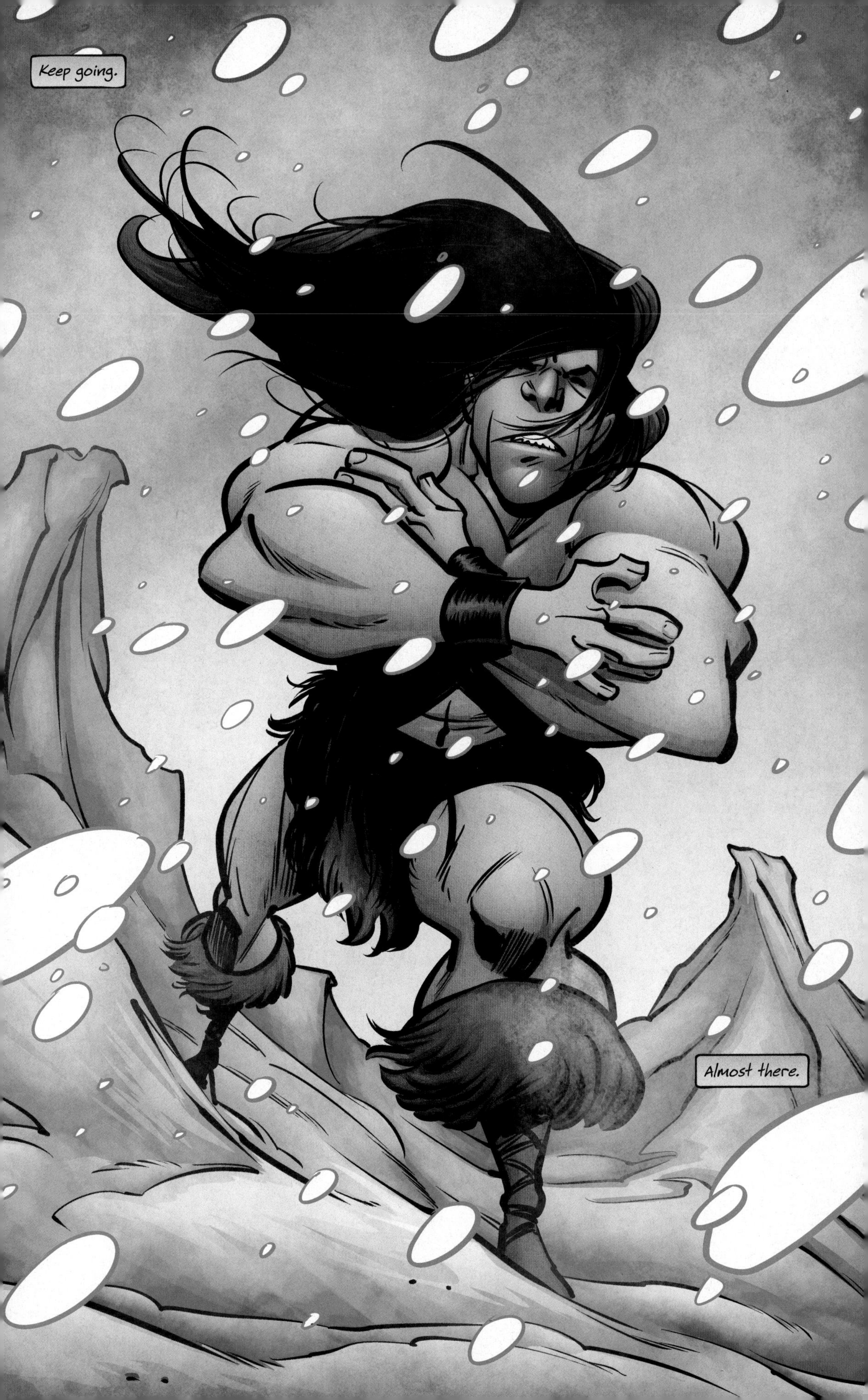
Keep going.
Almost there.

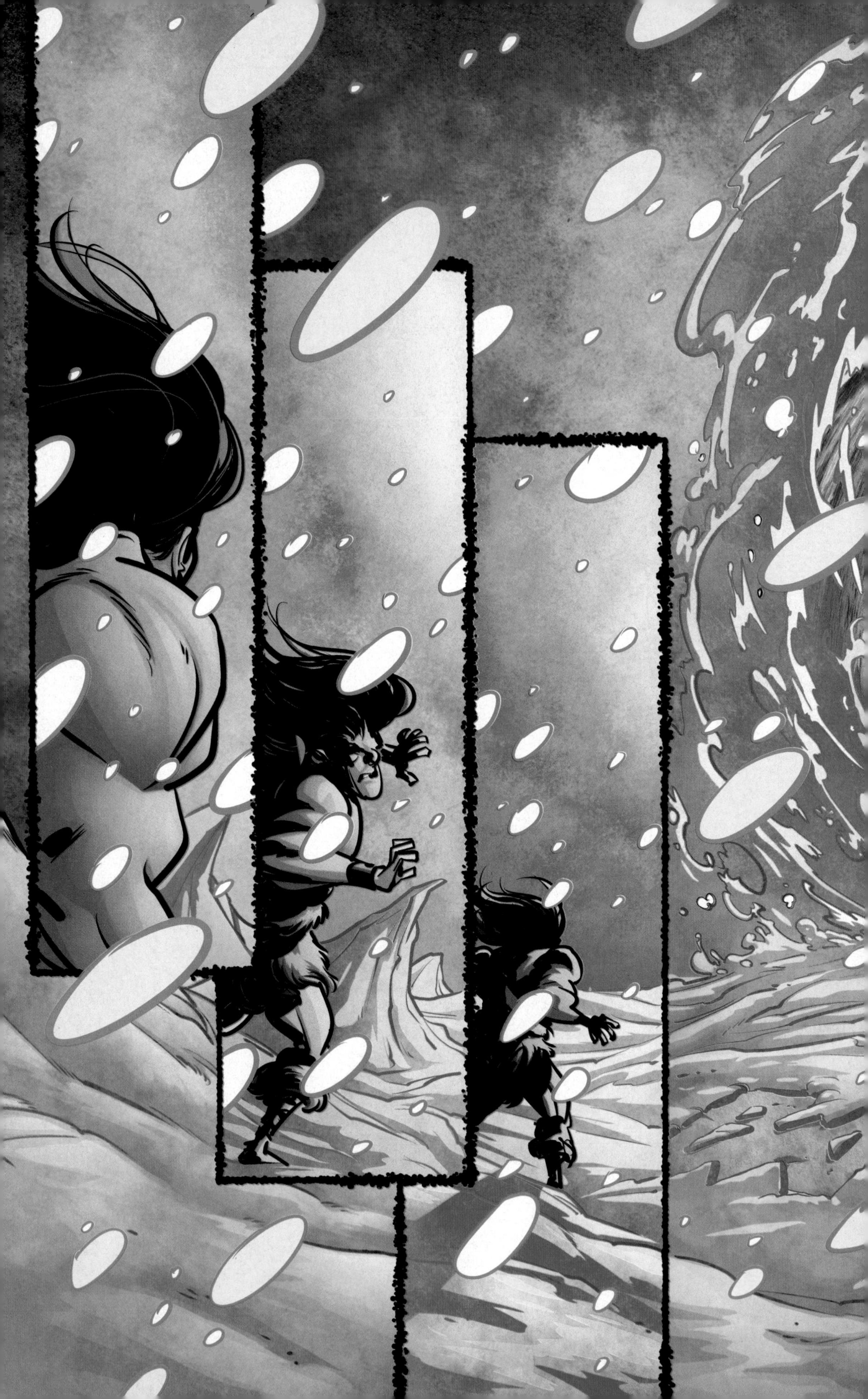

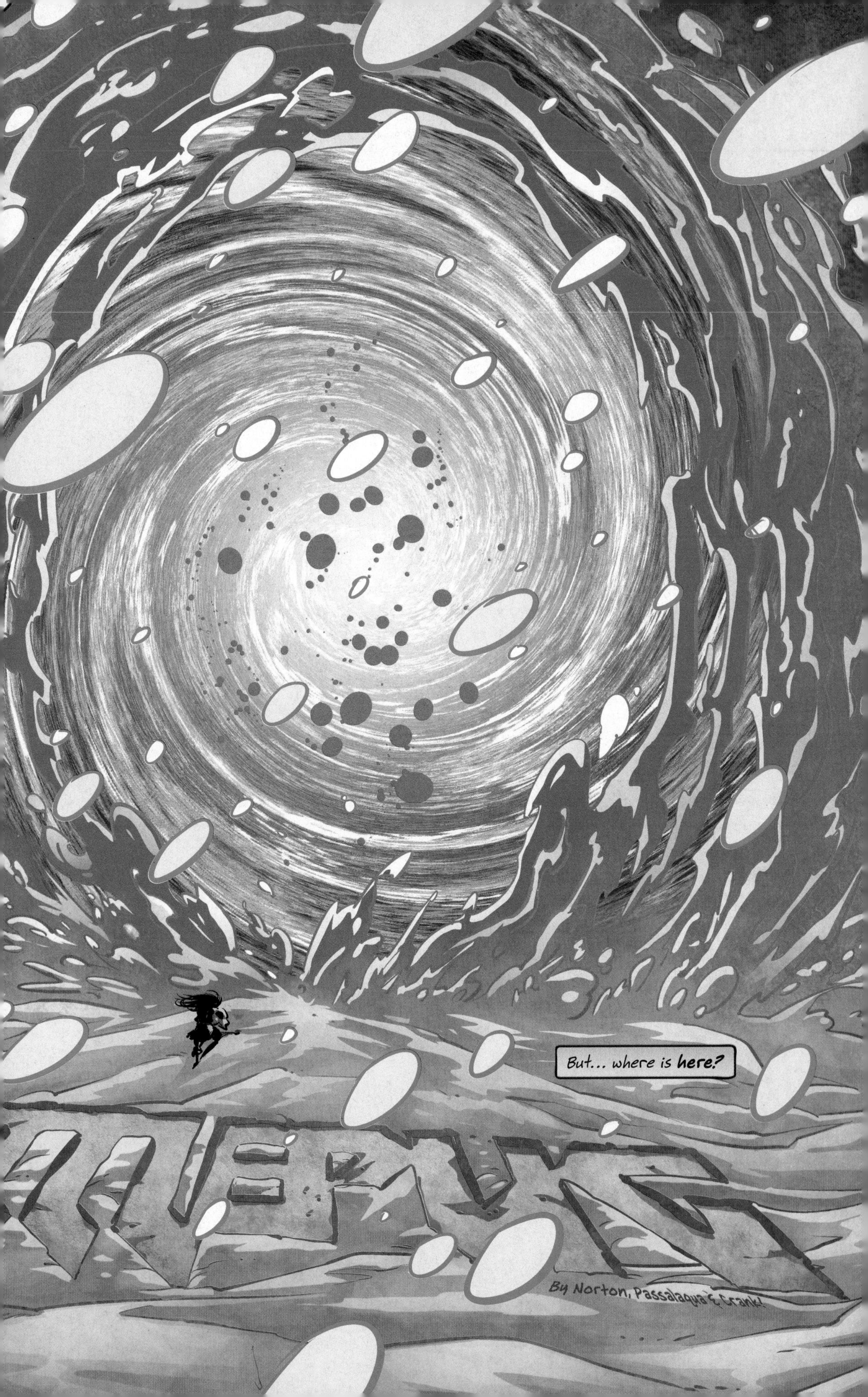
But... where is here?
By Norton, Passalaqua & Crank!

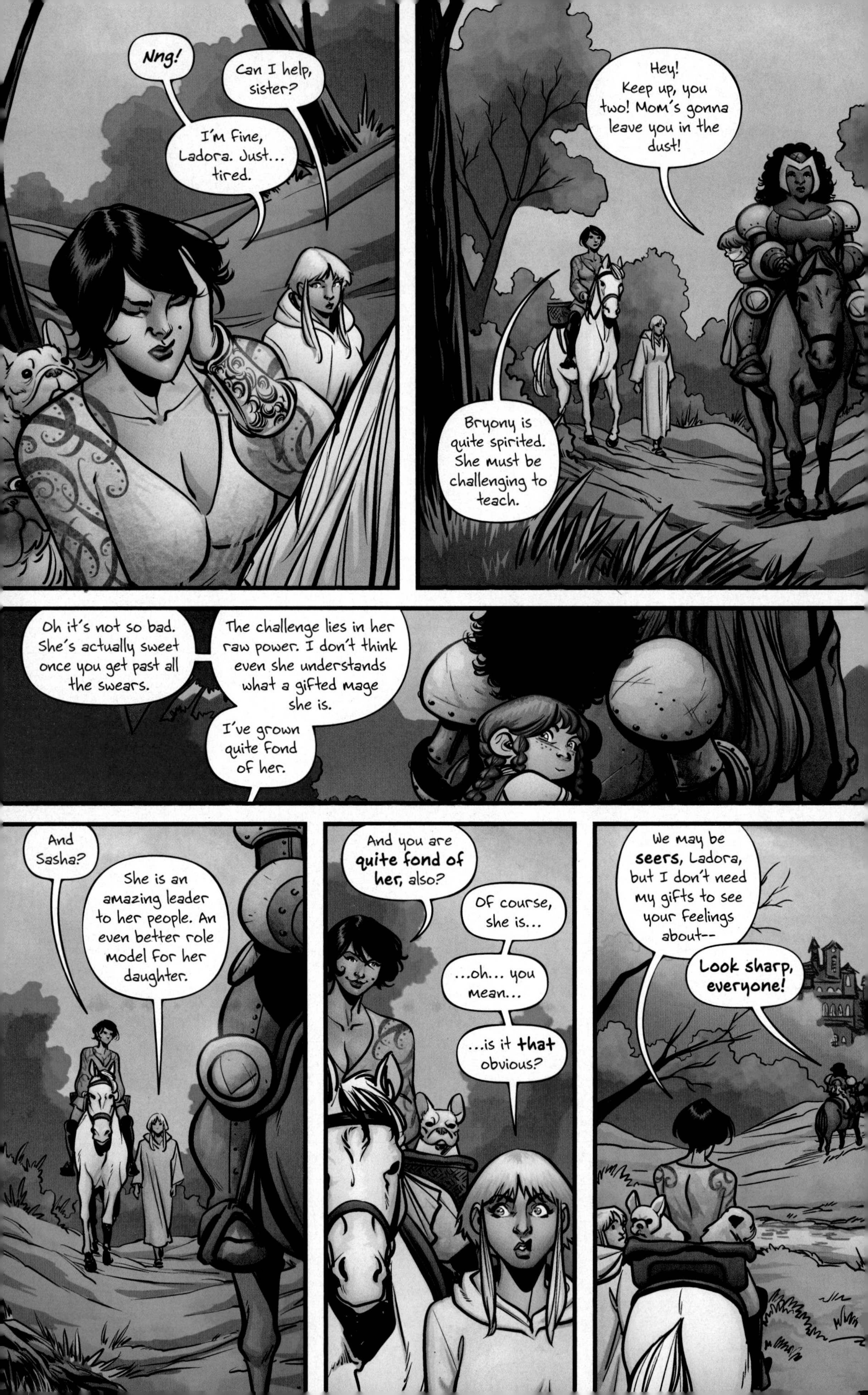
Nng!
Can I help, sister?
I'm fine, Ladora. Just... tired.
Hey! Keep up, you two! Mom's gonna leave you in the dust!
Bryony is quite spirited. She must be challenging to teach.
Oh it's not so bad. She's actually sweet once you get past all the swears.
The challenge lies in her raw power. I don't think even she understands what a gifted mage she is.
I've grown quite fond of her.
And Sasha?
She is an amazing leader to her people. An even better role model for her daughter.
And you are **quite fond of her,** also?
Of course, she is...
...oh... you mean...
...is it **that** obvious?
We may be **seers,** Ladora, but I don't need my gifts to see your feelings about--
Look sharp, everyone!

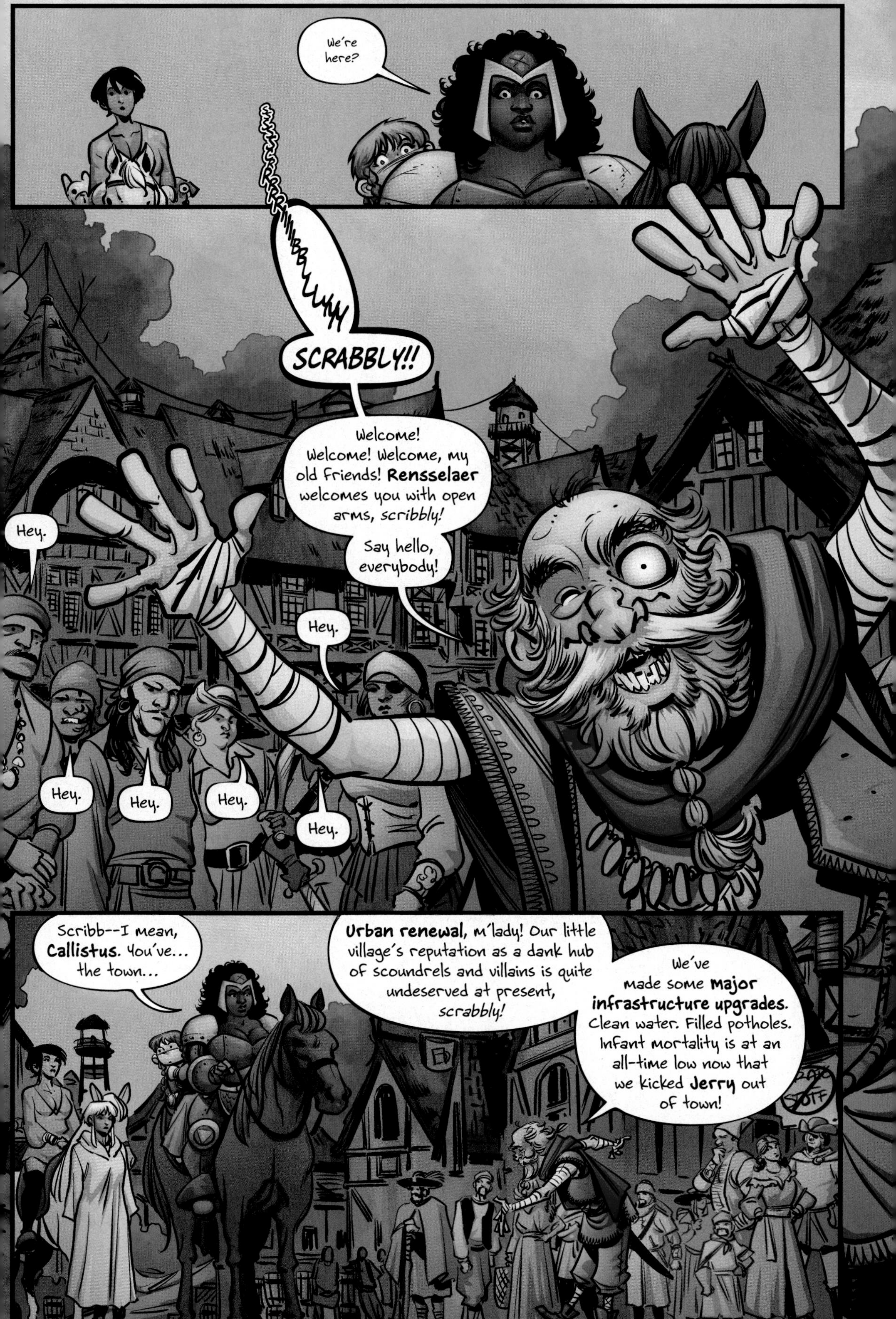
We're here?
SCRABBLY!!
Welcome! Welcome! Welcome, my old friends! **Rensselaer** welcomes you with open arms, *scribbly!*
Say hello, everybody!
Hey.
Hey.
Hey.
Hey.
Hey.
Hey.
Scribb--I mean, **Callistus**. You've... the town...
Urban renewal, m'lady! Our little village's reputation as a dank hub of scoundrels and villains is quite undeserved at present, *scrabbly!*
We've made some **major infrastructure upgrades**. Clean water. Filled potholes. Infant mortality is at an all-time low now that we kicked **Jerry** out of town!

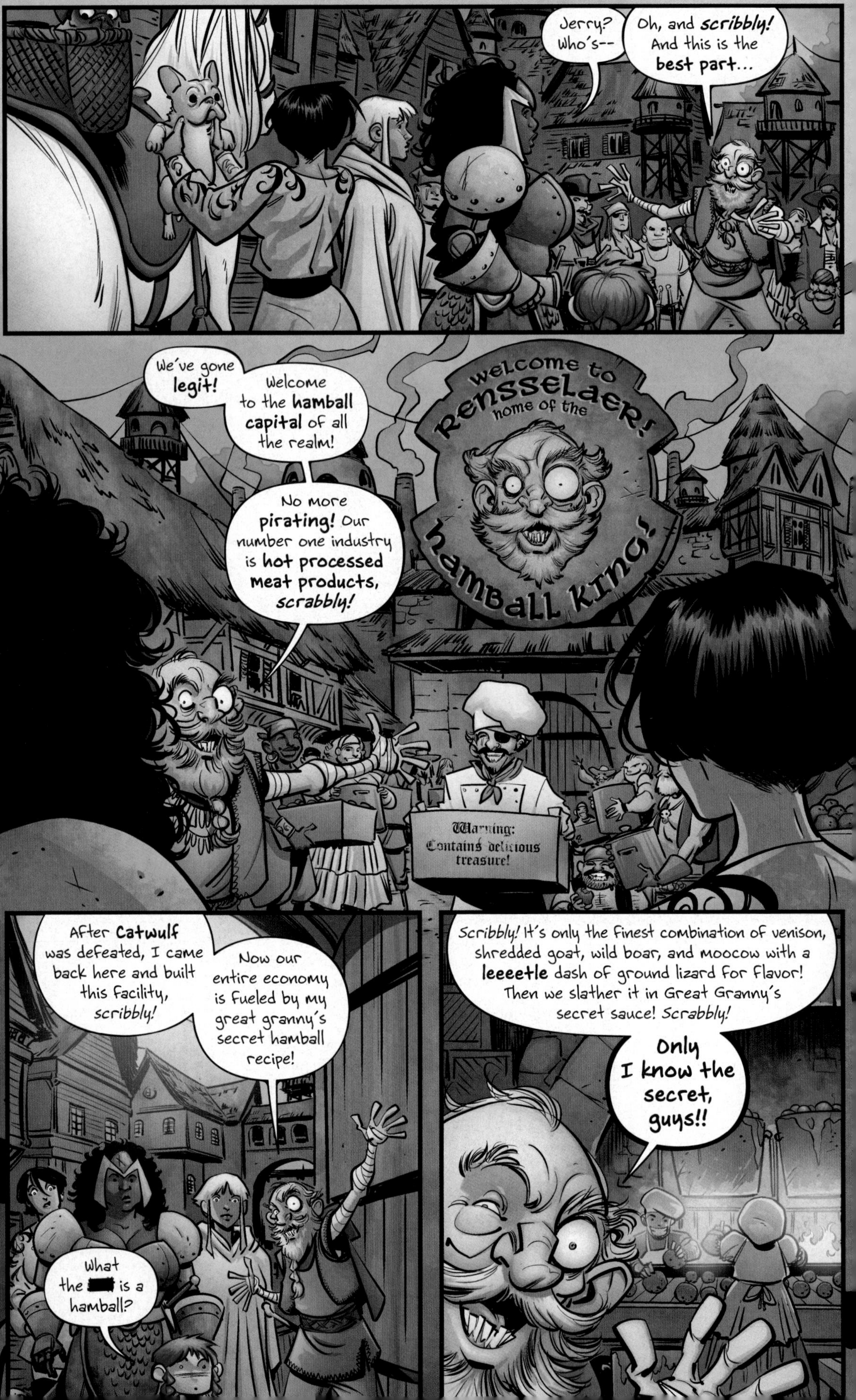
Jerry? Who's--
Oh, and scribbly! And this is the best part...
We've gone legit!
Welcome to the hamball capital of all the realm!
welcome to RENSSELAER! home of the HAMBALL KING!
No more pirating! Our number one industry is hot processed meat products, scrabbly!
Warning: Contains delicious treasure!
After Catwulf was defeated, I came back here and built this facility, scribbly!
Now our entire economy is fueled by my great granny's secret hamball recipe!
What the [redacted] is a hamball?
Scribbly! It's only the finest combination of venison, shredded goat, wild boar, and moocow with a leeeetle dash of ground lizard for flavor! Then we slather it in Great Granny's secret sauce! Scrabbly!
Only I know the secret, guys!!

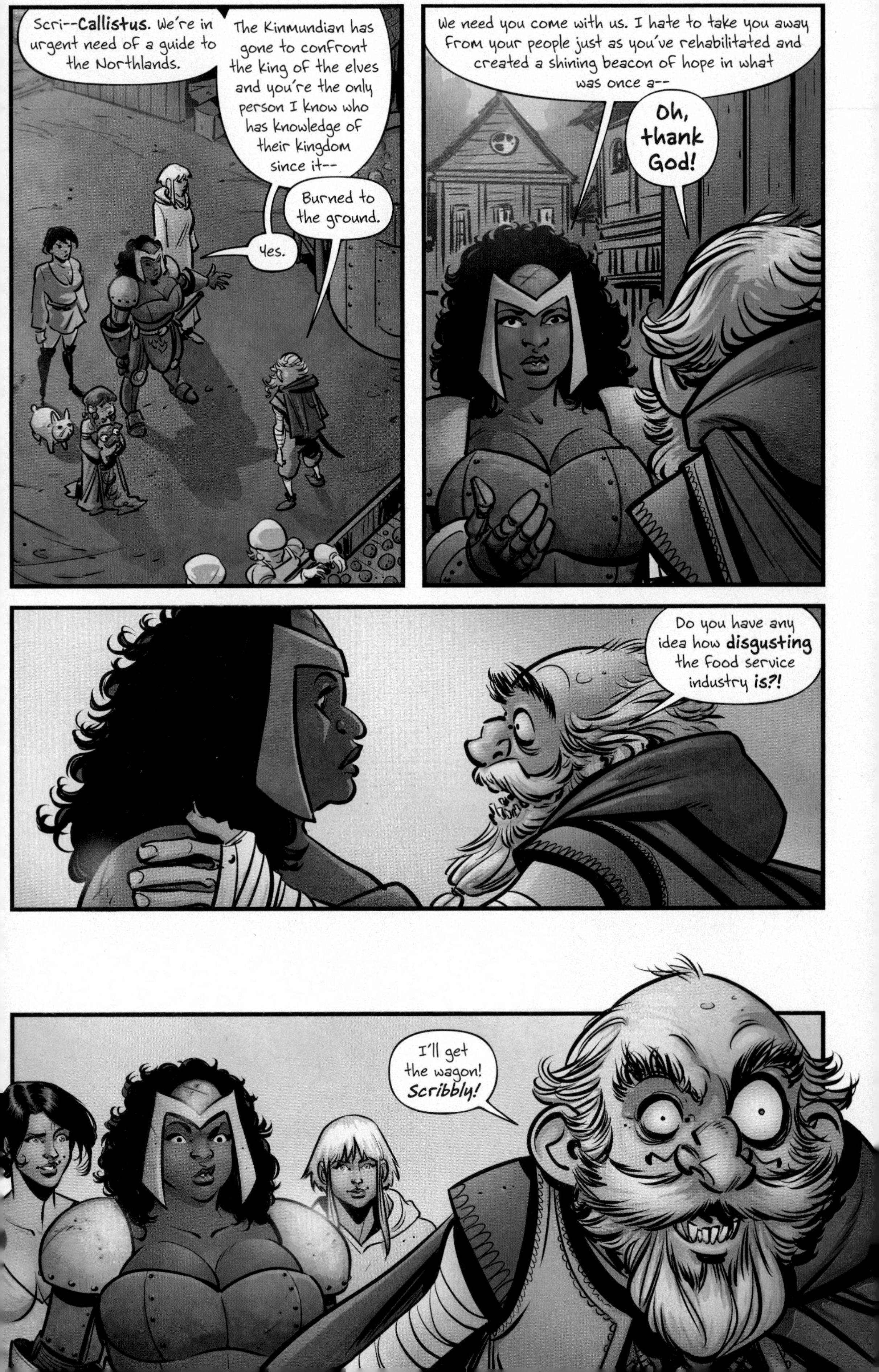
Scri--**Callistus**. We're in urgent need of a guide to the Northlands.
The Kinmundian has gone to confront the king of the elves and you're the only person I know who has knowledge of their kingdom since it--
Burned to the ground.
Yes.
We need you come with us. I hate to take you away from your people just as you've rehabilitated and created a shining beacon of hope in what was once a--
Oh, thank God!
Do you have any idea how **disgusting** the food service industry ***is?!***
I'll get the wagon! ***Scribbly!***

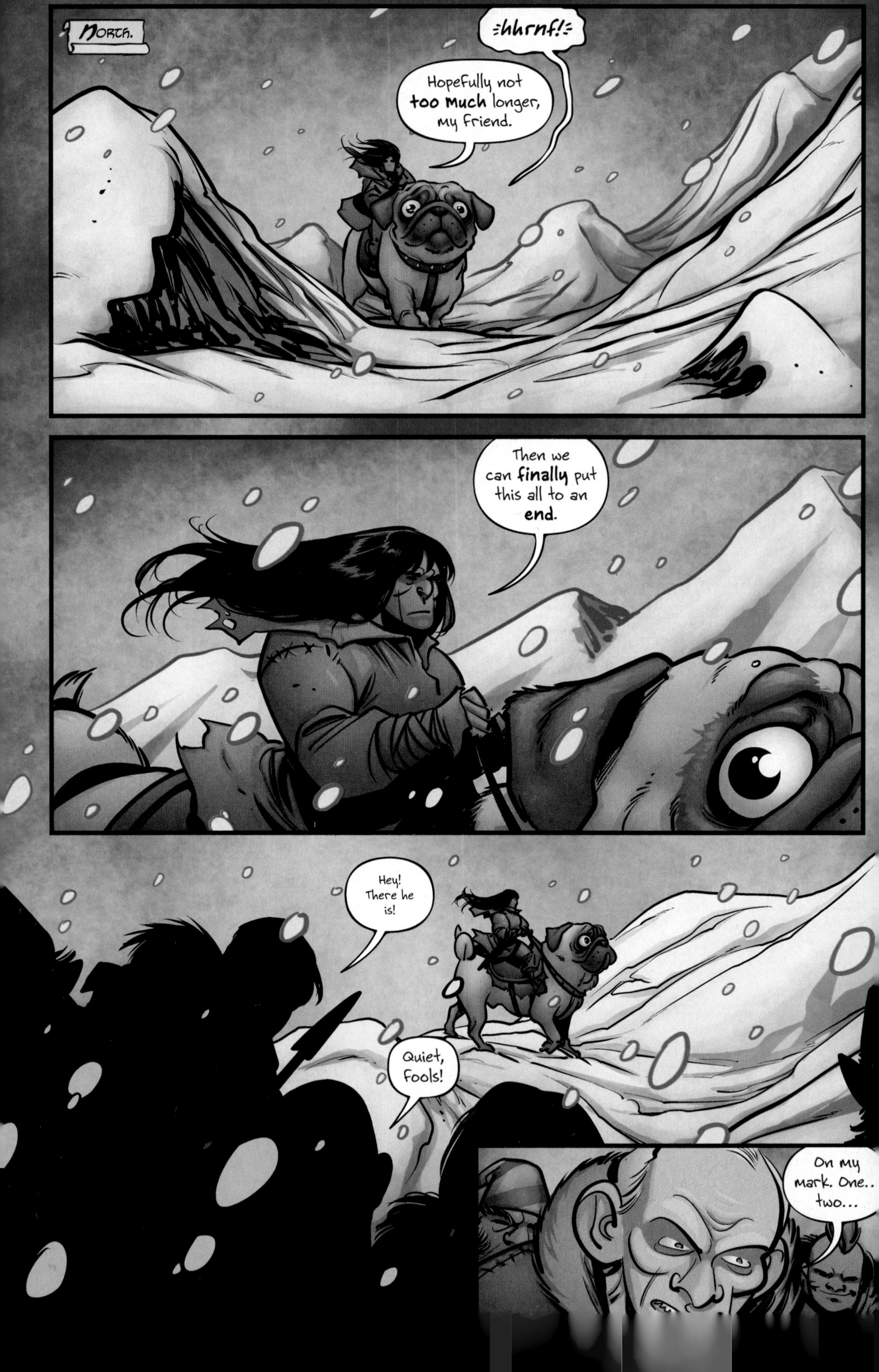
North.
hhrnf!
Hopefully not too much longer, my friend.
Then we can finally put this all to an end.
Hey! There he is!
Quiet, fools!
On my mark. One.. two...

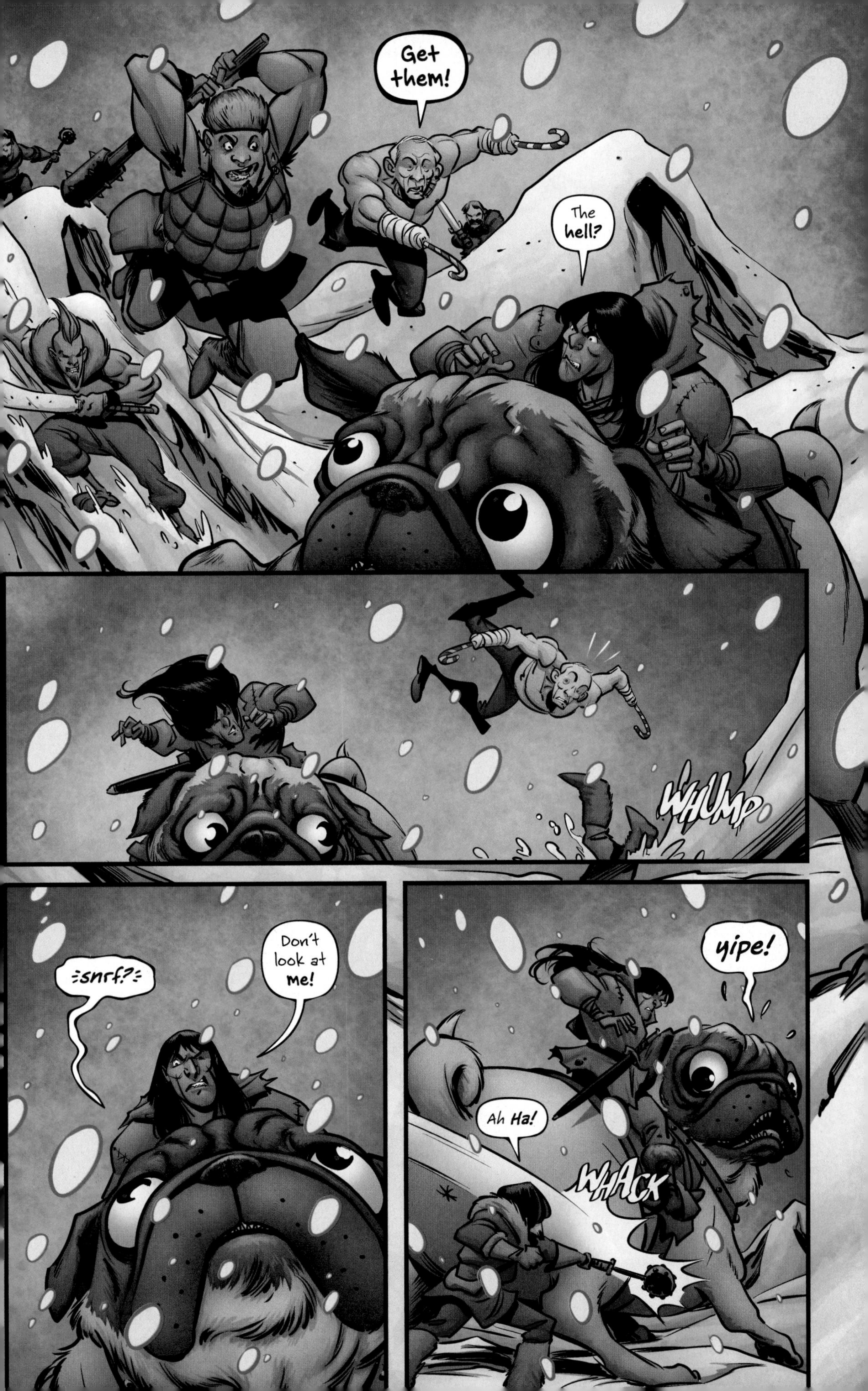
Get them!
The hell?
WHUMP
snrf?
Don't look at me!
yipe!
Ah Ha!
WHACK

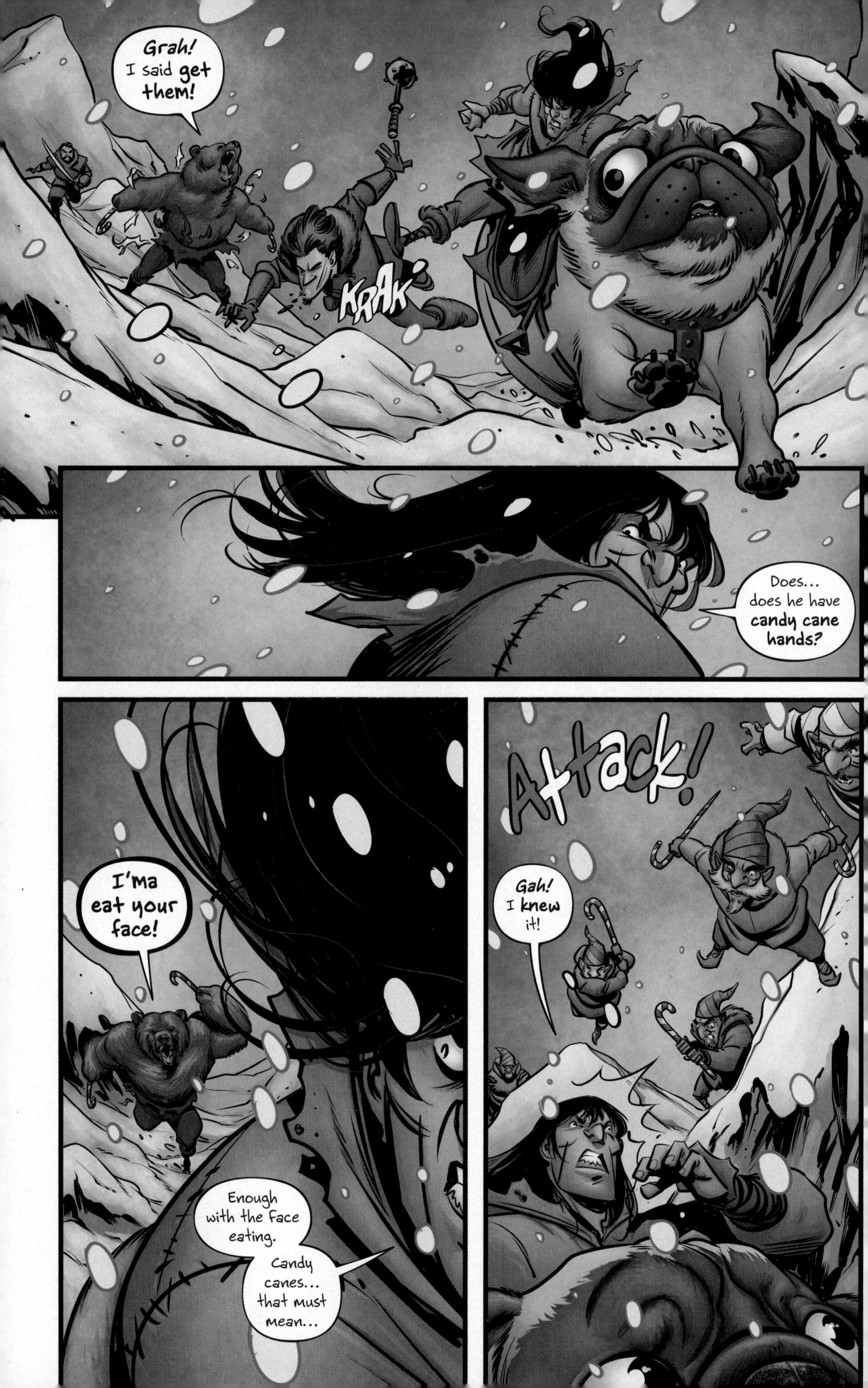
Grah! I said get them!
KRAK
Does... does he have candy cane hands?
I'ma eat your face!
Enough with the face eating.
Candy canes... that must mean...
Attack!
Gah! I knew it!

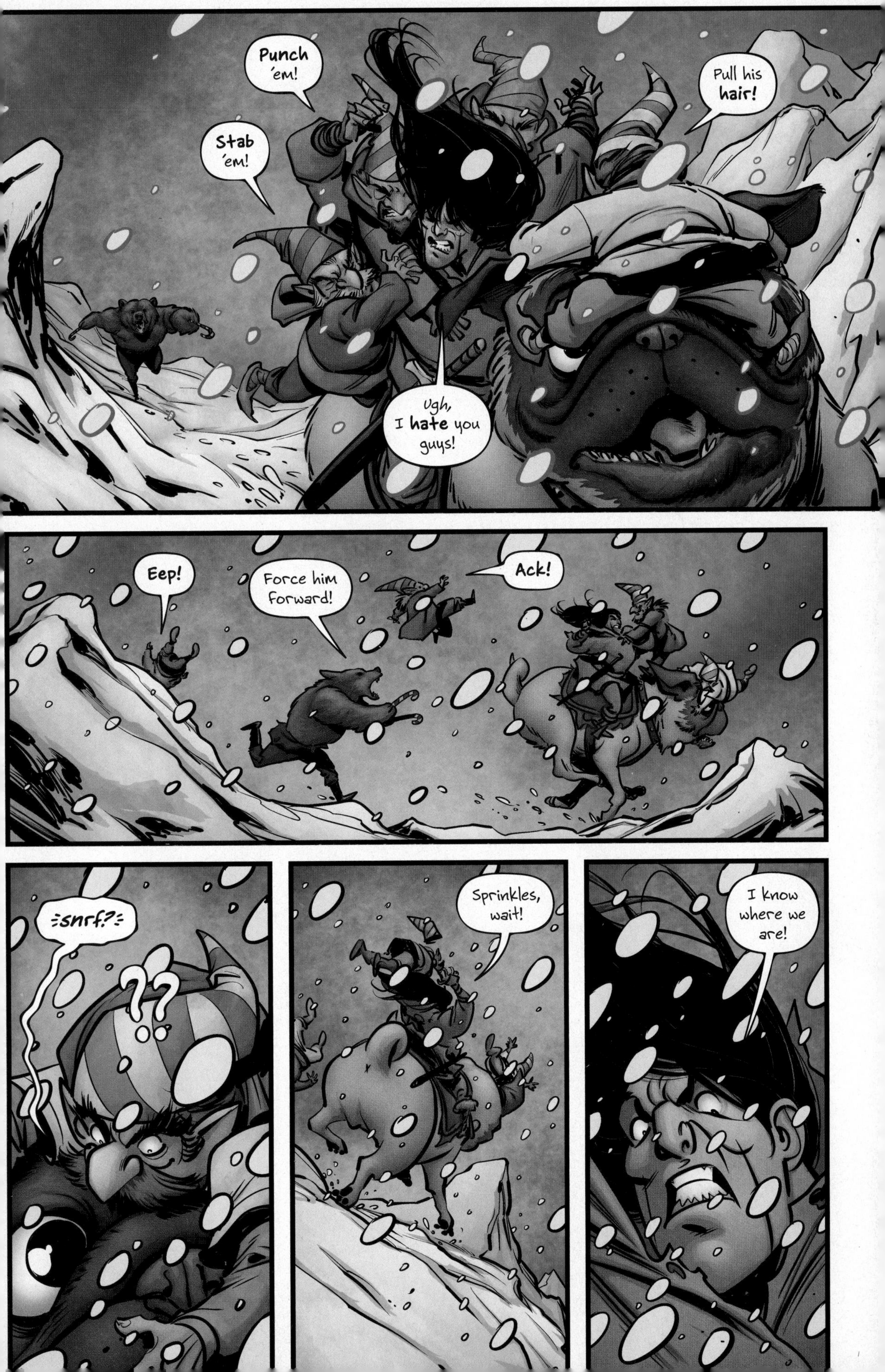
Punch 'em!
Stab 'em!
Pull his hair!
Ugh, I hate you guys!
Eep!
Force him forward!
Ack!
snrf?
??
Sprinkles, wait!
I know where we are!

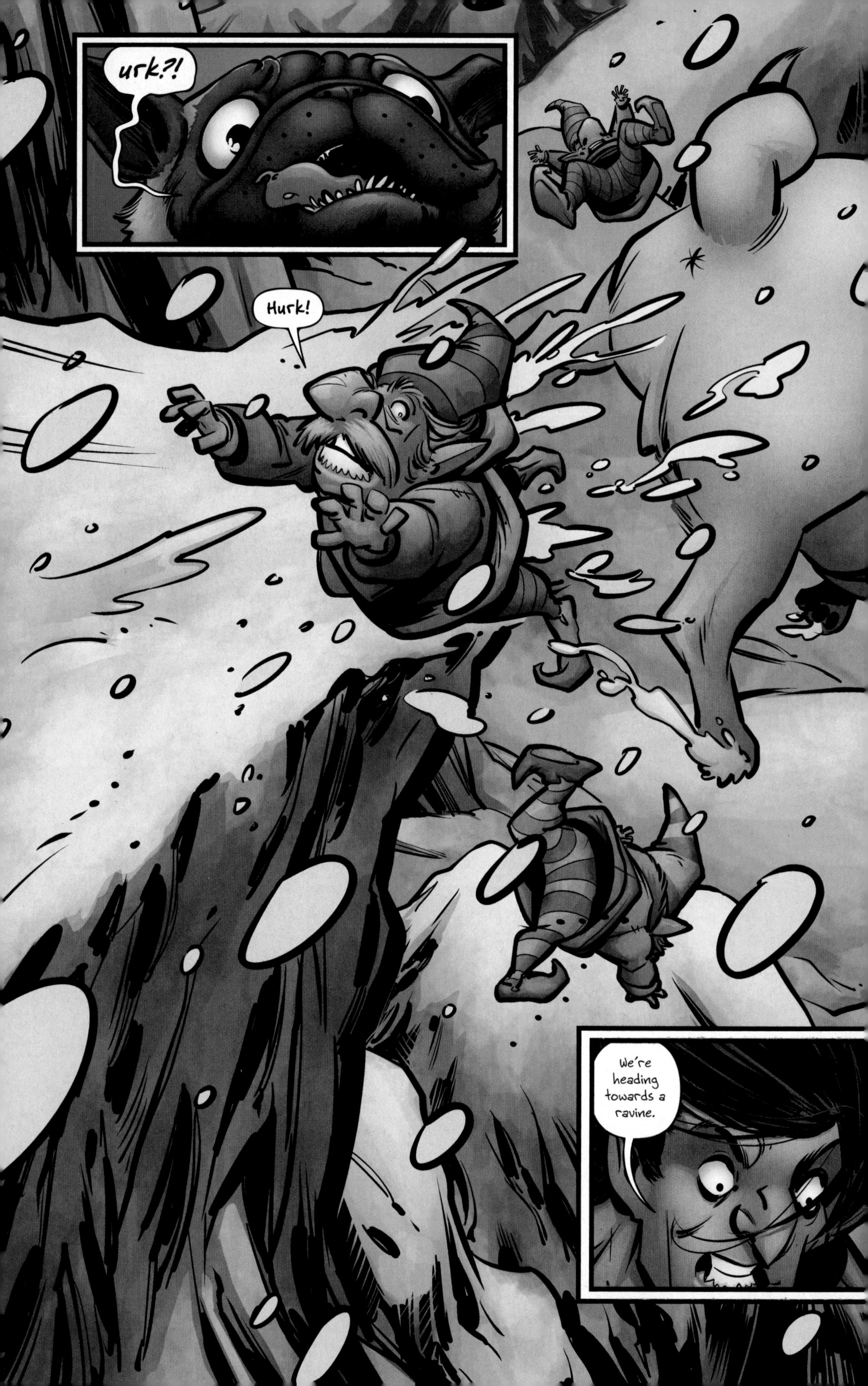
urk?!
Hurk!
We're heading towards a ravine.

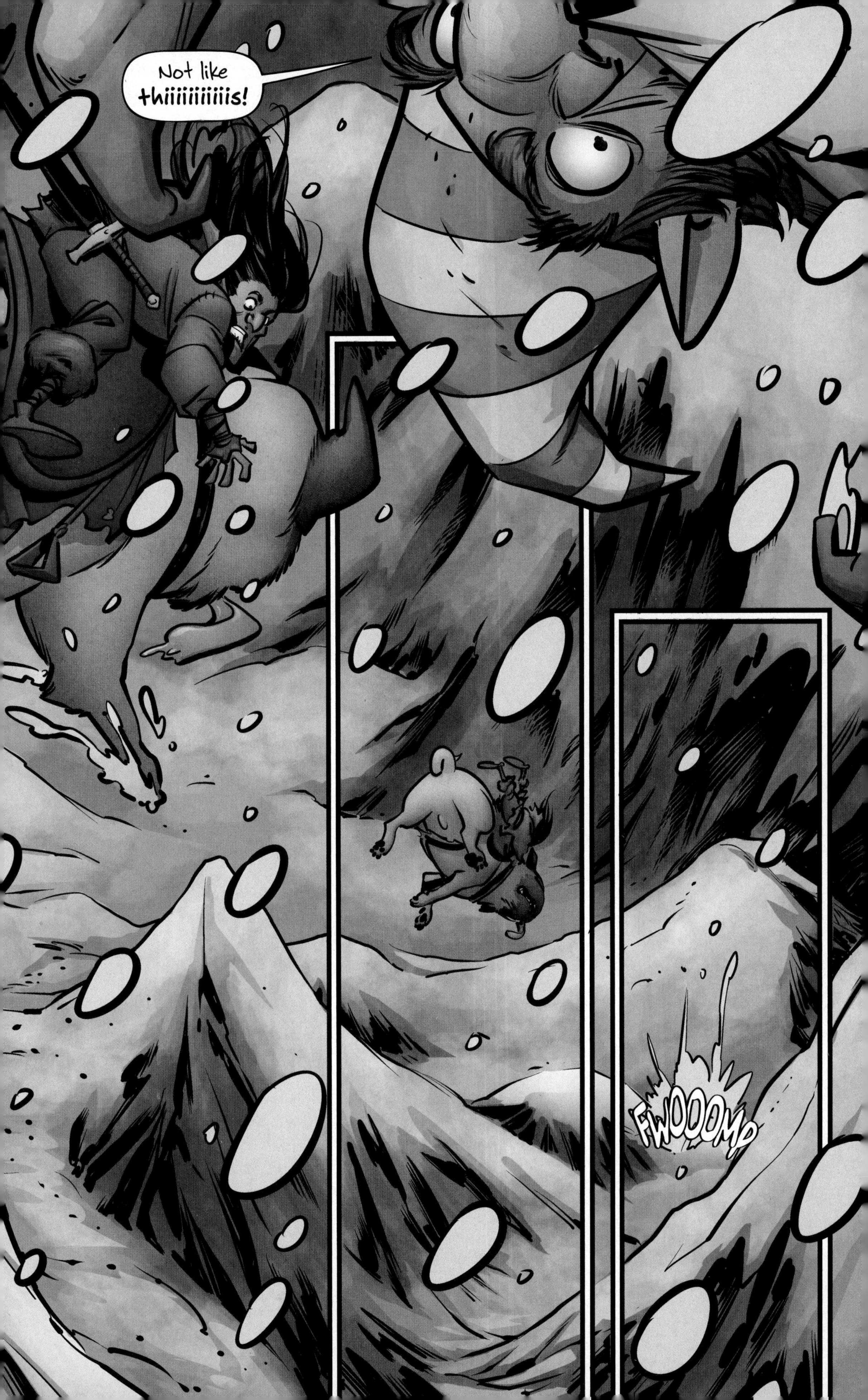
Not like thiiiiiiiiiis!
FWOOOMP

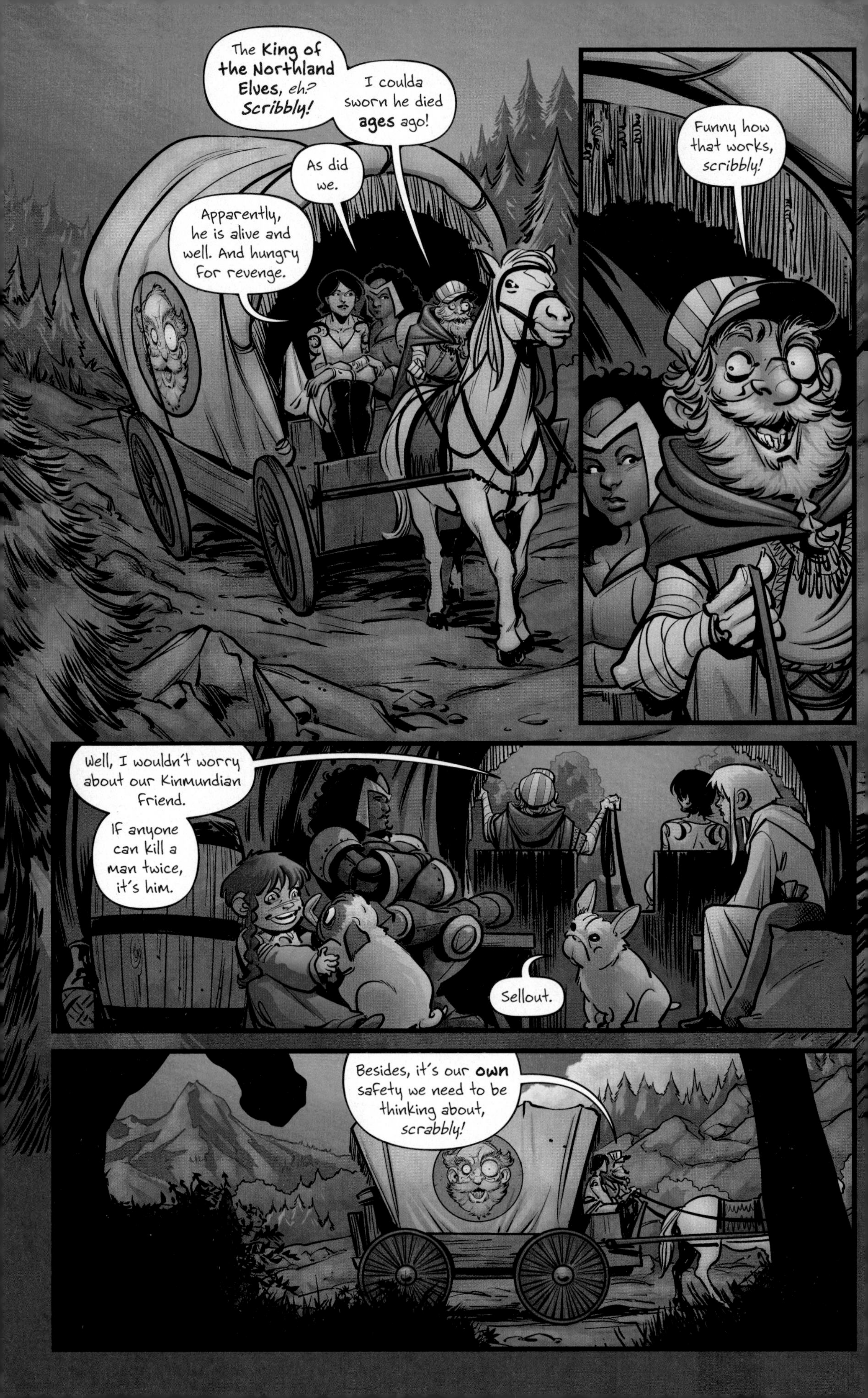
The **King of the Northland Elves**, *eh?* ***Scribbly!***
I coulda sworn he died **ages** ago!
As did we.
Apparently, he is alive and well. And hungry for revenge.
Funny how that works, *scribbly!*
Well, I wouldn't worry about our Kinmundian friend.
If anyone can kill a man twice, it's him.
Sellout.
Besides, it's our **own** safety we need to be thinking about, *scrabbly!*

These here woods are the stalking ground of one of the most vicious gangs I've ever heard tell of.

But you're the **pirate king.**

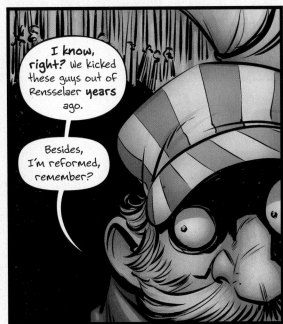

I know, right? We kicked these guys out of Rensselaer **years** ago.

Besides, I'm reformed, remember?

Apologies.

If we keep our heads down and move through quickly, I'm **sure** we'll be okay, scribbly.

Too late, **pirate wuss.**

Callistus?

It's them!

Ssqqqqqquuuueeeeee!

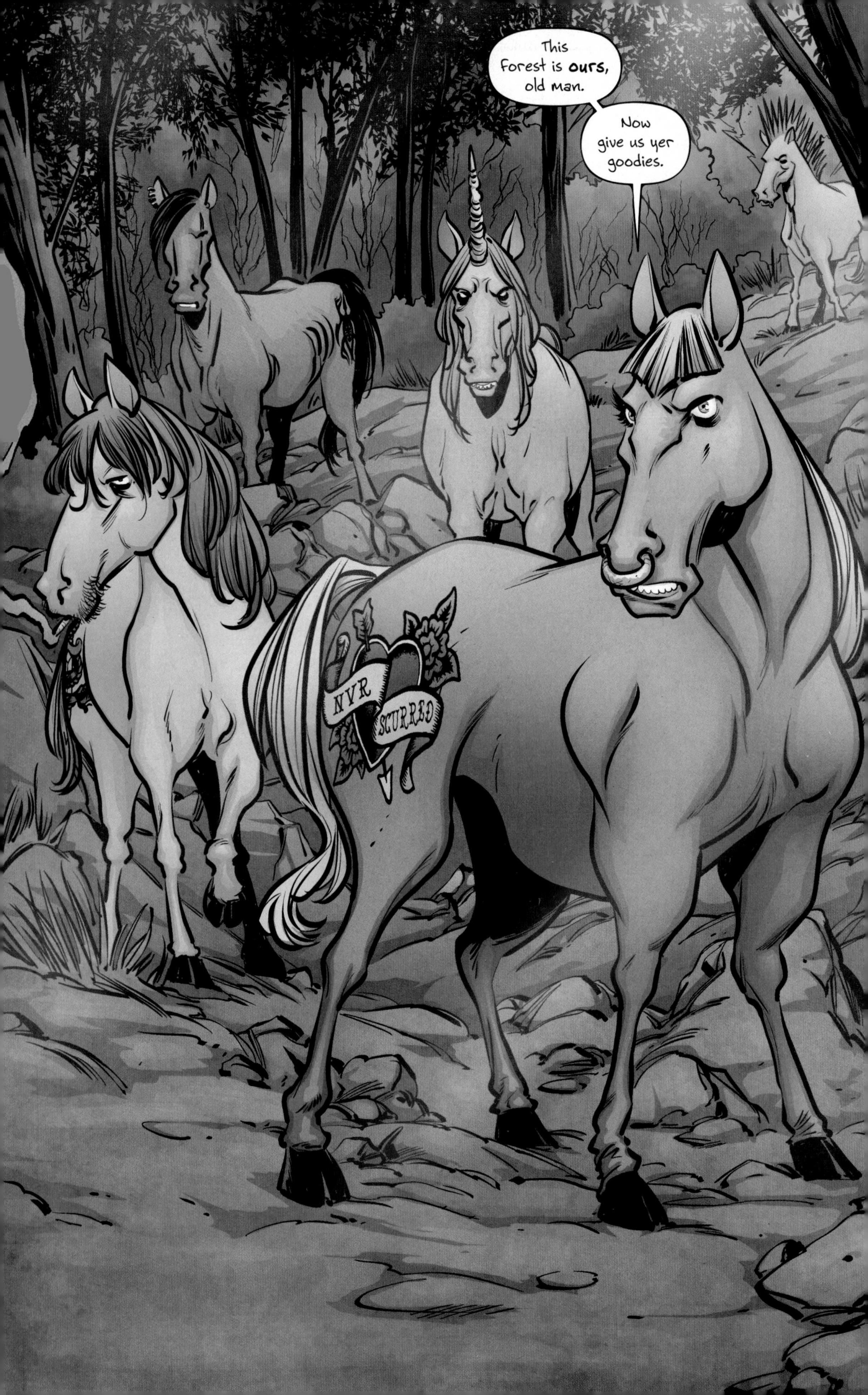
This Forest is **ours,** old man.
Now give us yer goodies.
NVR SCURRED

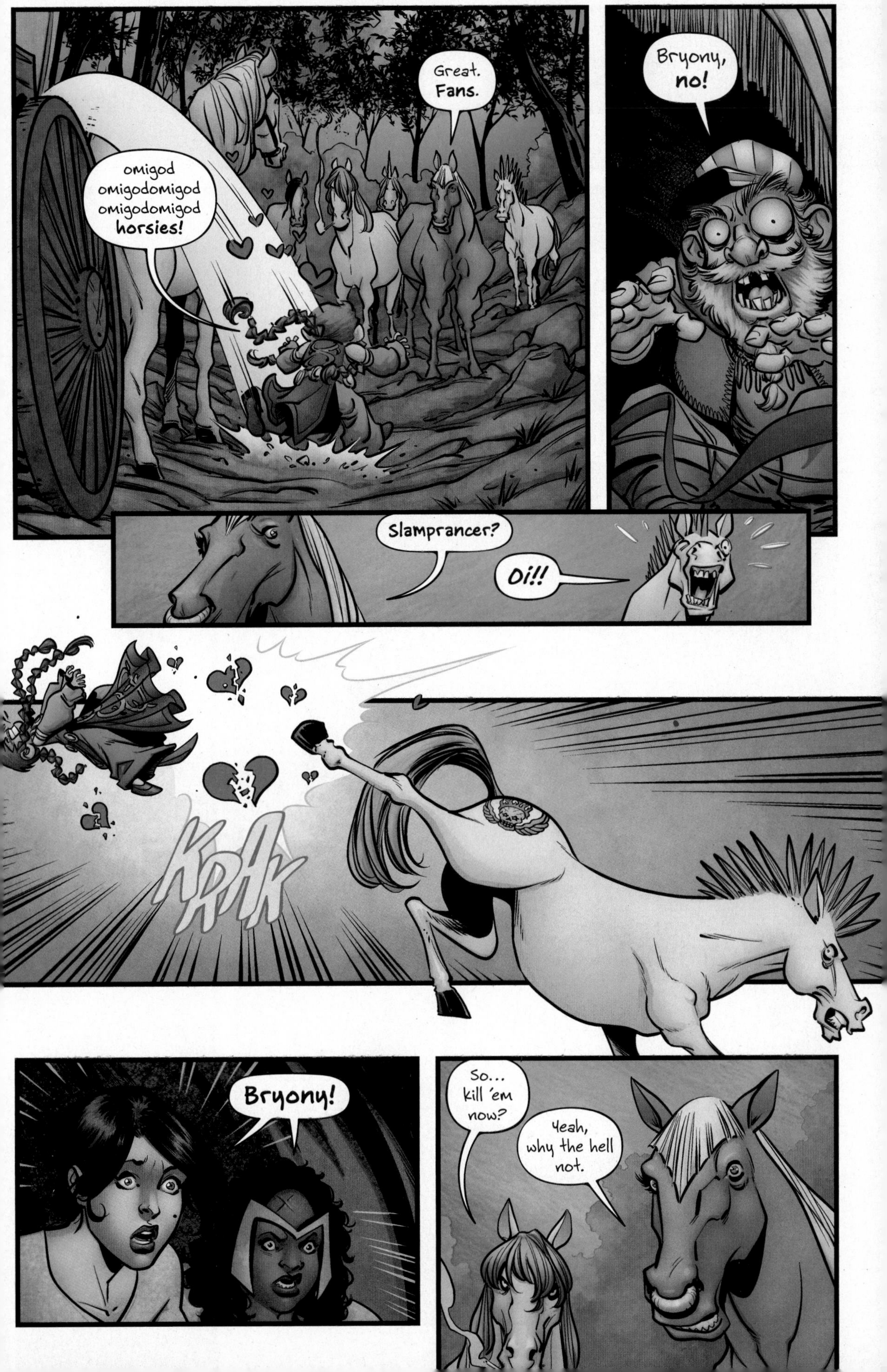

omigod omigodomigod omigodomigod horsies!
Great. Fans.
Bryony, no!
Slamprancer?
Oi!!
KRAK
Bryony!
So... kill 'em now?
Yeah, why the hell not.

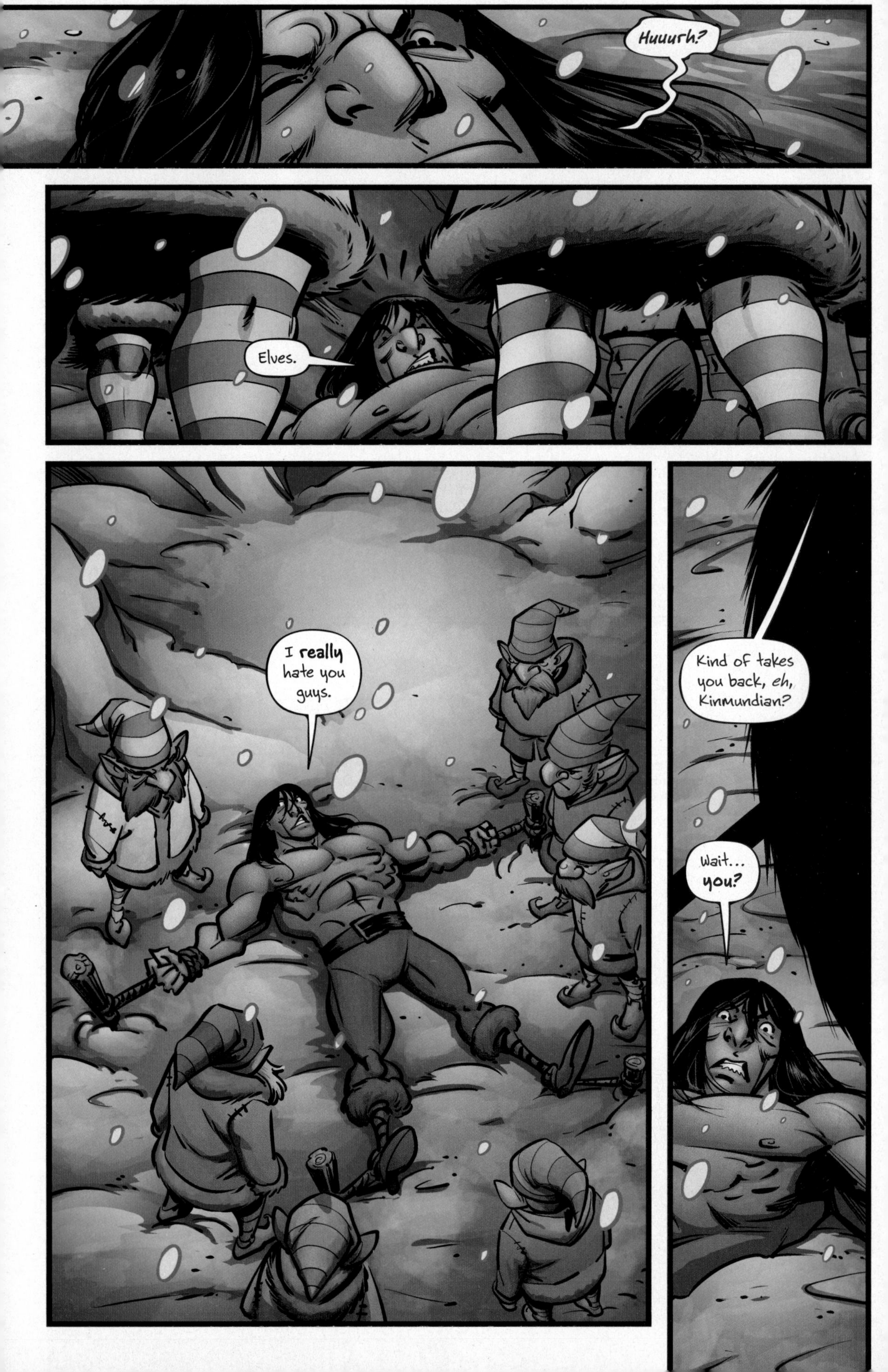
Huuurh?
Elves.
I really hate you guys.
Kind of takes you back, eh, Kinmundian?
Wait... you?

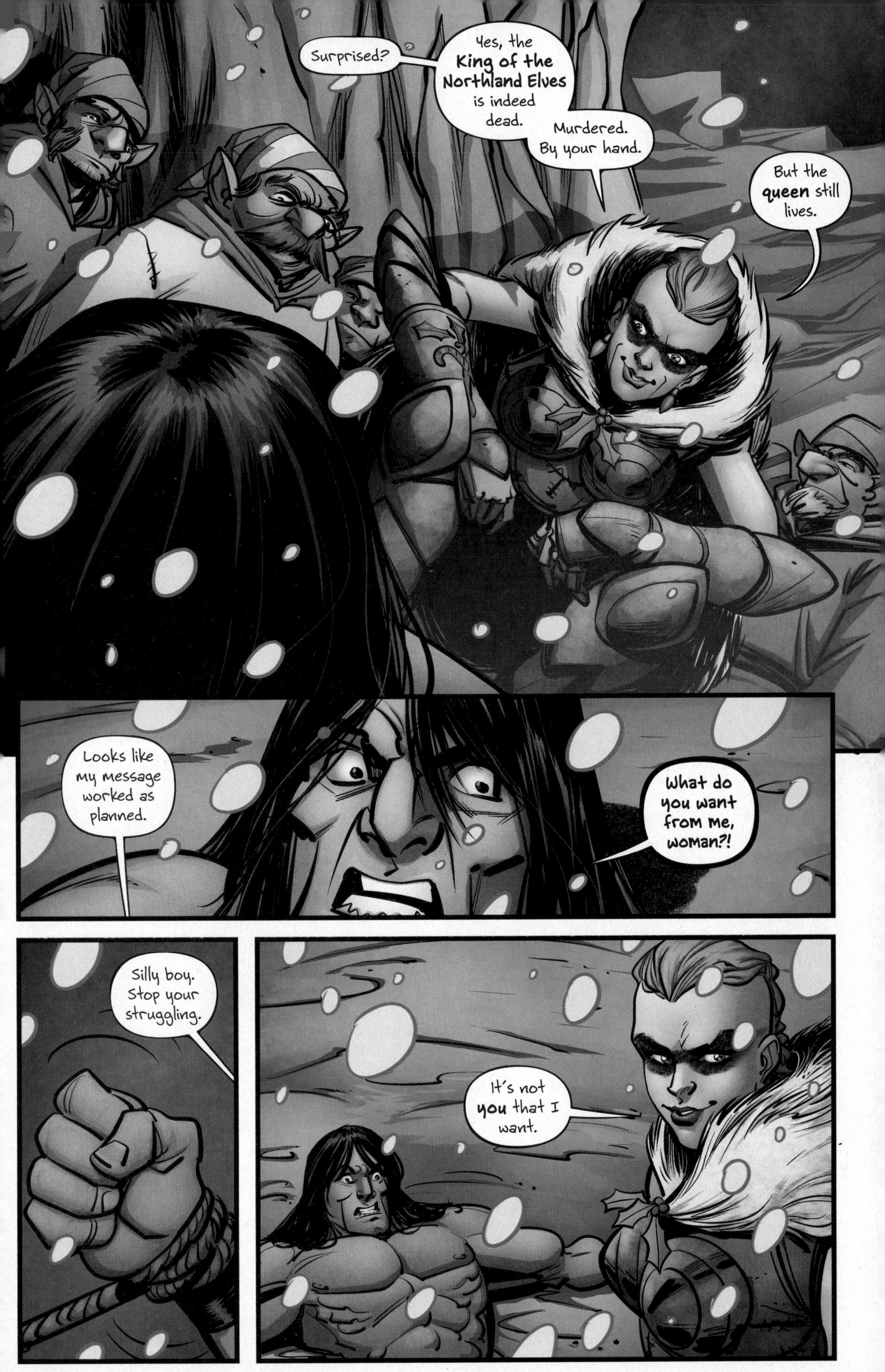
Surprised?
Yes, the King of the Northland Elves is indeed dead.
Murdered. By your hand.
But the queen still lives.
Looks like my message worked as planned.
What do you want from me, woman?!
Silly boy. Stop your struggling.
It's not you that I want.

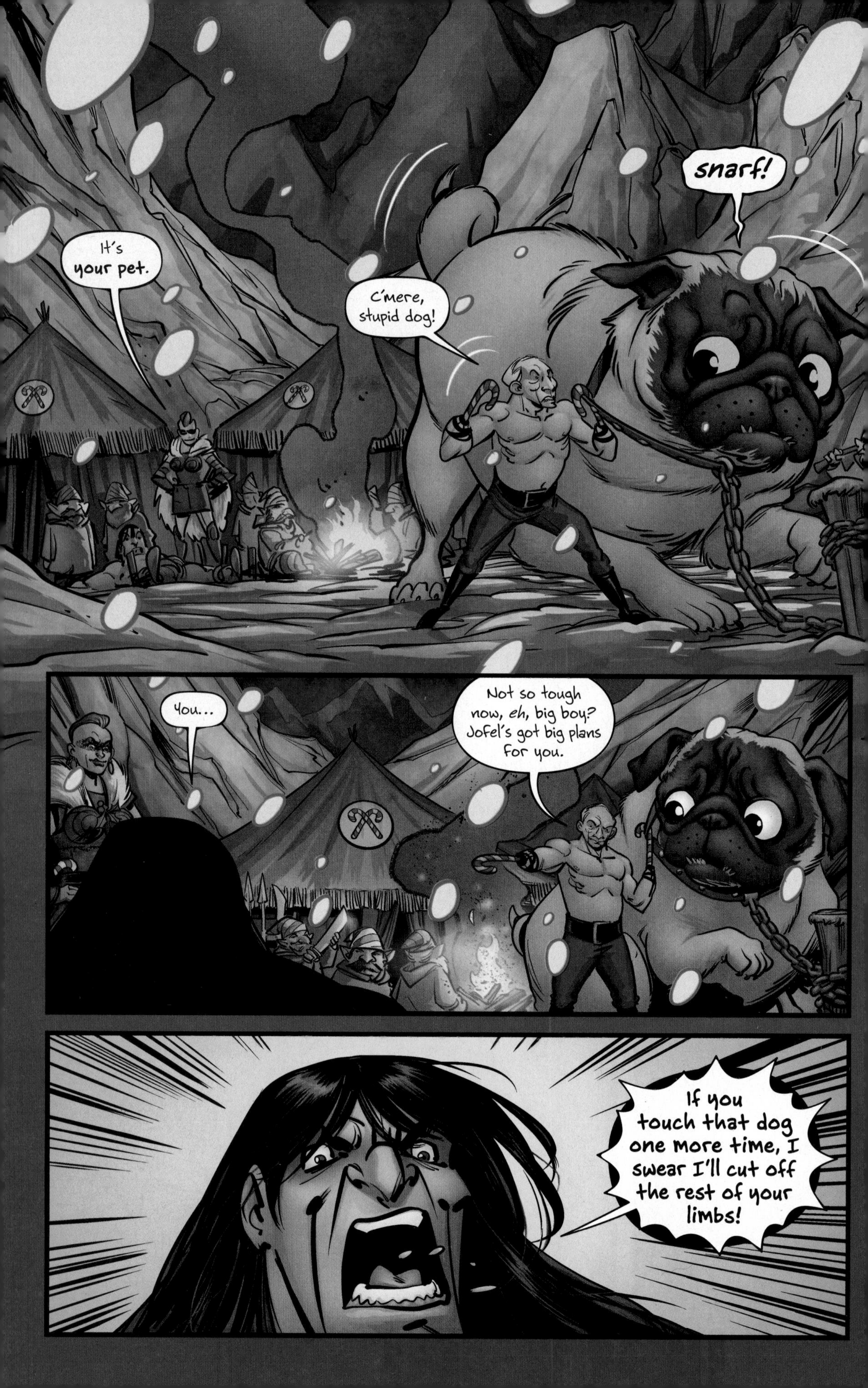
It's your pet.
C'mere, stupid dog!
snarf!
You...
Not so tough now, *eh*, big boy? Jofel's got big plans for you.
If you touch that dog one more time, I swear I'll cut off the rest of your limbs!

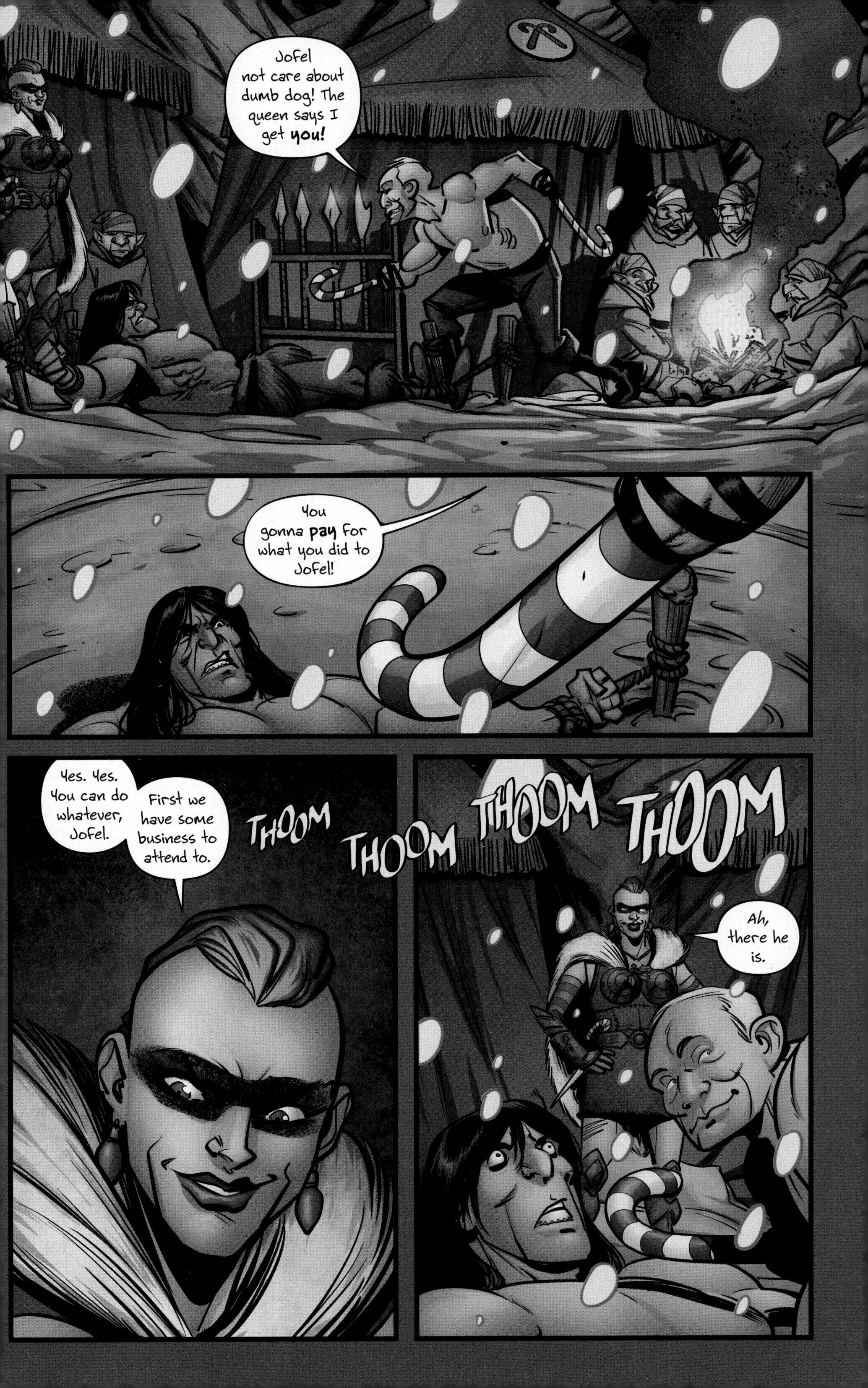

Jofel not care about dumb dog! The queen says I get **you!**
You gonna **pay** for what you did to Jofel!
Yes. Yes. You can do whatever, Jofel.
First we have some business to attend to.
THOOM
THOOM THOOM THOOM
Ah, there he is.

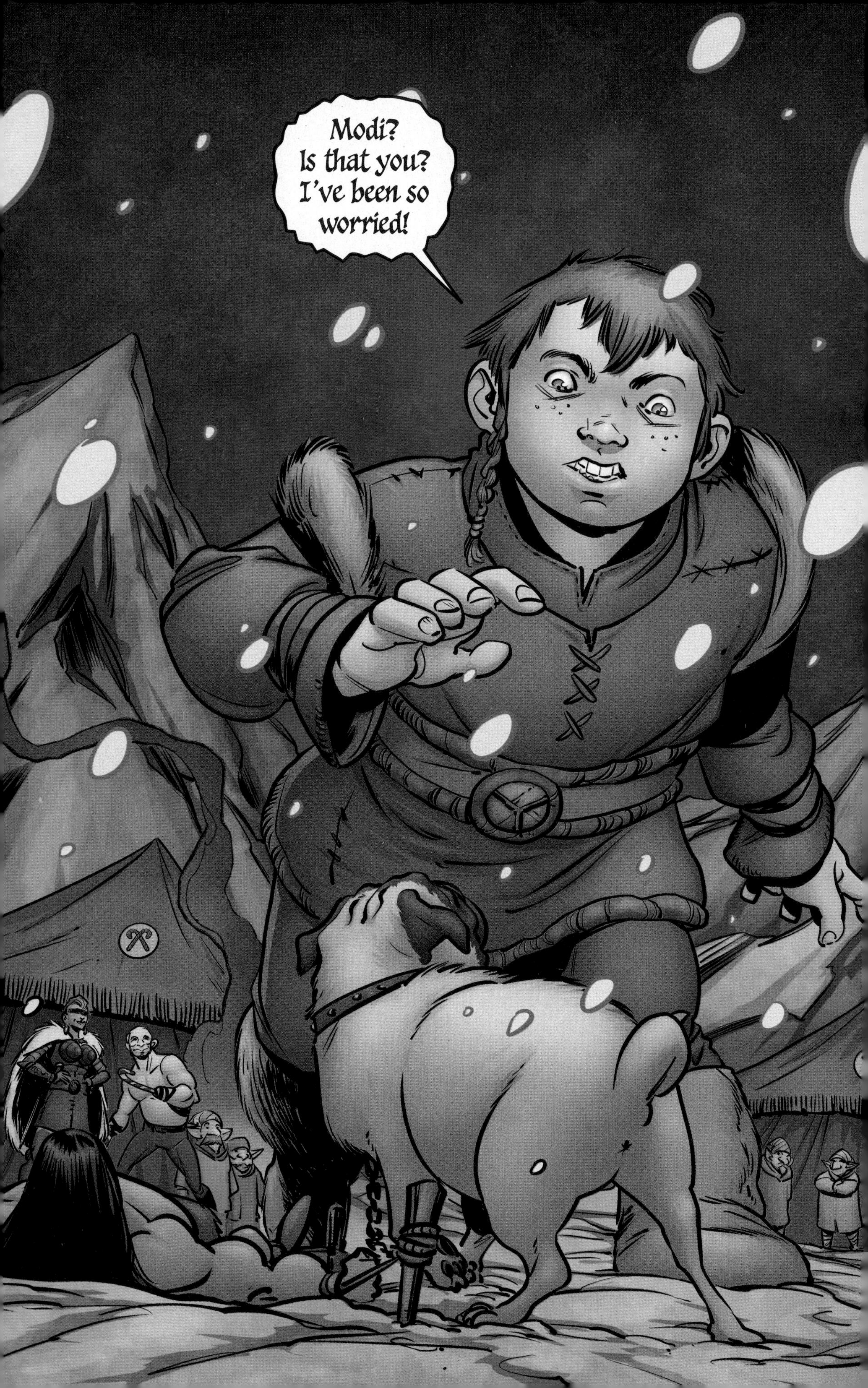
Modi? Is that you? I've been so worried!

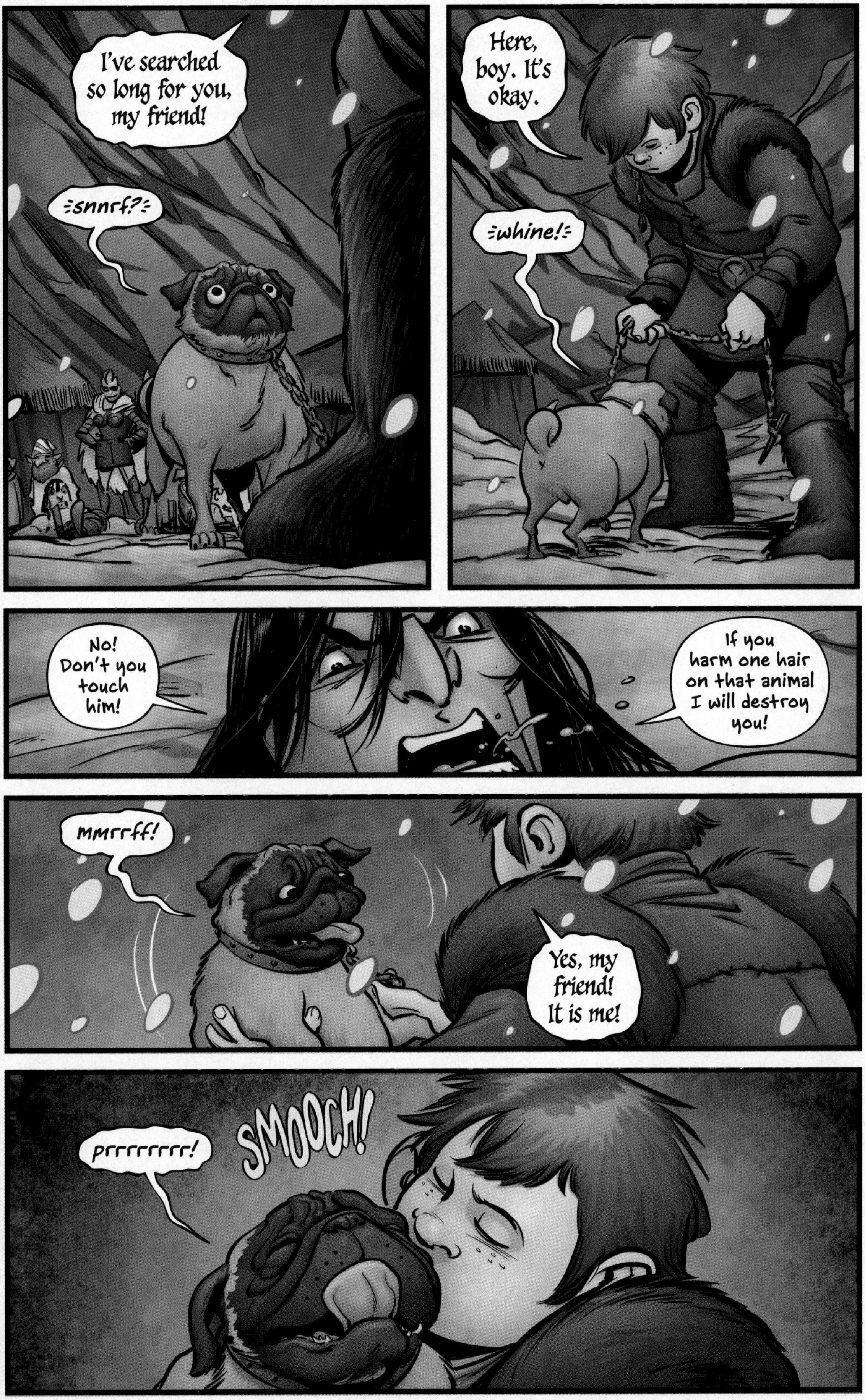
I've searched so long for you, my friend!
=snnrf?=
Here, boy. It's okay.
=whine!=
No! Don't you touch him!
If you harm one hair on that animal I will destroy you!
mmrrff!
Yes, my friend! It is me!
prrrrrrrr!
SMOOCH!

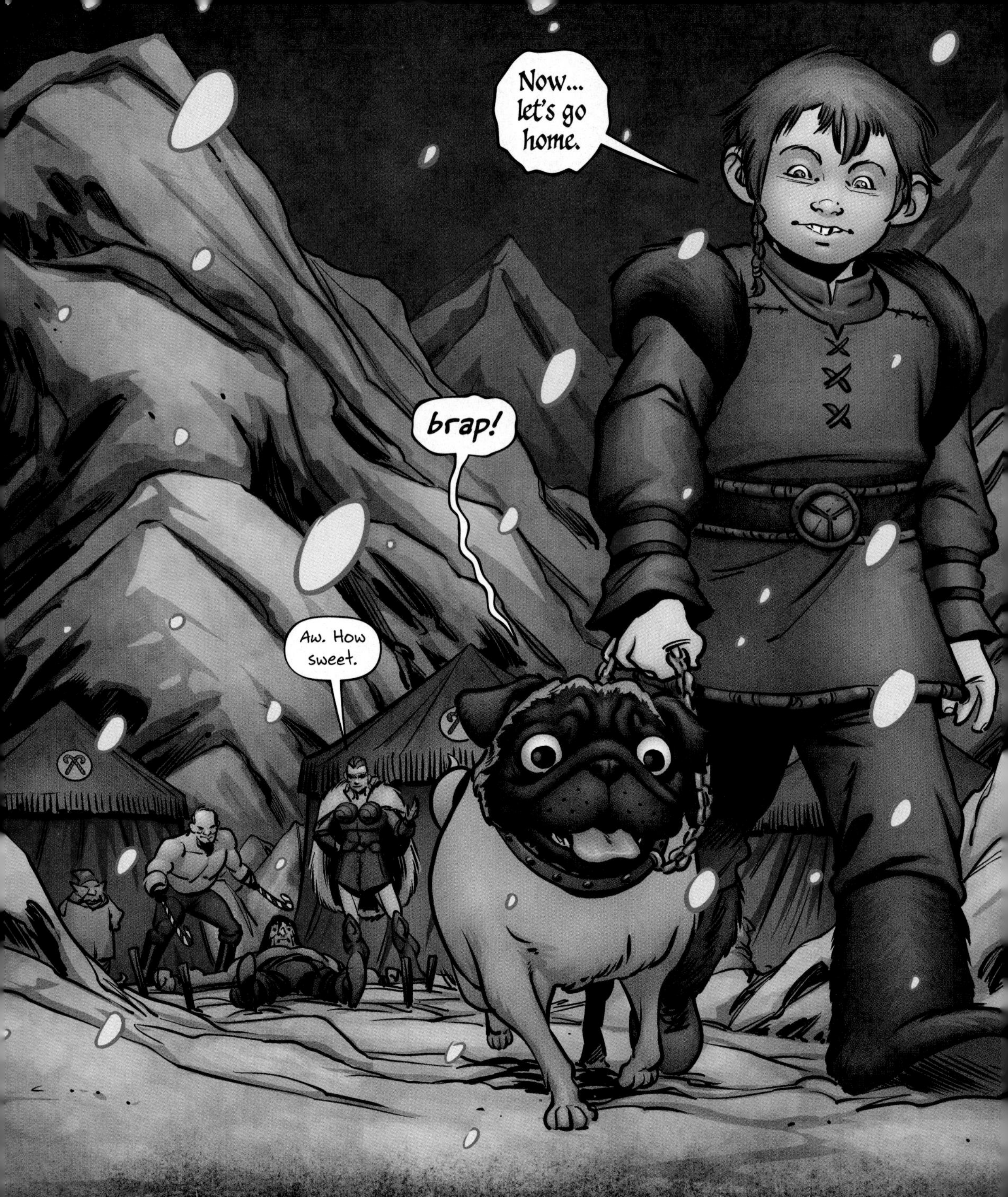
Now... let's go home.
brap!
Aw. How sweet.

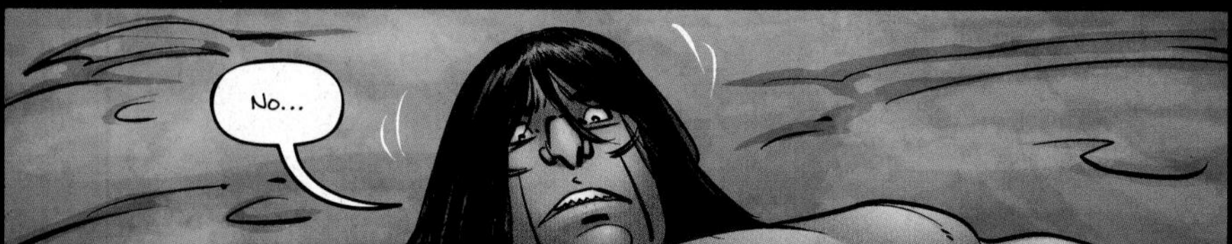
No...

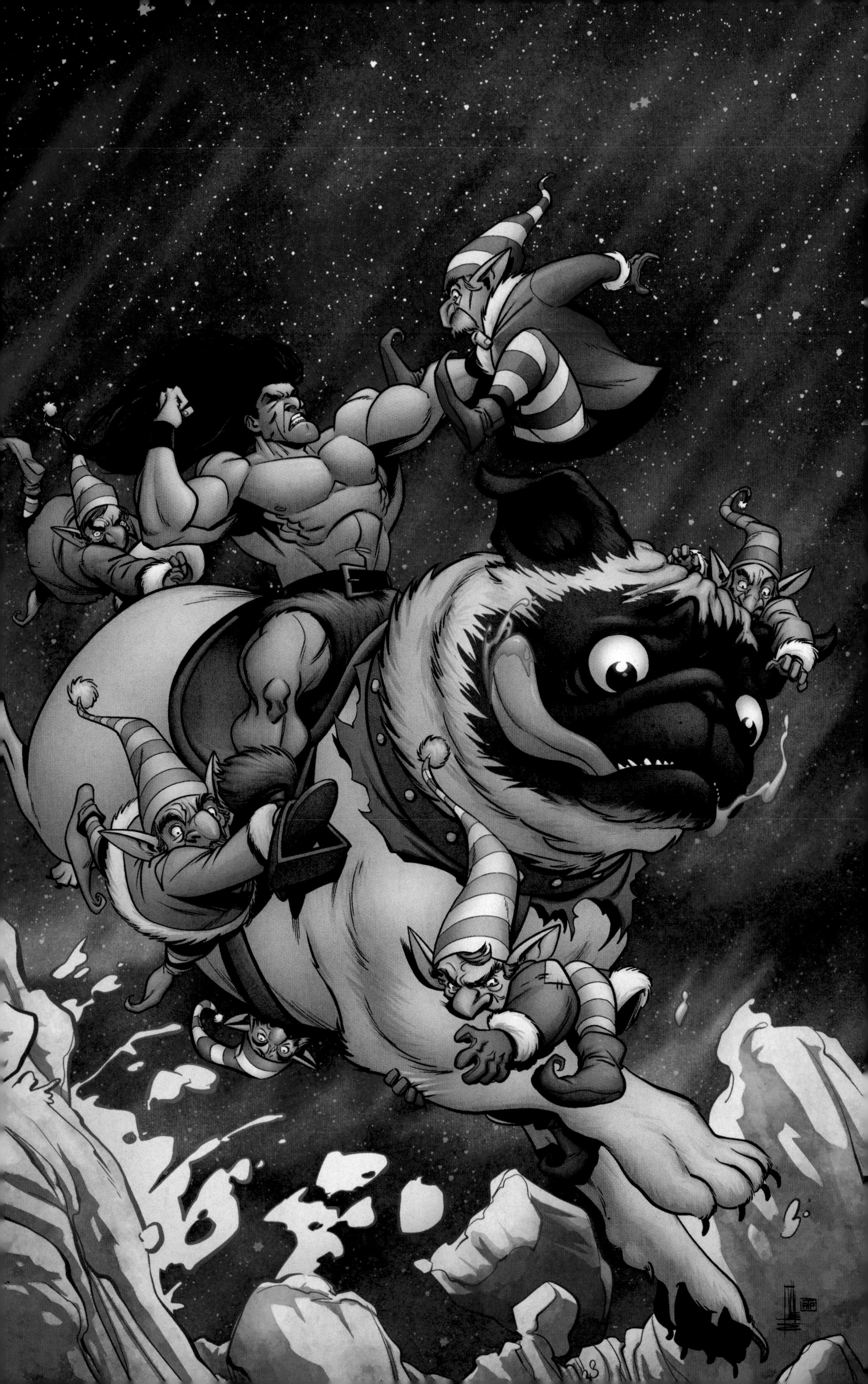

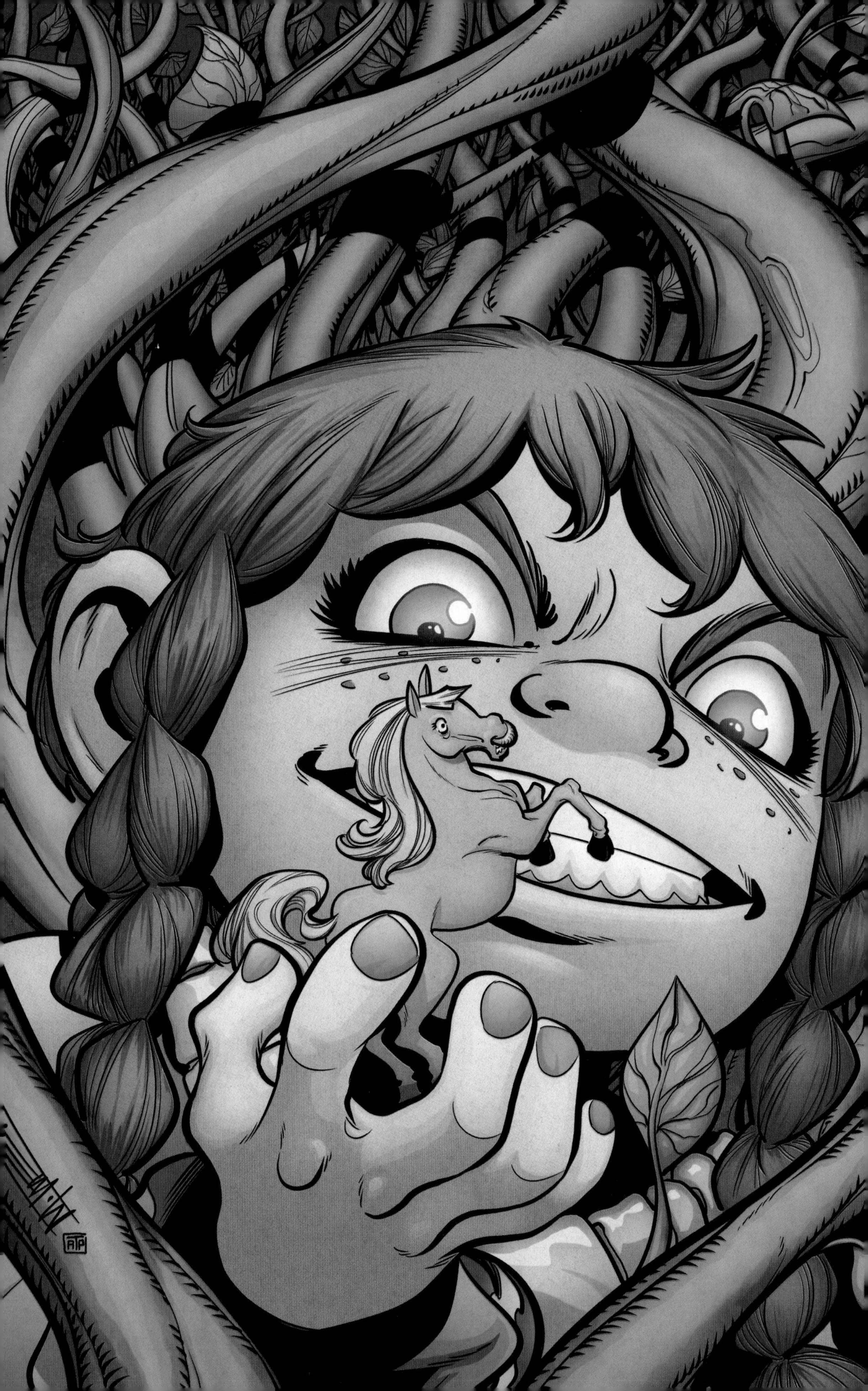

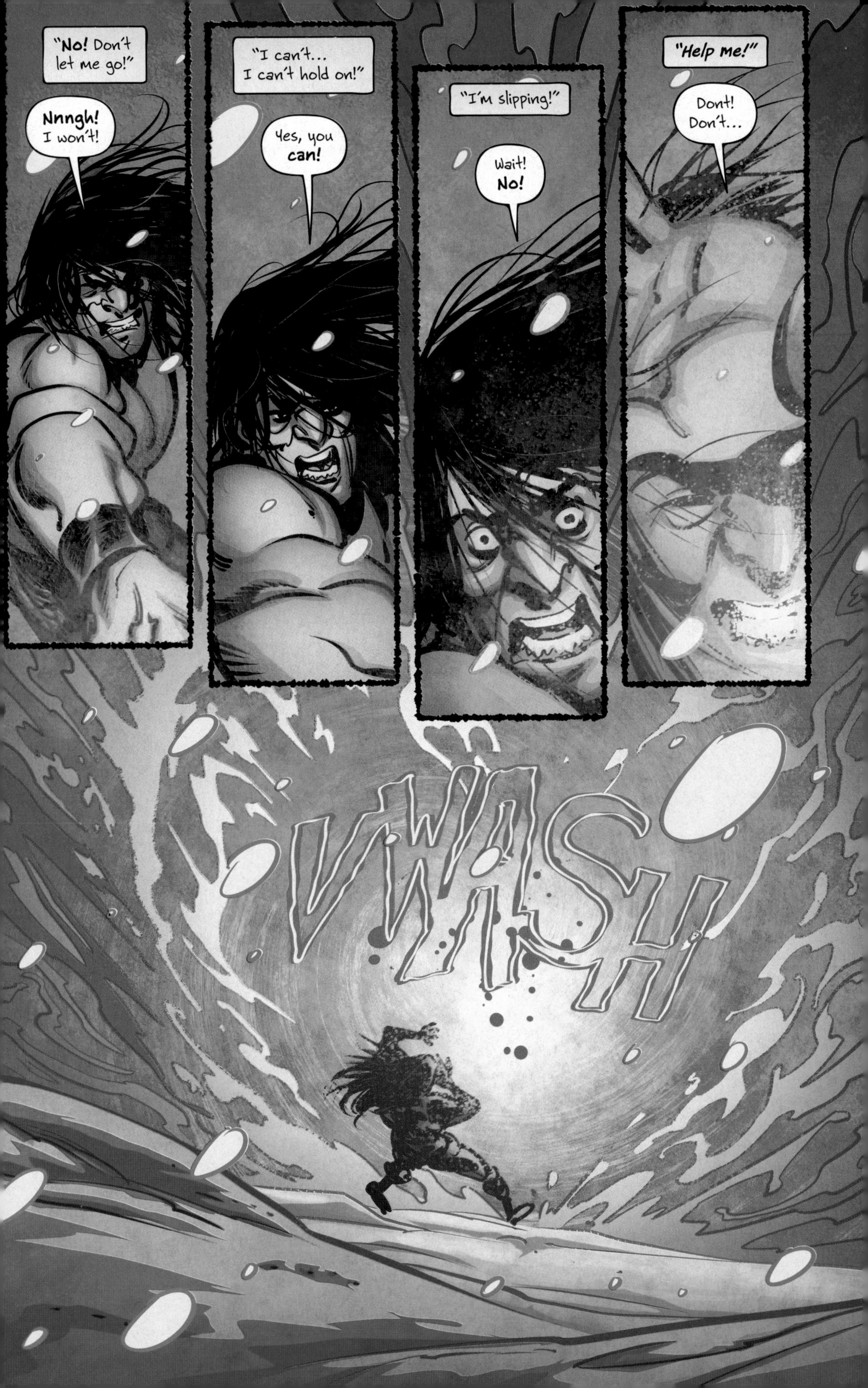
"No! Don't let me go!"
Nnngh! I won't!
"I can't... I can't hold on!"
Yes, you can!
"I'm slipping!"
Wait! No!
"Help me!"
Dont! Don't...
VWOOSH

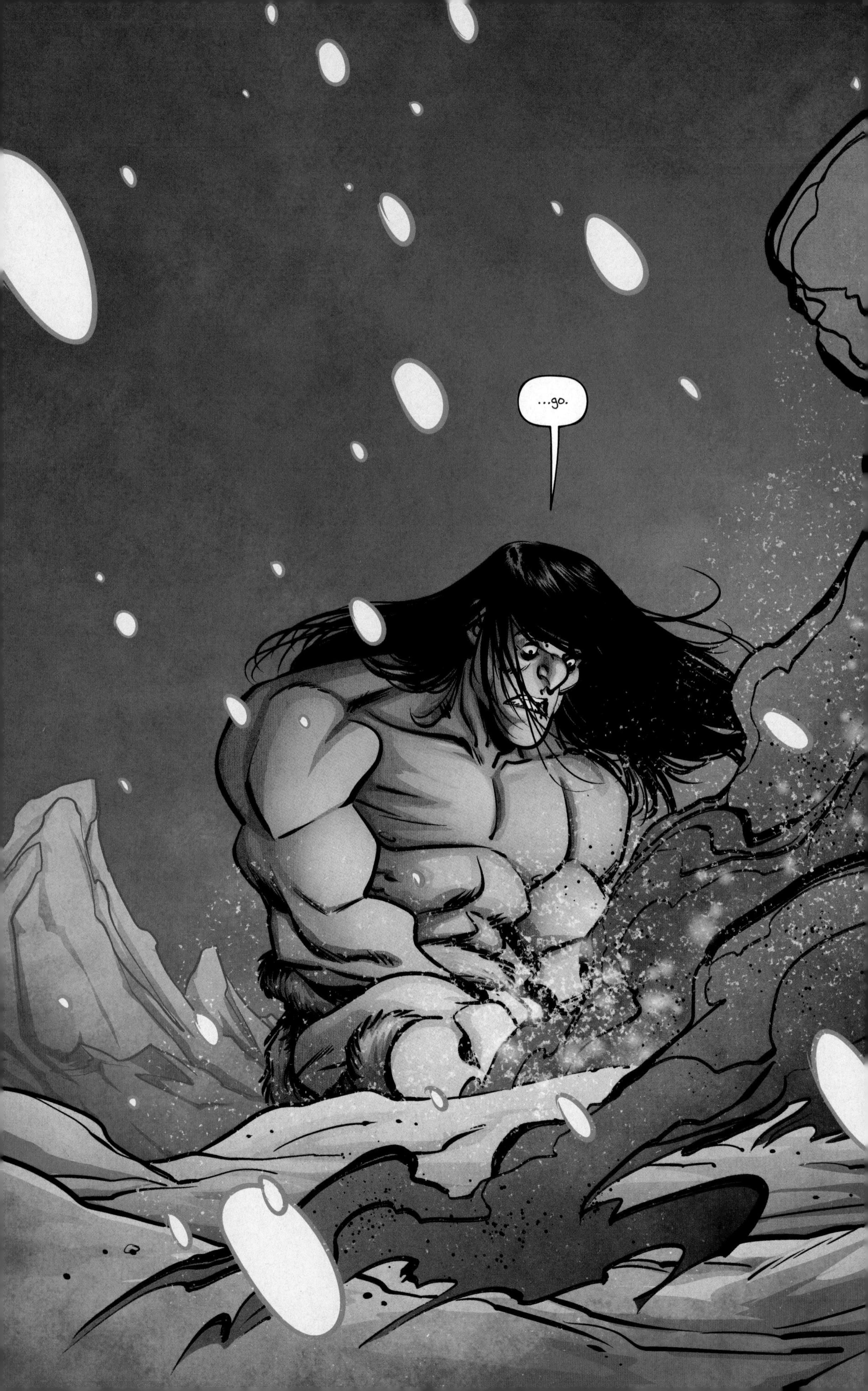
...go.

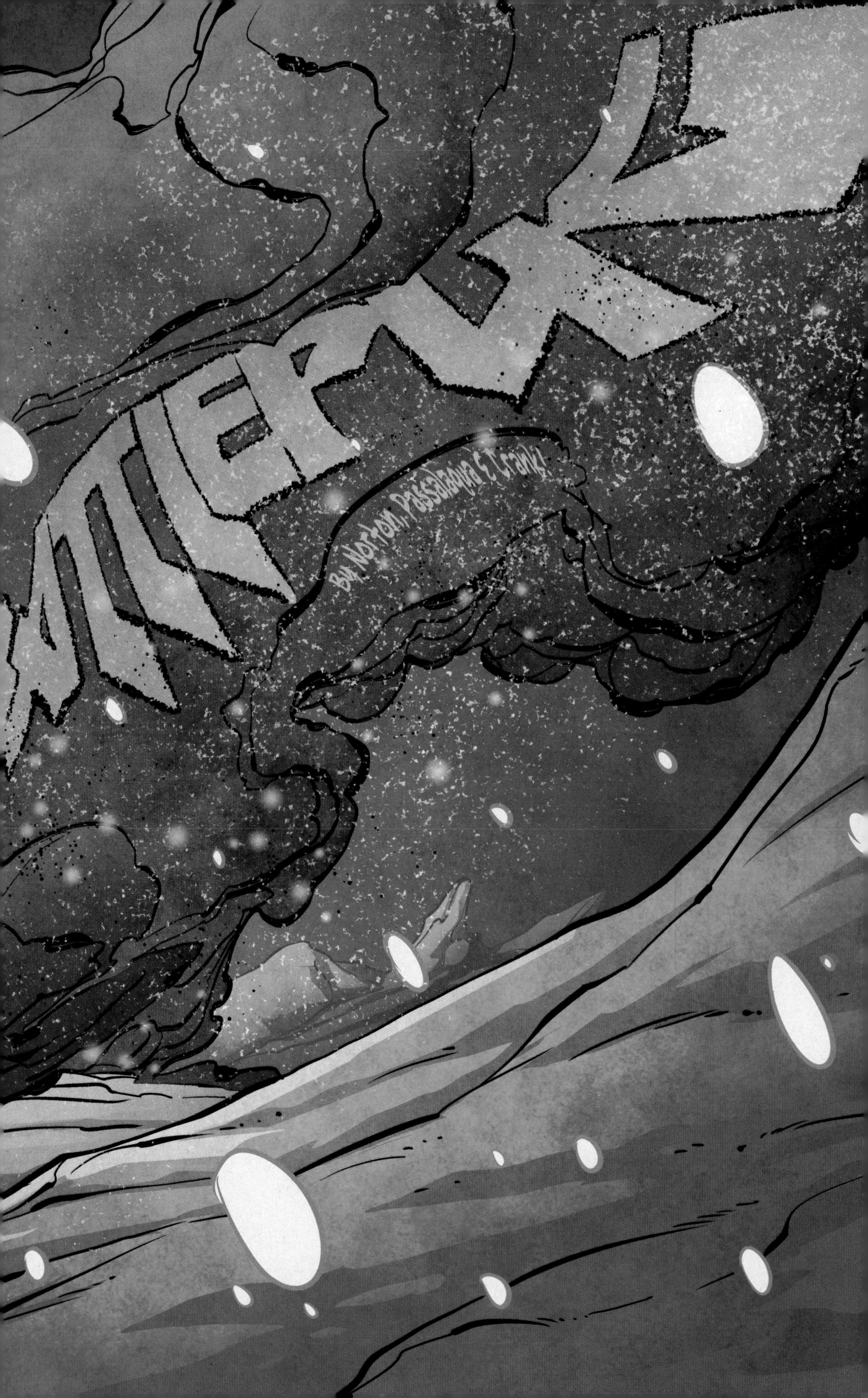
By Norton, Passalaqua & Crank!

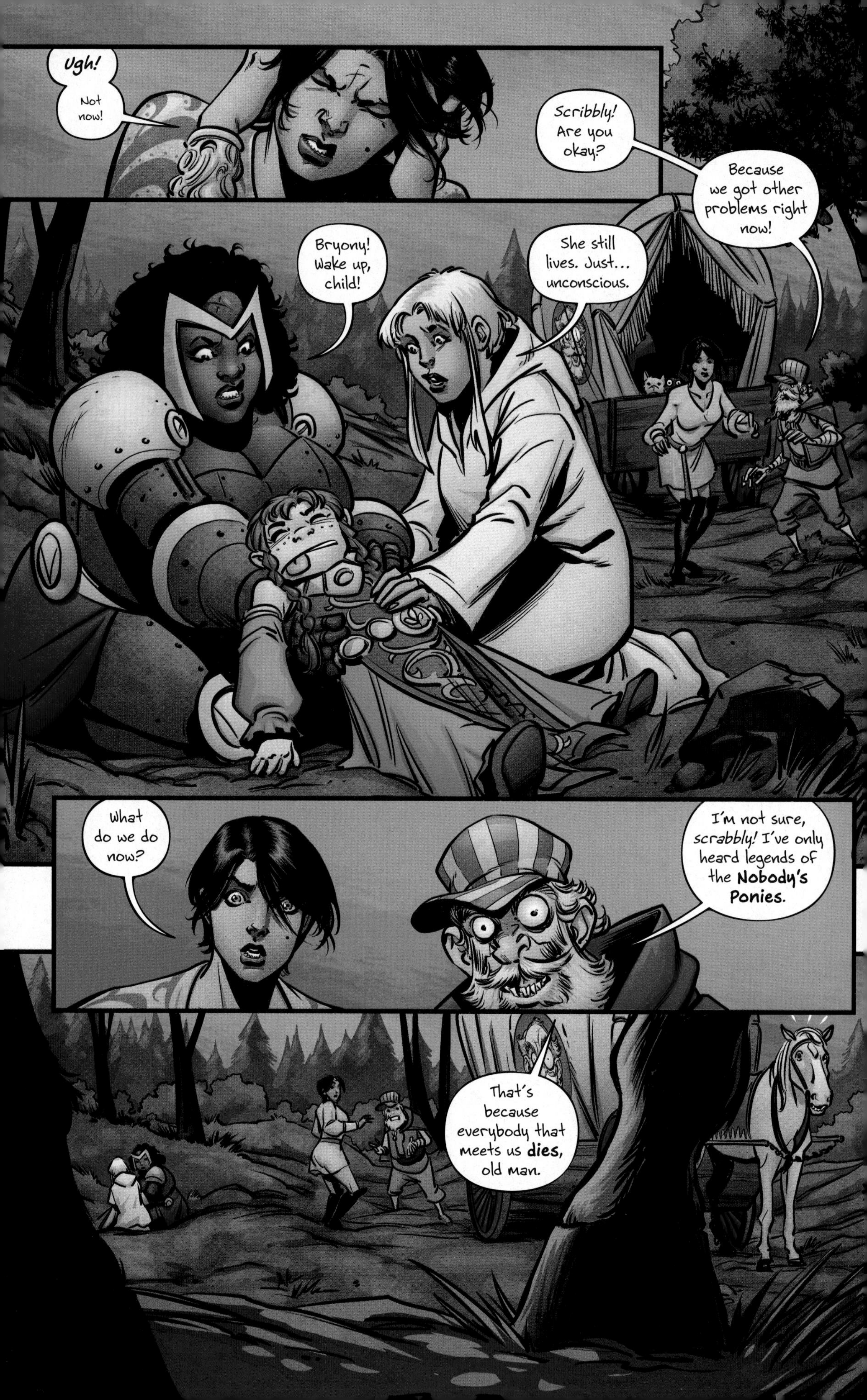
Ugh!
Not now!
Scribbly! Are you okay?
Because we got other problems right now!
Bryony! Wake up, child!
She still lives. Just... unconscious.
What do we do now?
I'm not sure, scrabbly! I've only heard legends of the **Nobody's Ponies**.
That's because everybody that meets us **dies**, old man.

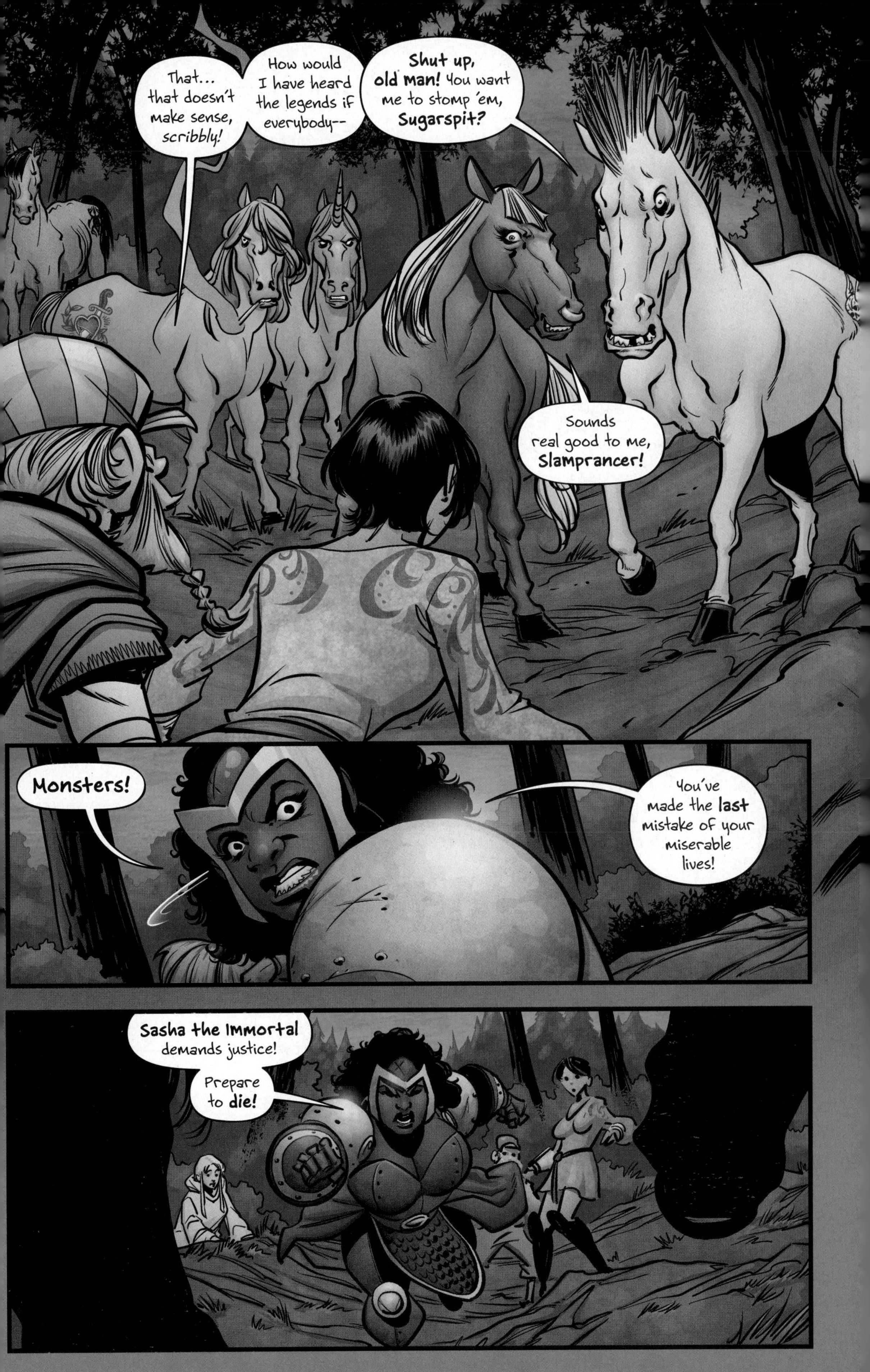
That... that doesn't make sense, scribbly!
How would I have heard the legends if everybody--
Shut up, old man! You want me to stomp 'em, Sugarspit?
Sounds real good to me, Slamprancer!
Monsters!
You've made the last mistake of your miserable lives!
Sasha the Immortal demands justice!
Prepare to die!

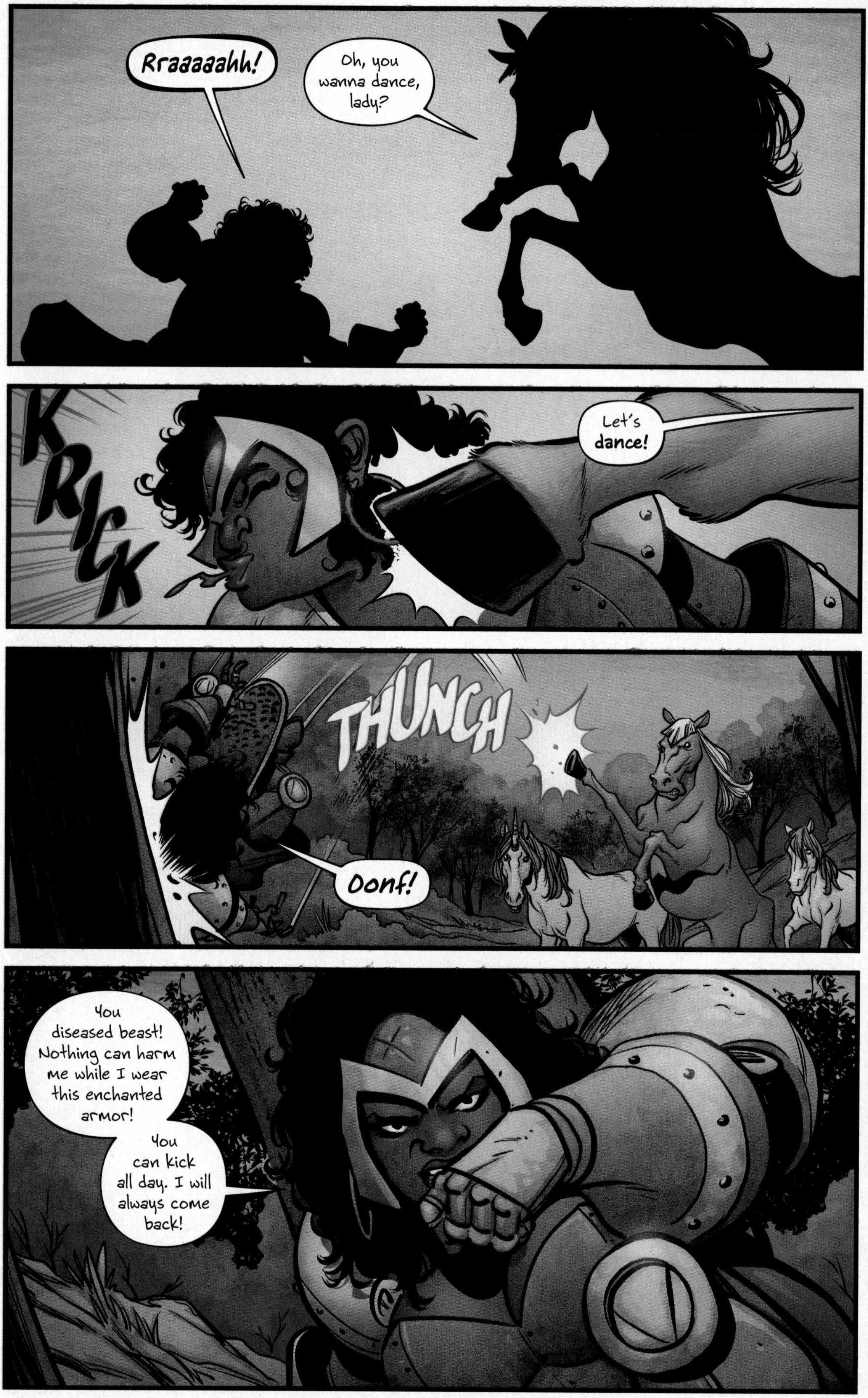
Rraaaaahh!
Oh, you wanna dance, lady?
KRICK
Let's dance!
THUNCH
Oonf!
You diseased beast! Nothing can harm me while I wear this enchanted armor!
You can kick all day. I will always come back!

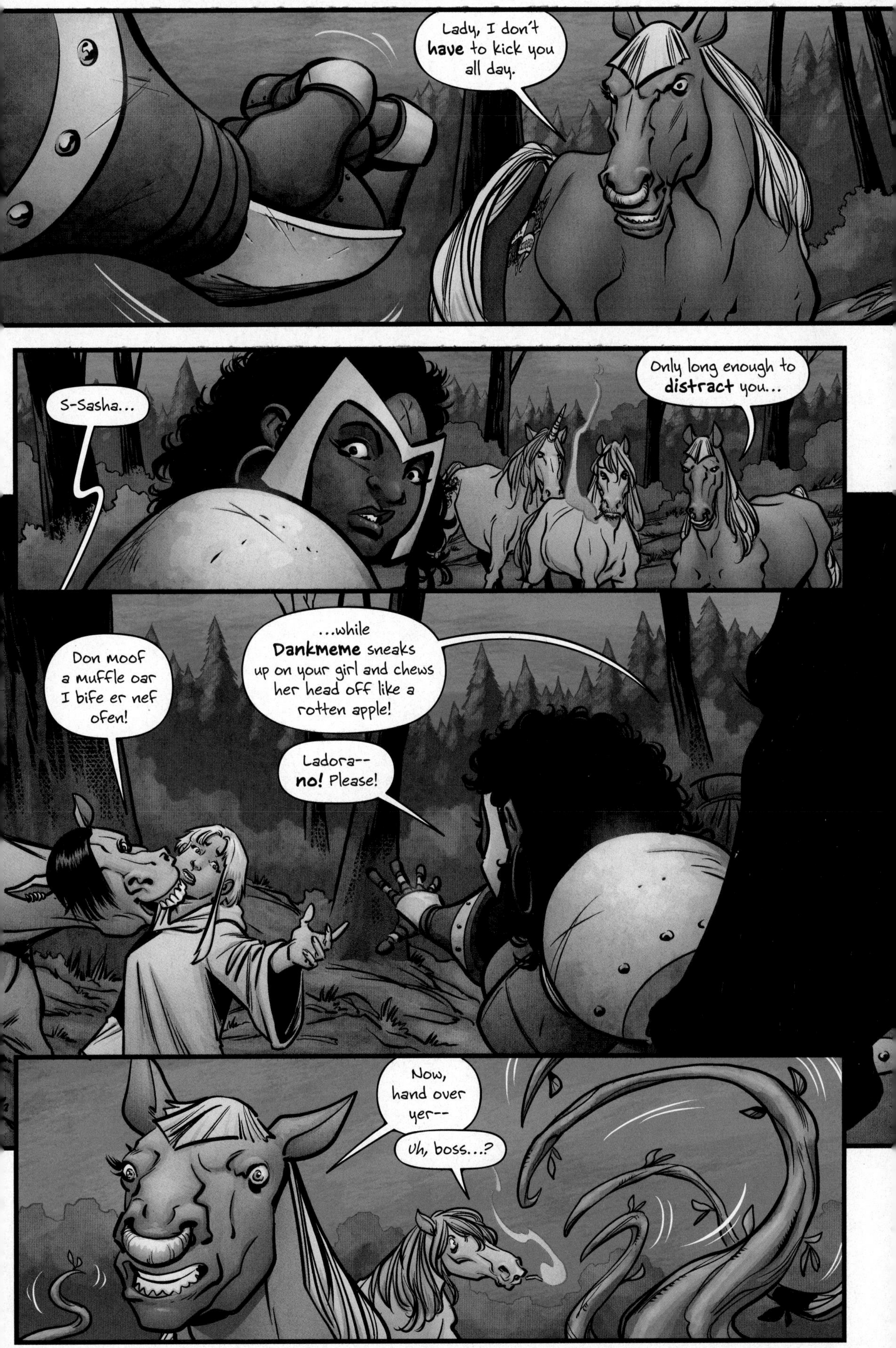

Lady, I don't **have** to kick you all day.
S-Sasha...
Only long enough to **distract** you...
...while **Dankmeme** sneaks up on your girl and chews her head off like a rotten apple!
Don moof a muffle oar I bife er nef ofen!
Ladora-- **no!** Please!
Now, hand over yer--
Uh, boss...?

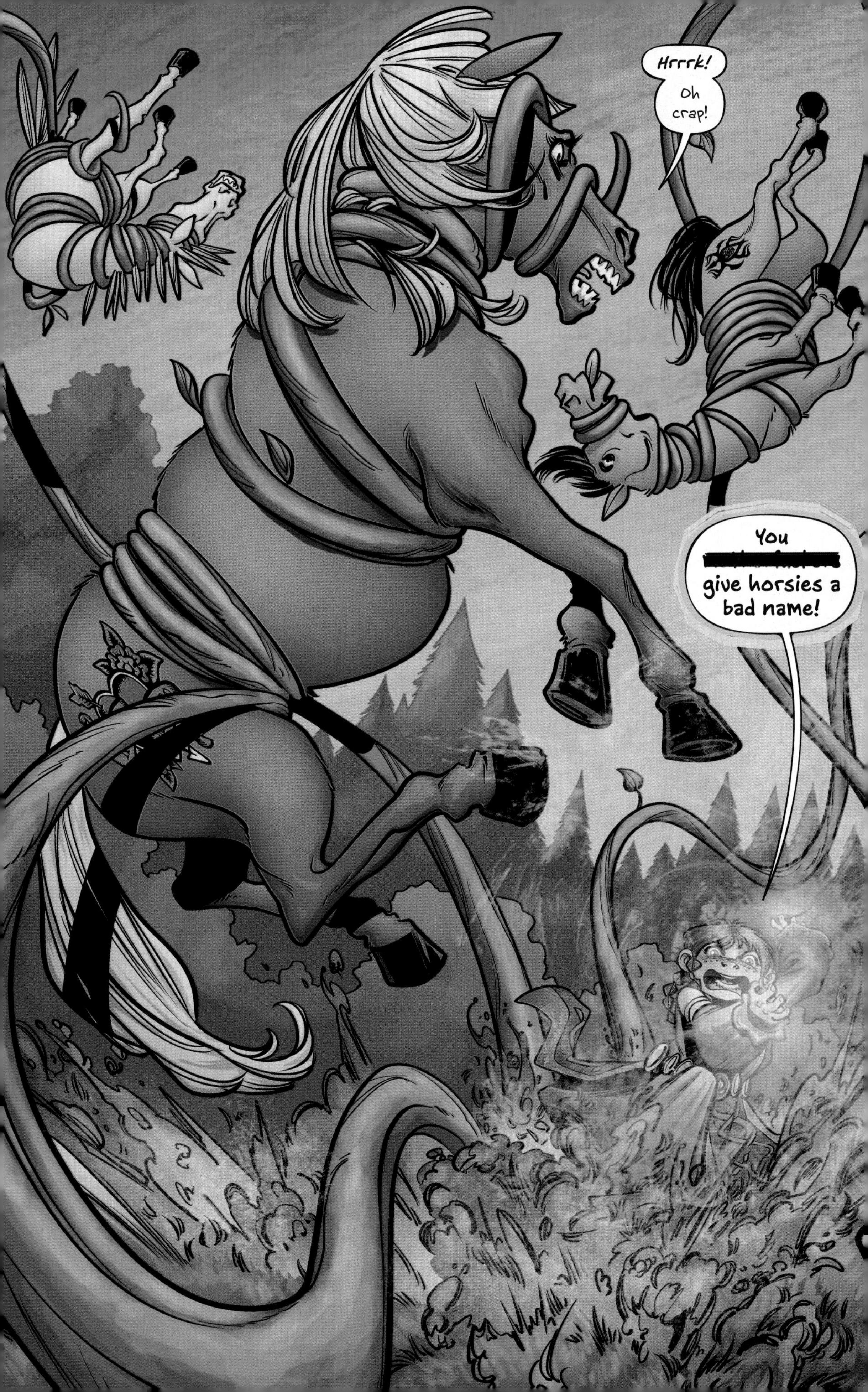
Hrrrk!
Oh crap!
You [redacted] give horsies a bad name!

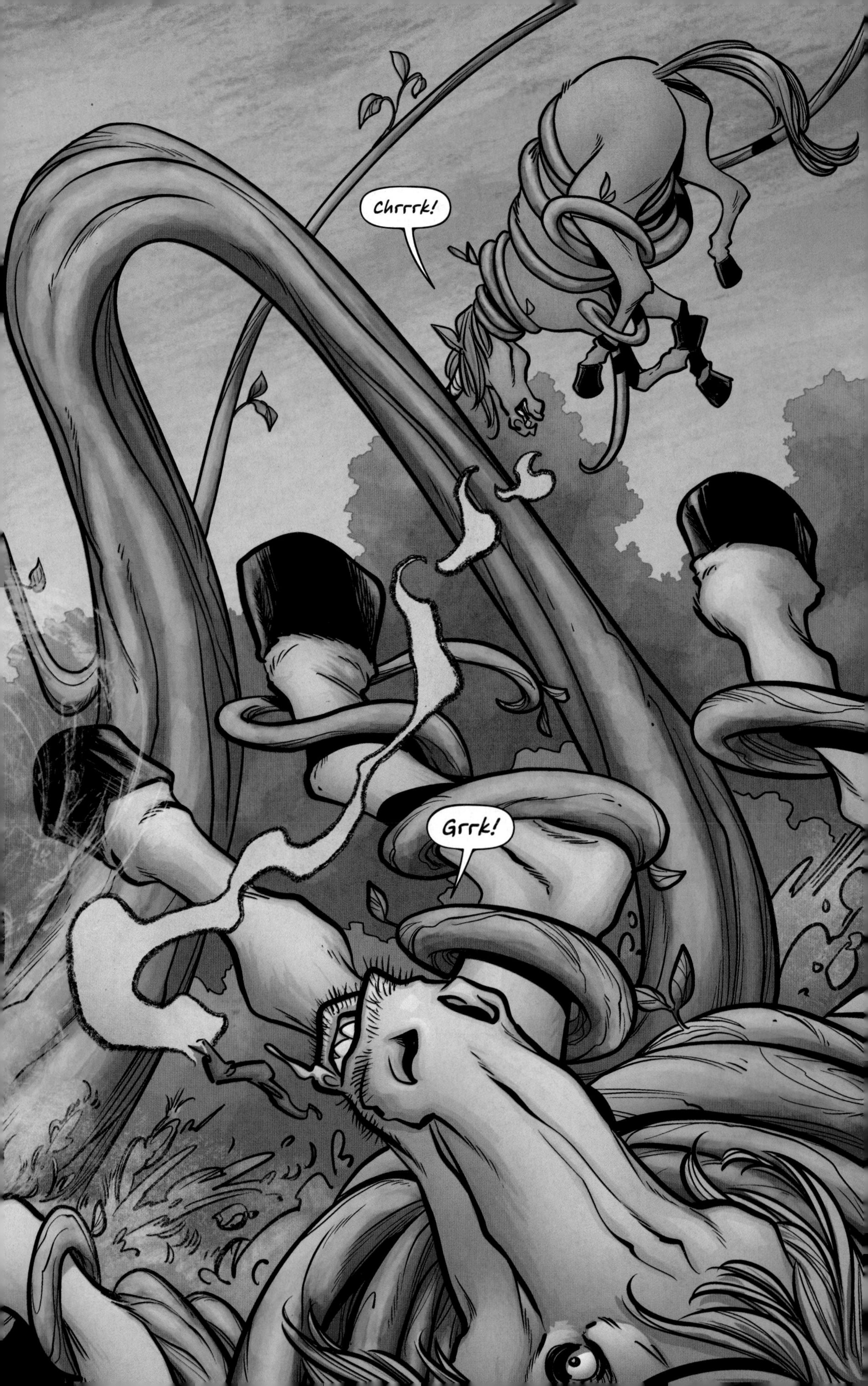
Chrrrk!
Grrk!

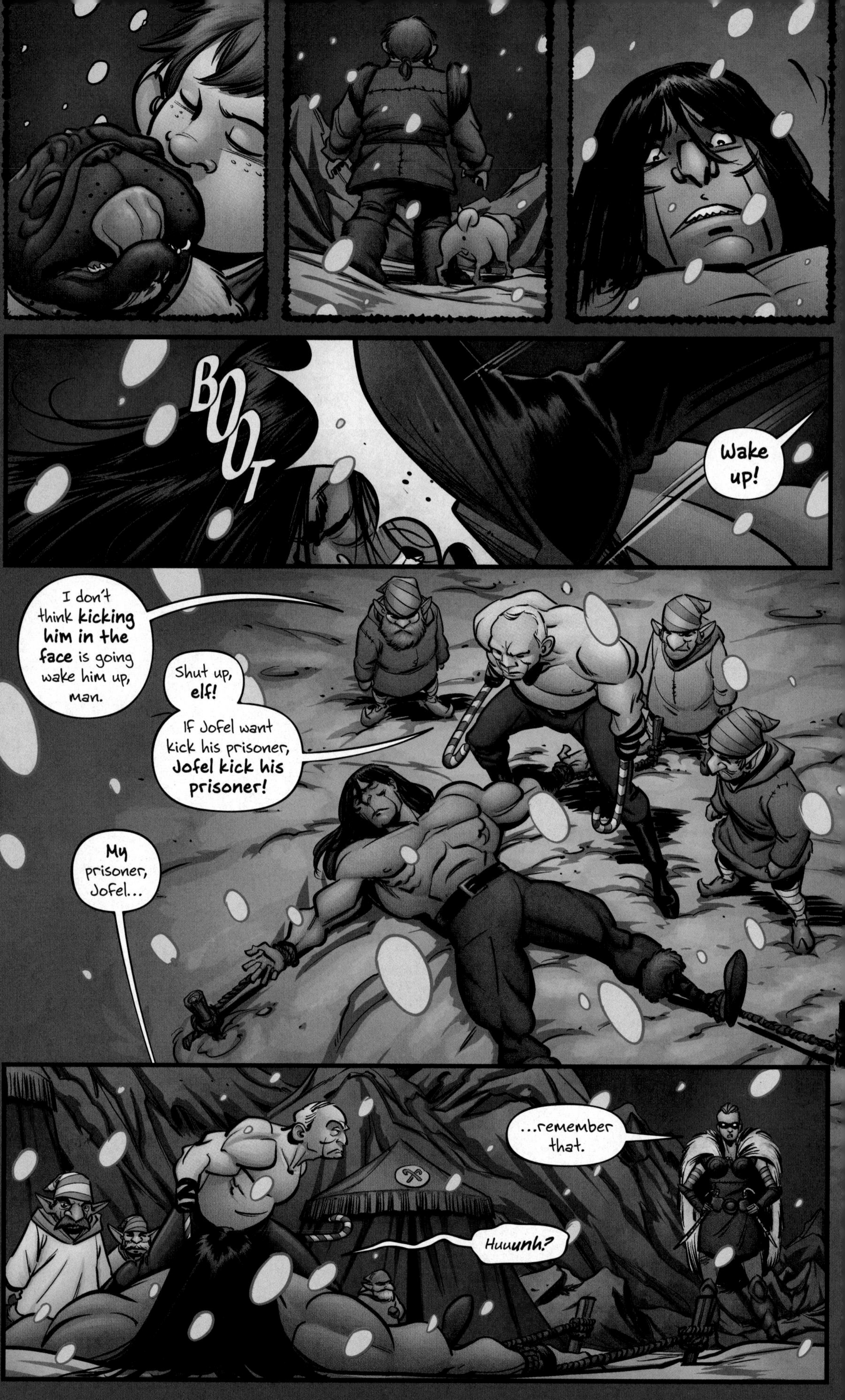
BOOT
Wake up!
I don't think kicking him in the face is going wake him up, man.
Shut up, elf!
If Jofel want kick his prisoner, Jofel kick his prisoner!
My prisoner, Jofel...
...remember that.
Huuunh?

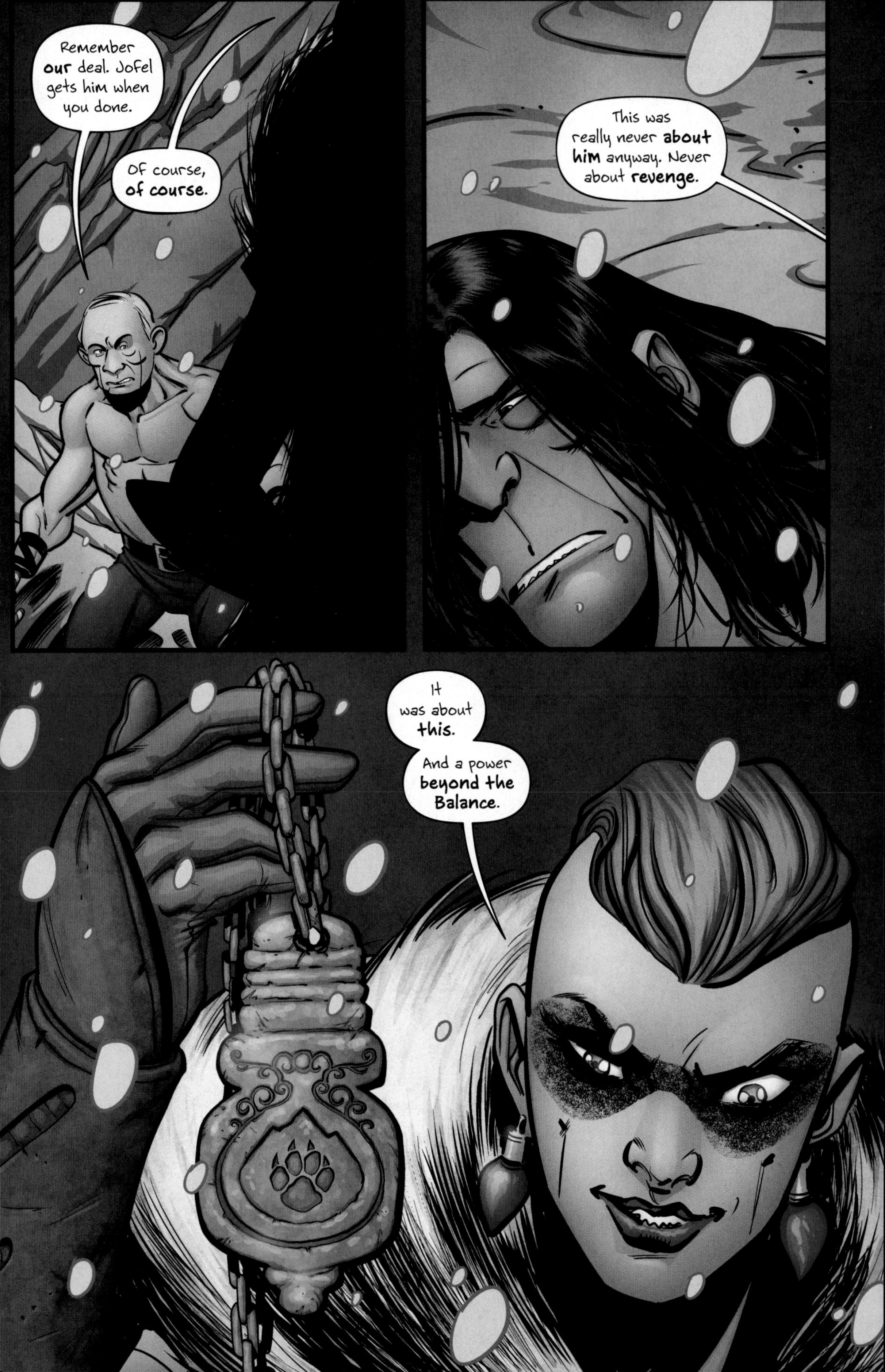
Remember our deal. Jofel gets him when you done.
Of course, of course.
This was really never about him anyway. Never about revenge.
It was about this.
And a power beyond the Balance.

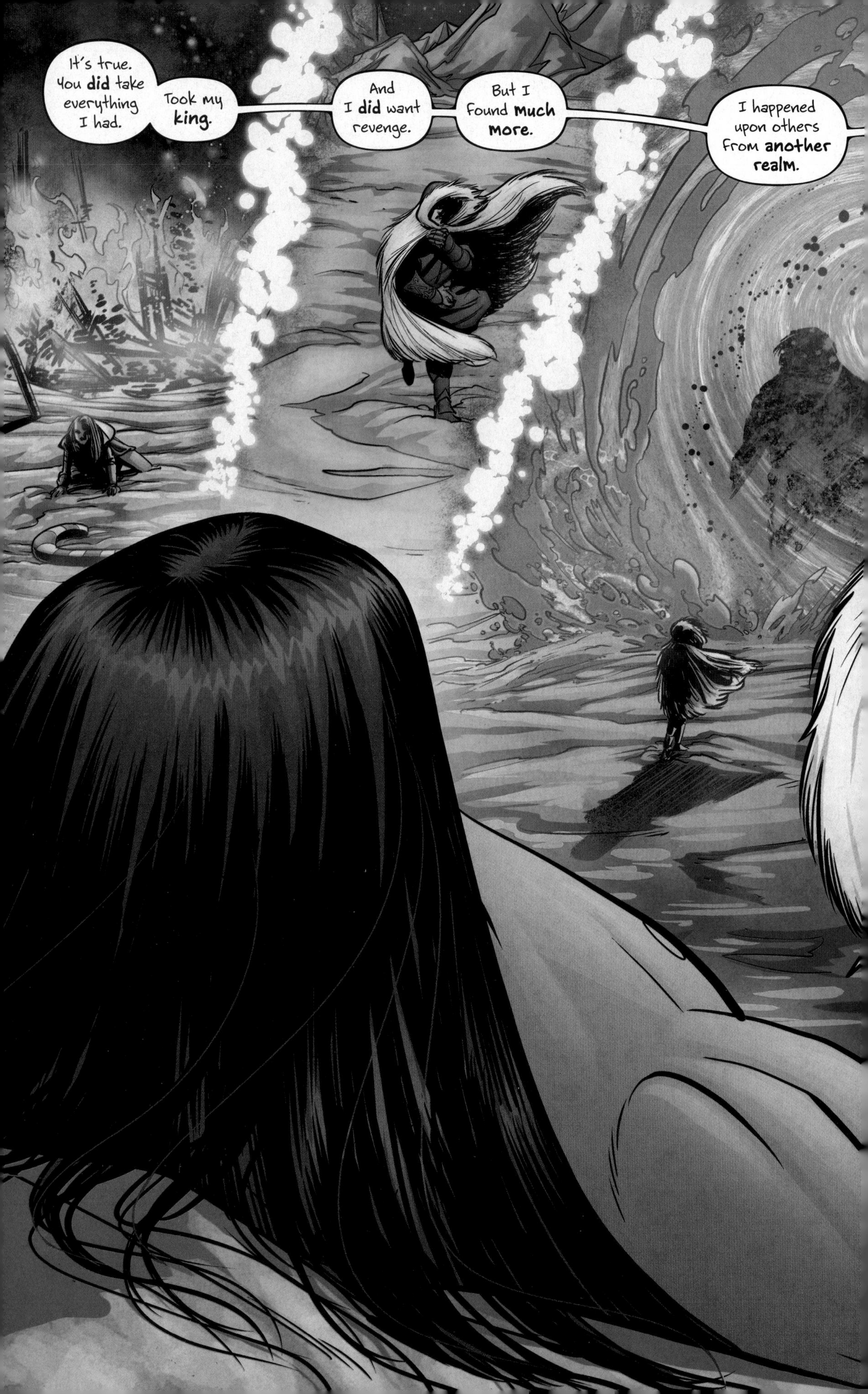
It's true. You **did** take everything I had.
Took my **king**.
And I **did** want revenge.
But I found **much more**.
I happened upon others from **another realm**.

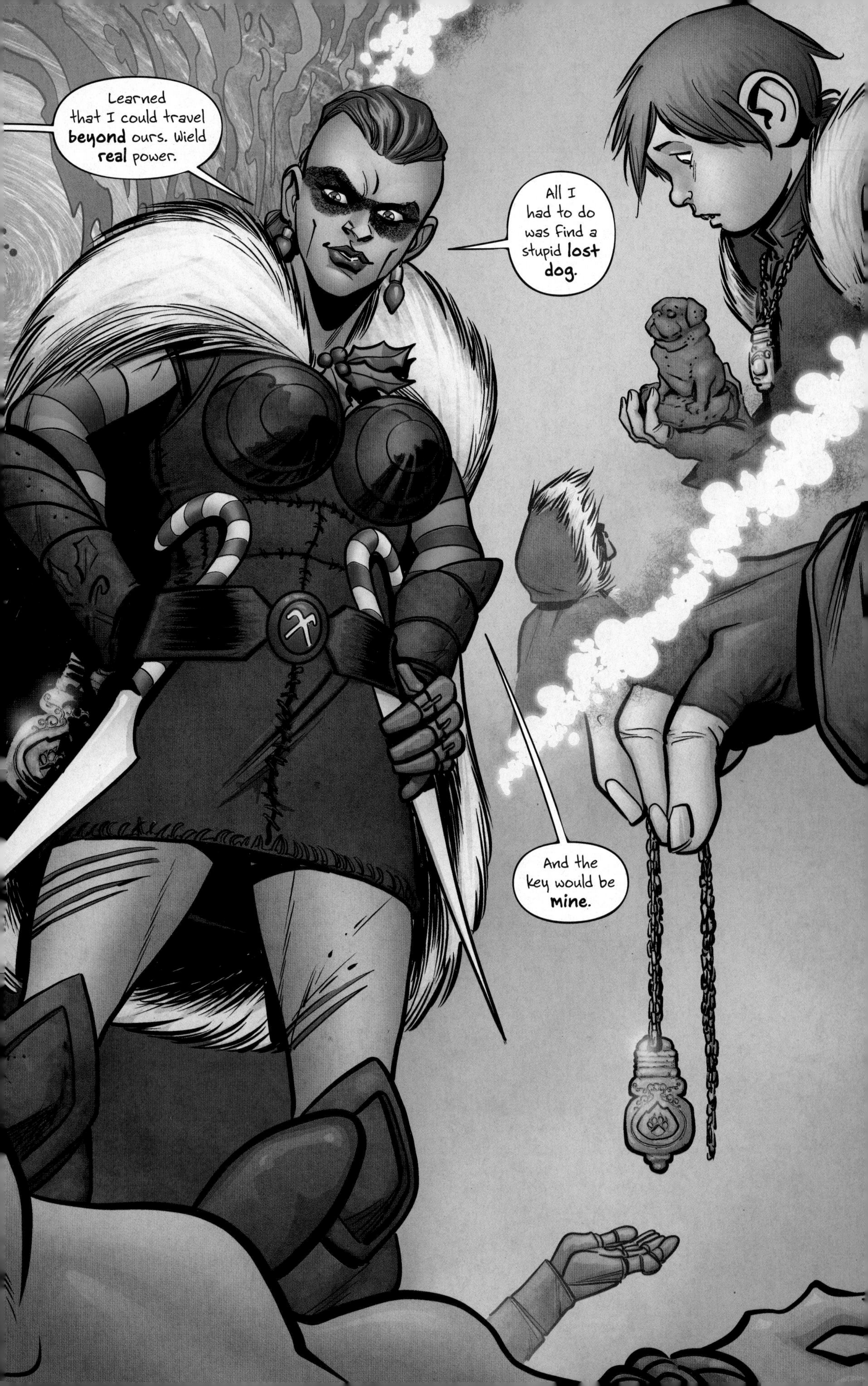
Learned that I could travel **beyond** ours. Wield **real** power.
All I had to do was find a stupid **lost dog**.
And the key would be **mine**.

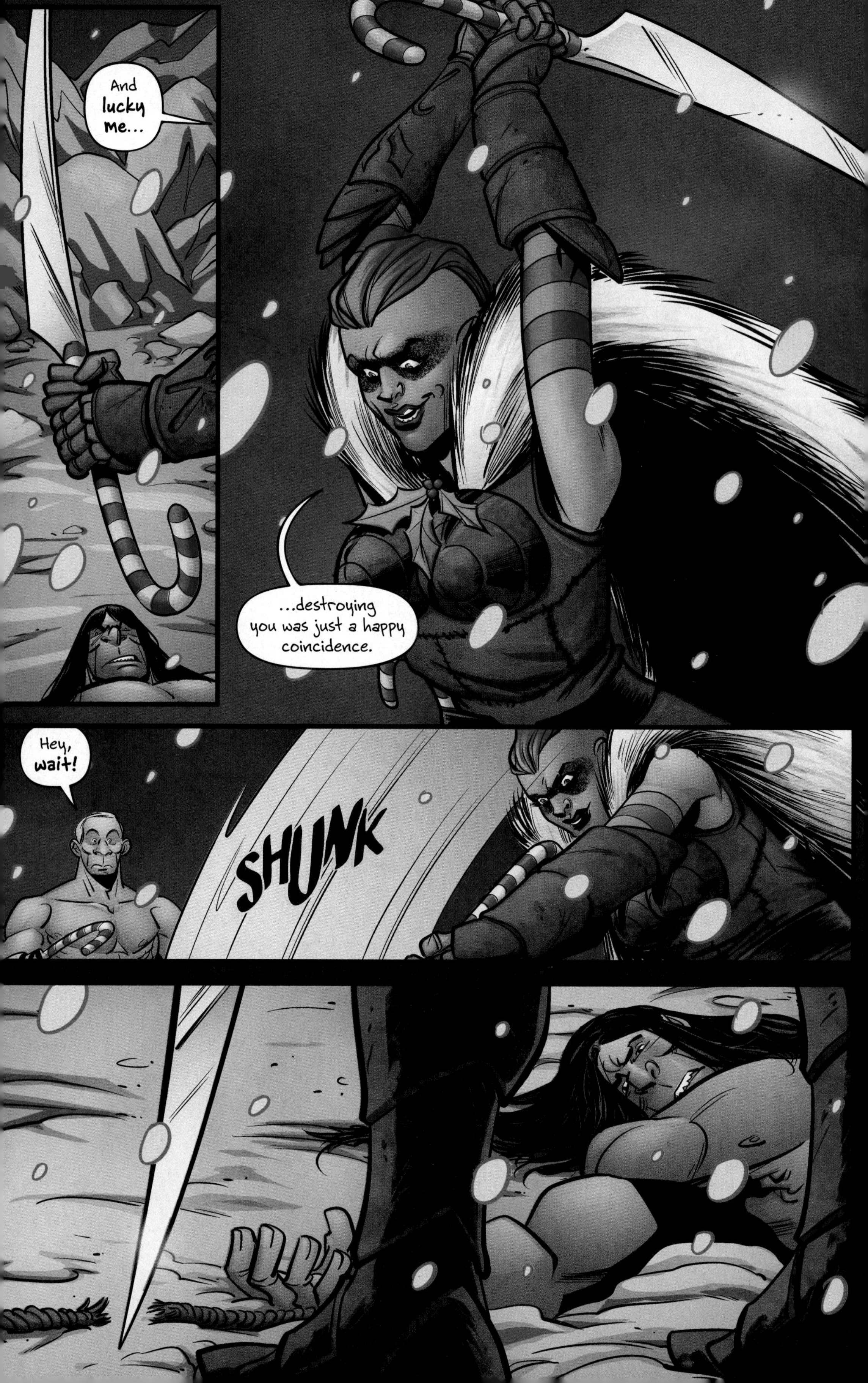
And lucky me...
...destroying you was just a happy coincidence.
Hey, wait!
SHUNK

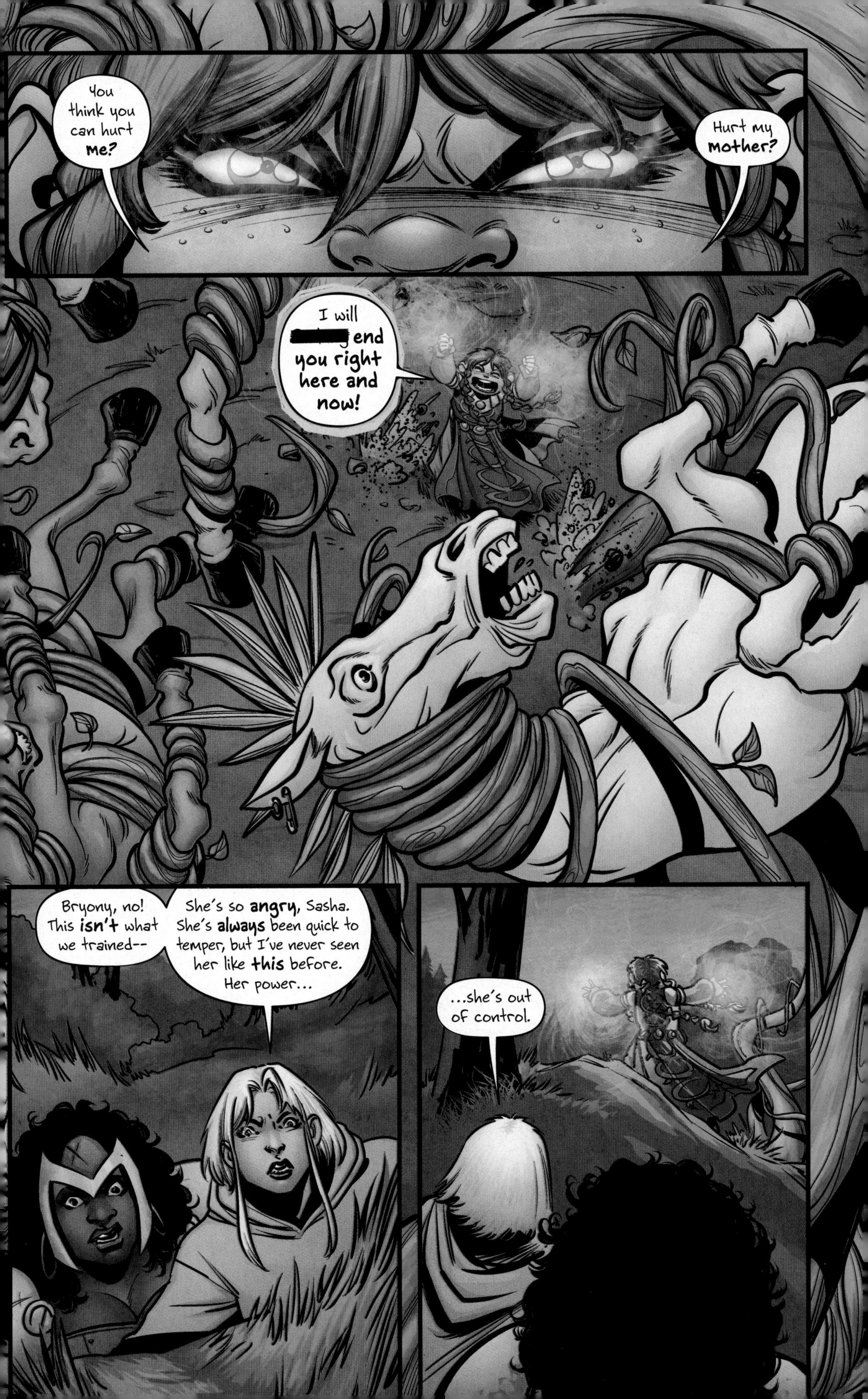
You think you can hurt **me?**
Hurt my **mother?**
I will [redacted] end you right here and now!
Bryony, no! This **isn't** what we trained--
She's so **angry,** Sasha. She's **always** been quick to temper, but I've never seen her like **this** before. Her power...
...she's out of control.

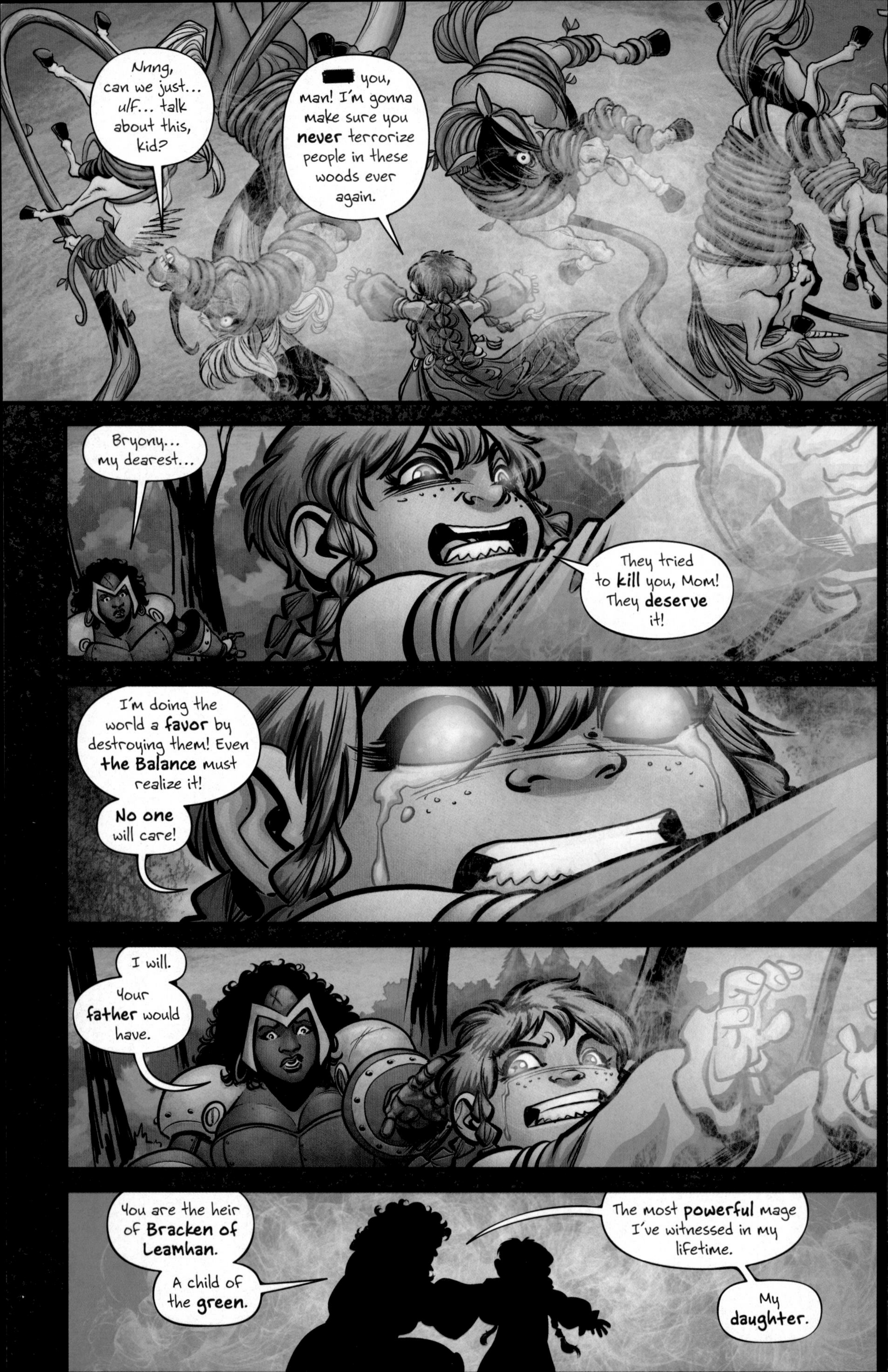
Nnng, can we just... ulf... talk about this, kid?
[redacted] you, man! I'm gonna make sure you **never** terrorize people in these woods ever again.
Bryony... my dearest...
They tried to **kill** you, Mom! They **deserve** it!
I'm doing the world a **favor** by destroying them! Even **the Balance** must realize it!
No one will care!
I will.
Your **father** would have.
You are the heir of **Bracken of Leamhan**.
A child of the **green**.
The most **powerful** mage I've witnessed in my lifetime.
My **daughter**.

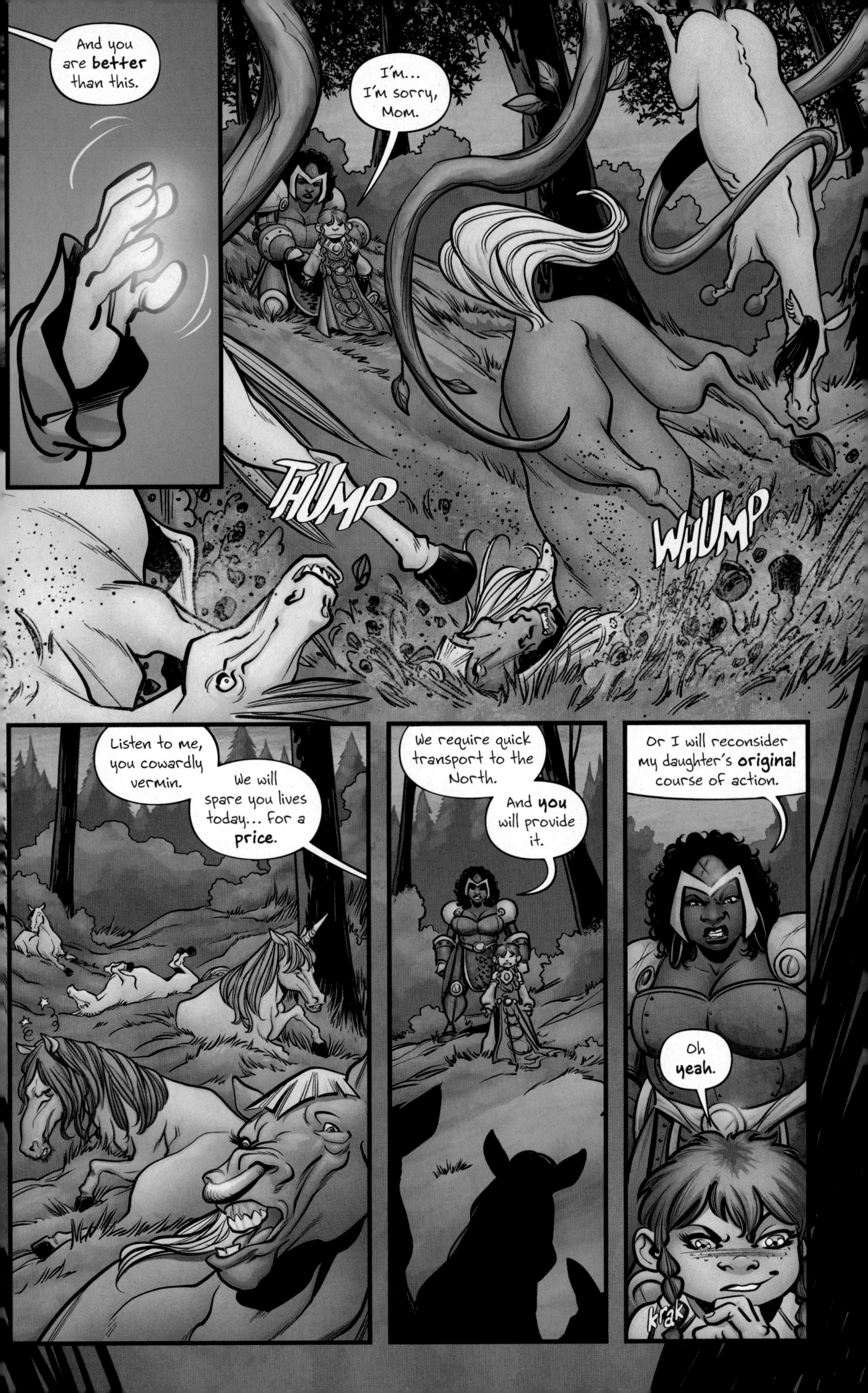

And you are **better** than this.
I'm... I'm sorry, Mom.
THUMP
WHUMP
Listen to me, you cowardly vermin.
We will spare you lives today... for a **price**.
We require quick transport to the North.
And **you** will provide it.
Or I will reconsider my daughter's **original** course of action.
Oh **yeah**.
krak

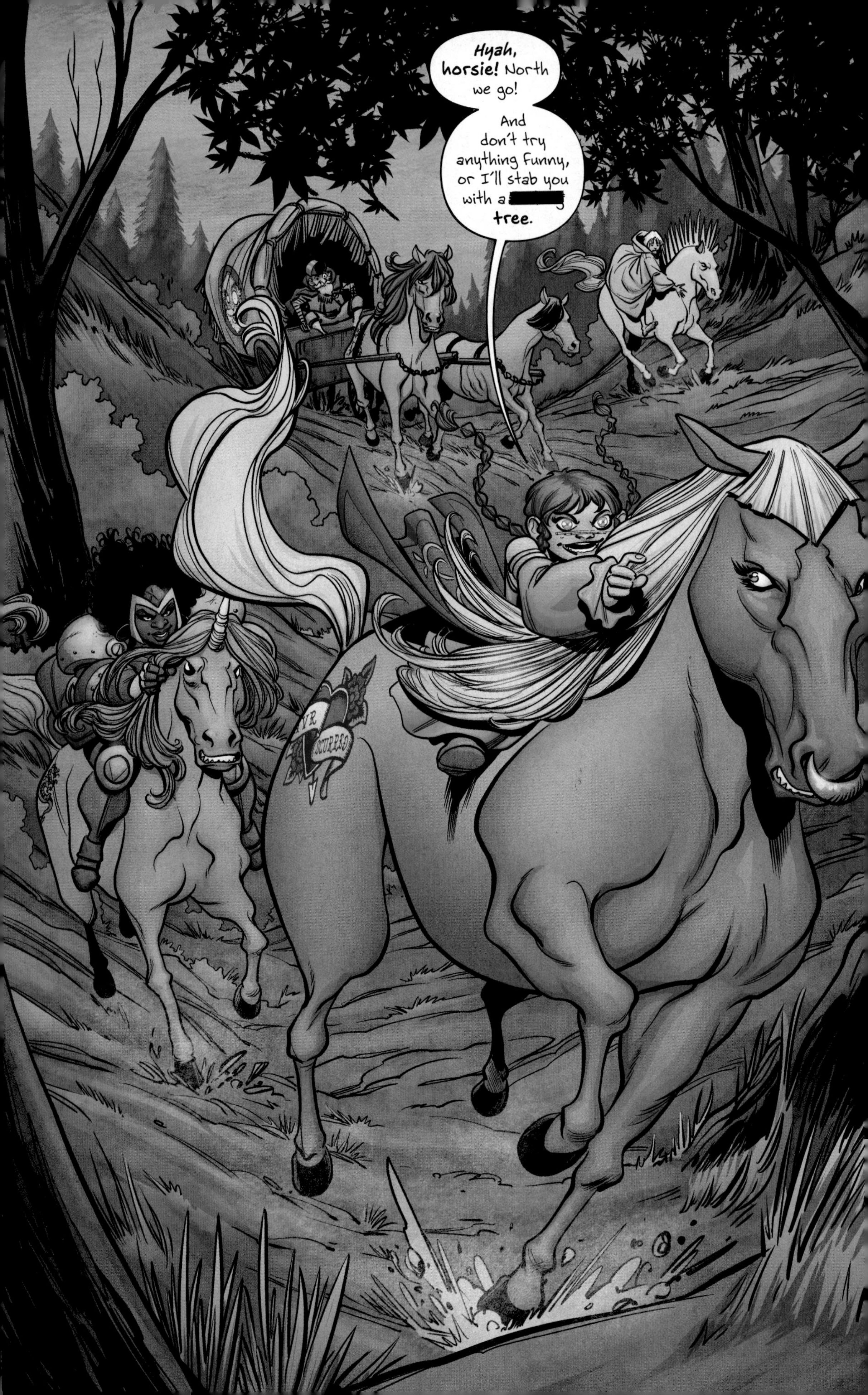
Hyah, horsie! North we go!
And don't try anything funny, or I'll stab you with a [redacted] tree.

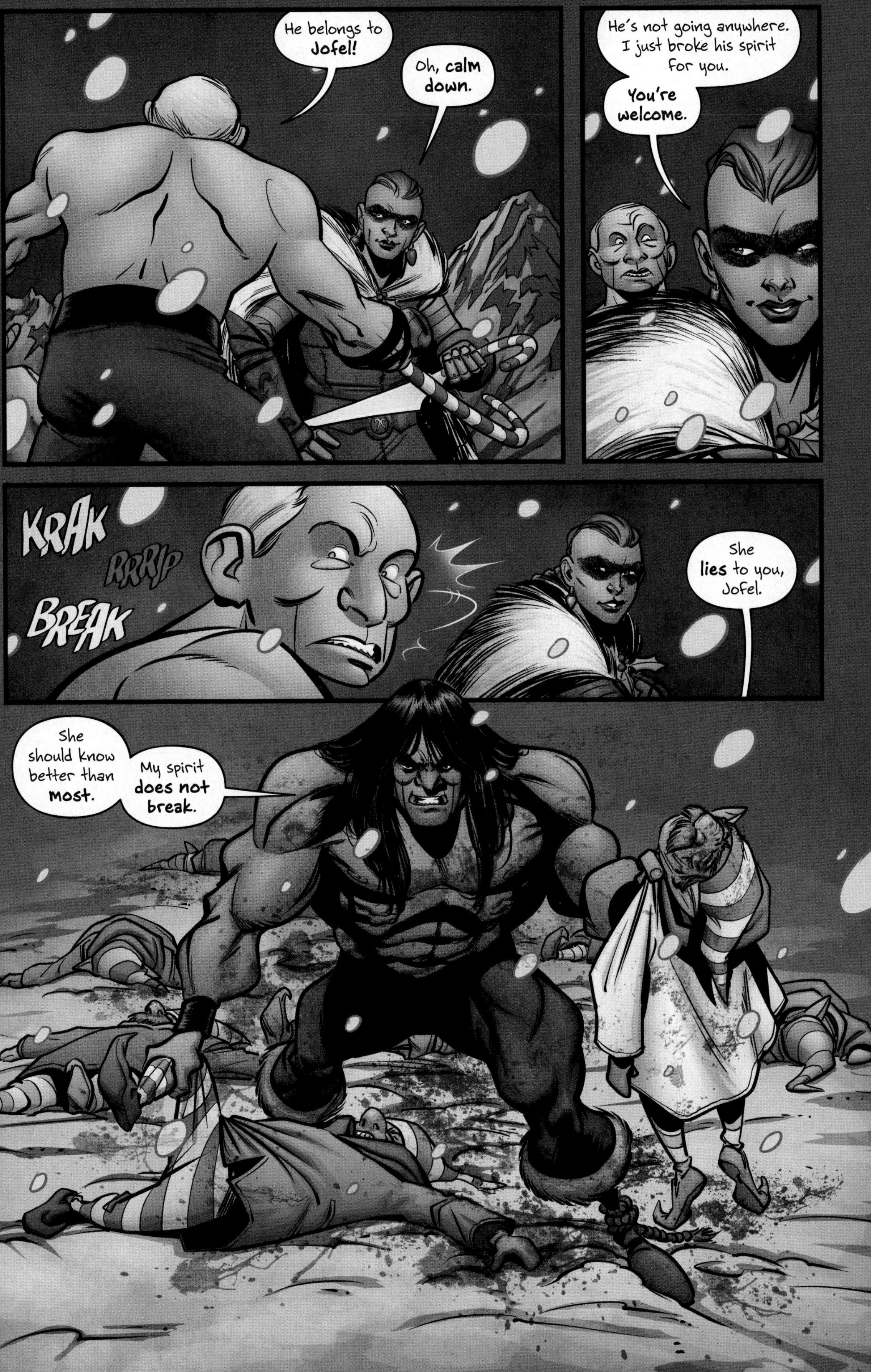
He belongs to Jofel!
Oh, calm down.
He's not going anywhere. I just broke his spirit for you.
You're welcome.
KRAK
RRRIP
BREAK
She lies to you, Jofel.
She should know better than most.
My spirit does not break.

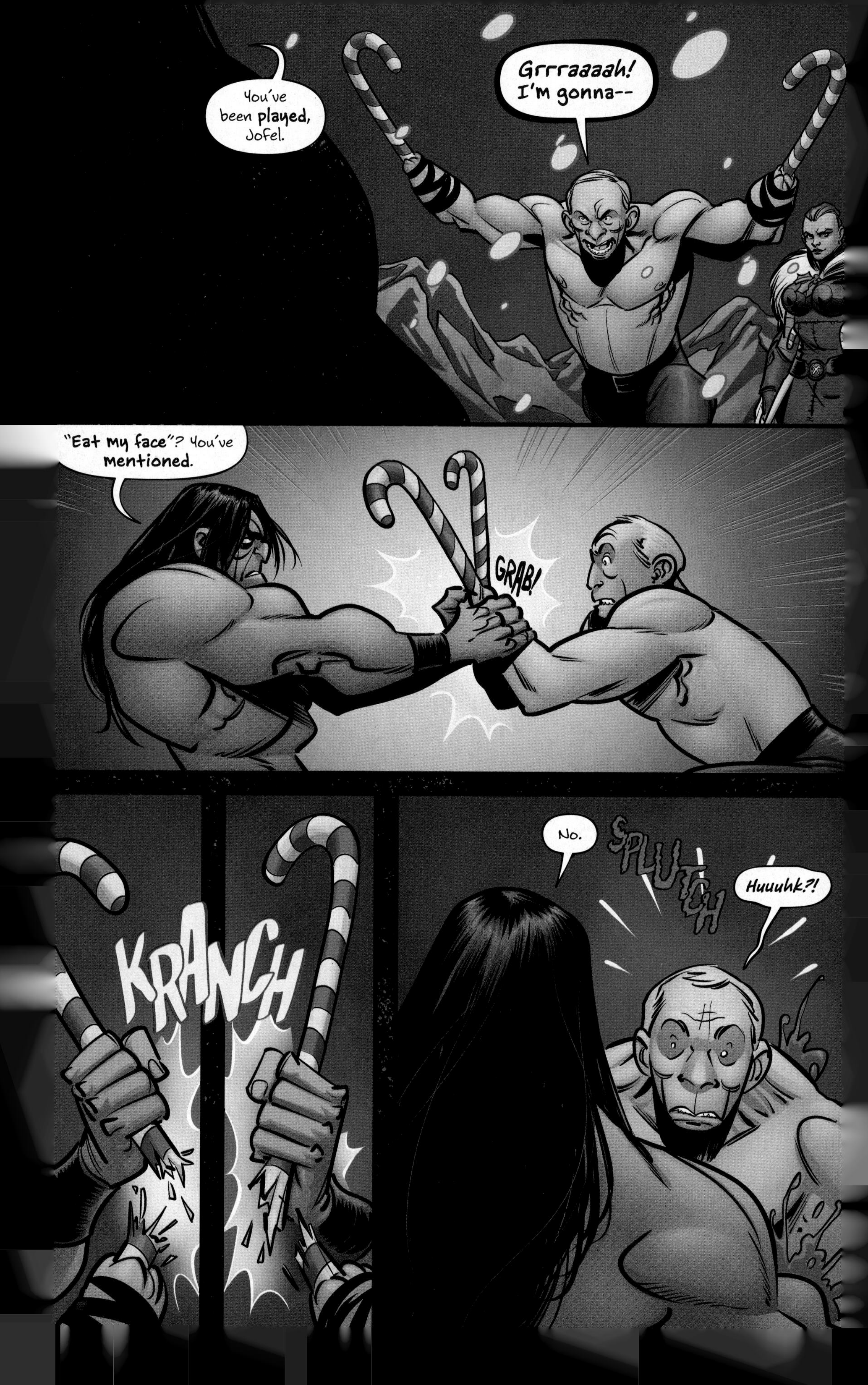
You've been played, Jofel.
Grrraaaah! I'm gonna--
"Eat my face"? You've mentioned.
GRAB!
KRANCH
No.
SPLUTCH
Huuuhk?!

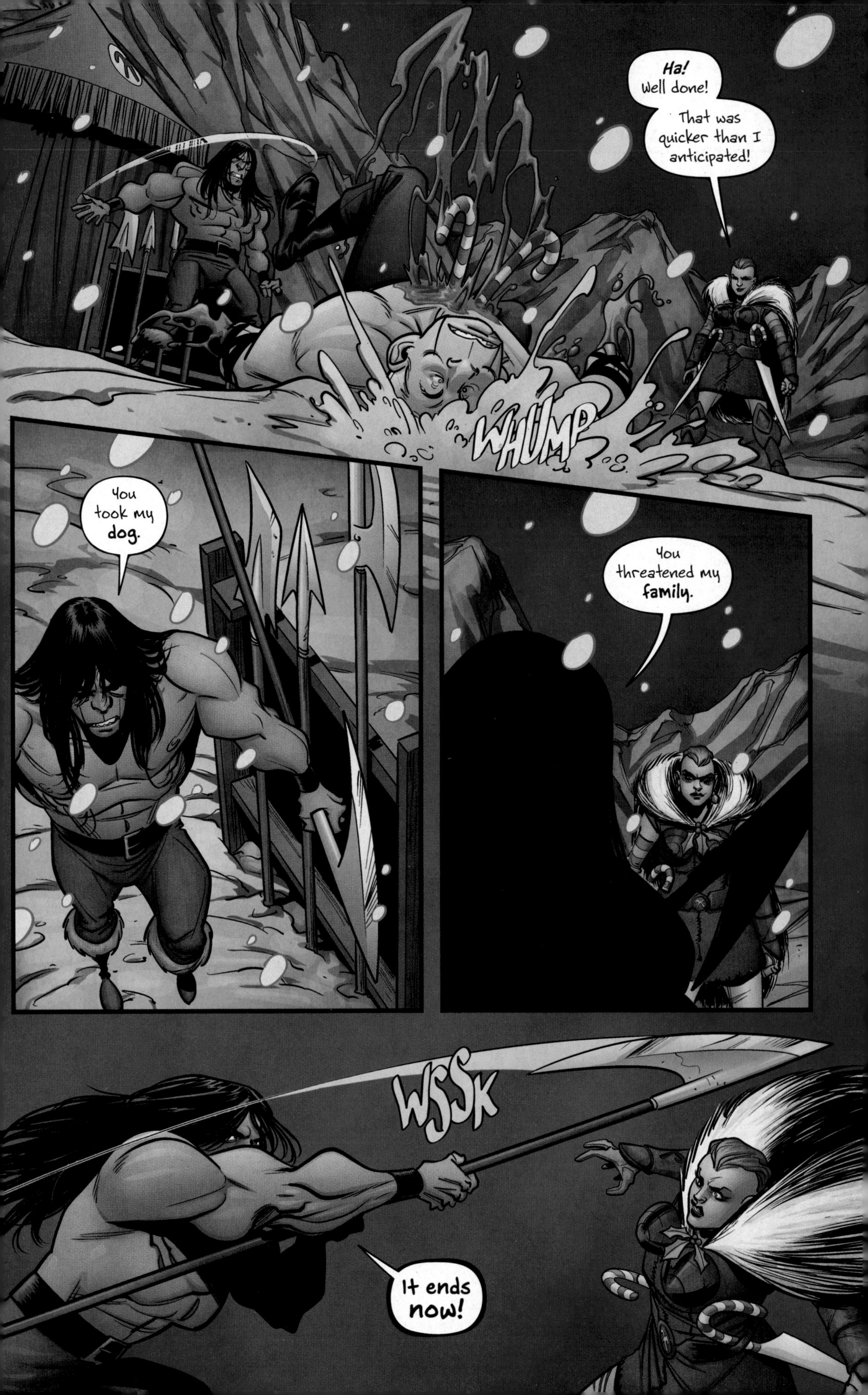

Ha! Well done!
That was quicker than I anticipated!
WHUMP
You took my dog.
You threatened my family.
WSSK
It ends now!

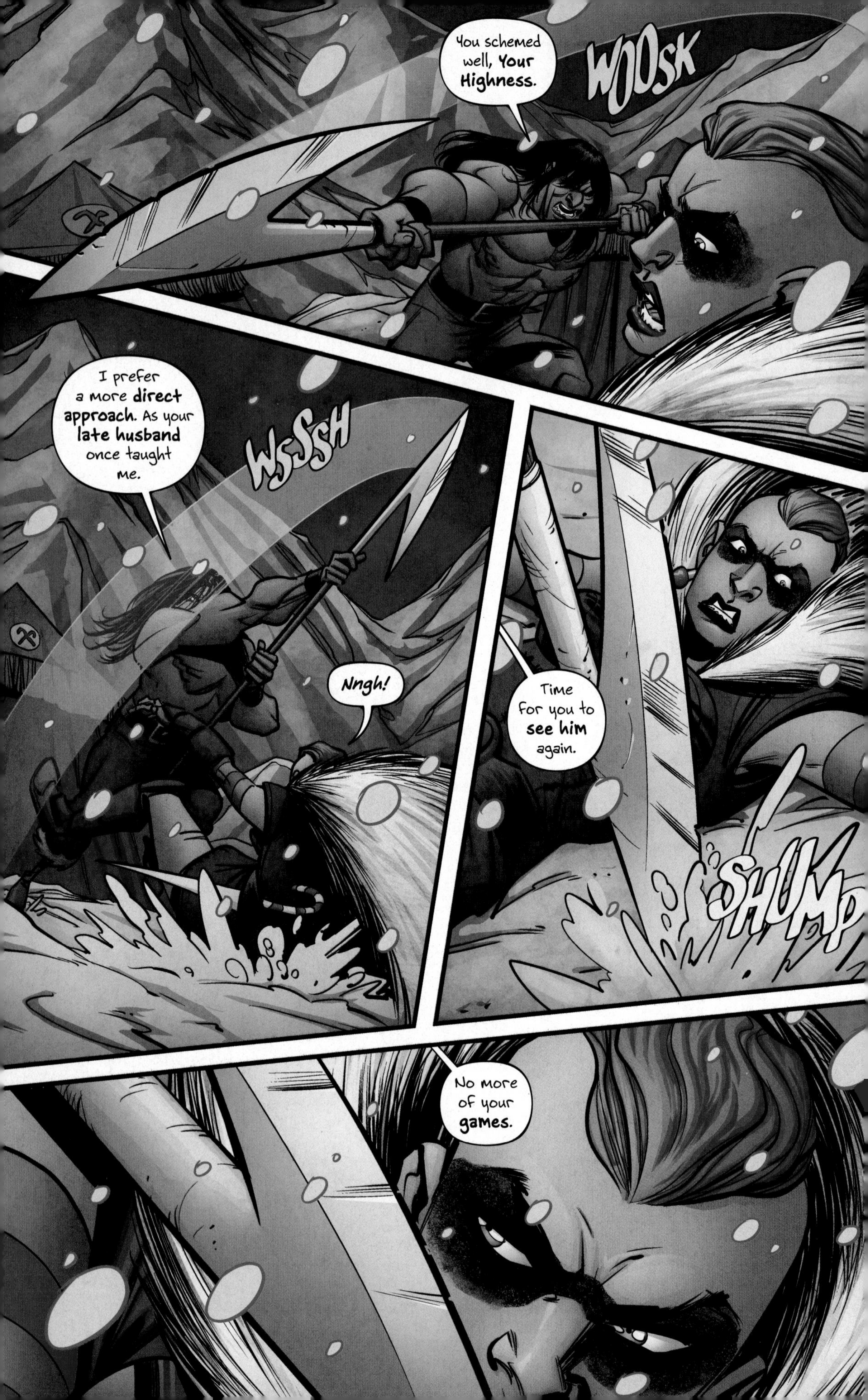
You schemed well, Your Highness.
WOOSK
I prefer a more direct approach. As your late husband once taught me.
WSSSH
Nngh!
Time for you to see him again.
SHUMP
No more of your games.

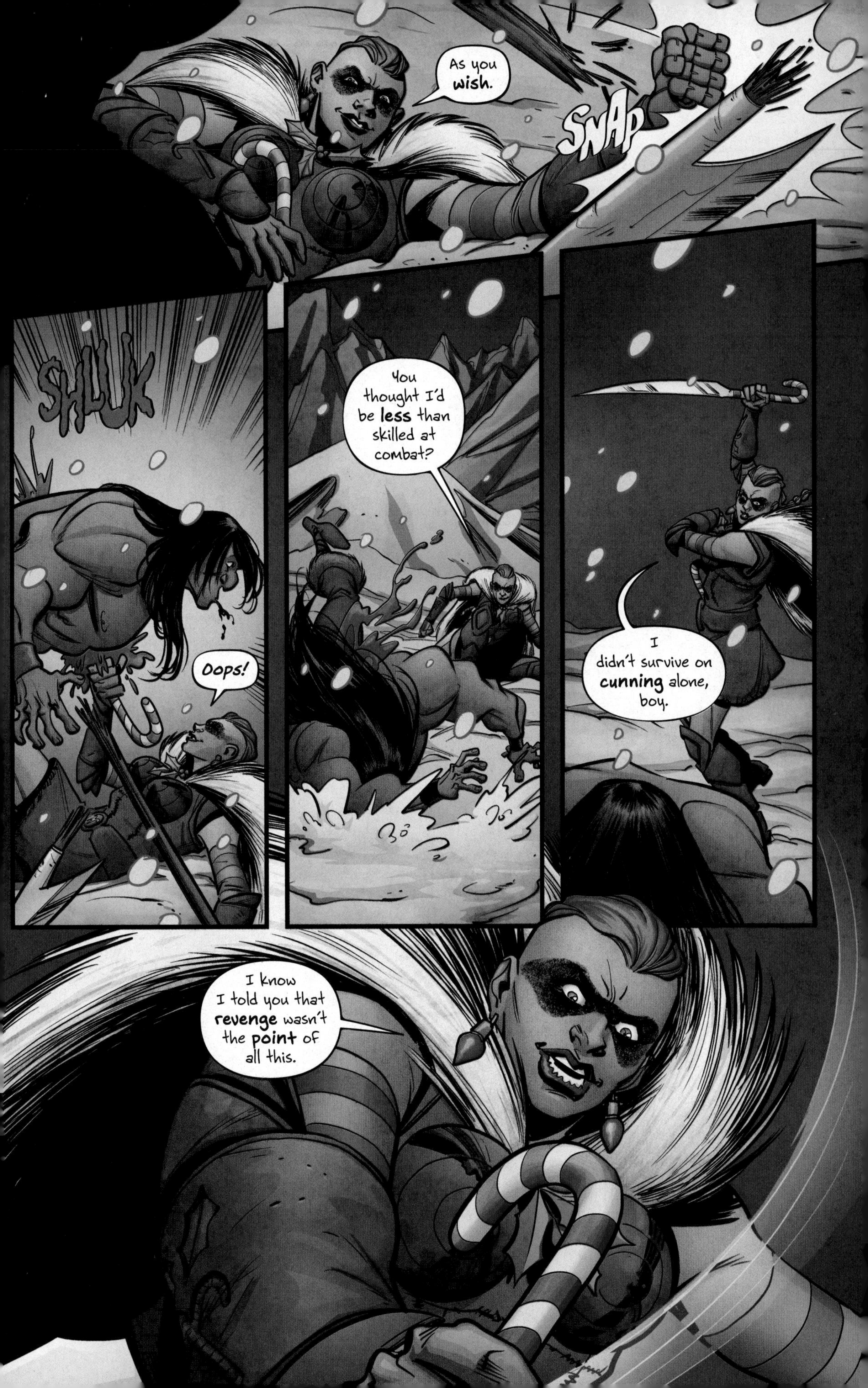
As you **wish.**
SNAP
SHLUK
Oops!
You thought I'd be **less** than skilled at combat?
I didn't survive on **cunning** alone, boy.
I know I told you that **revenge** wasn't the **point** of all this.

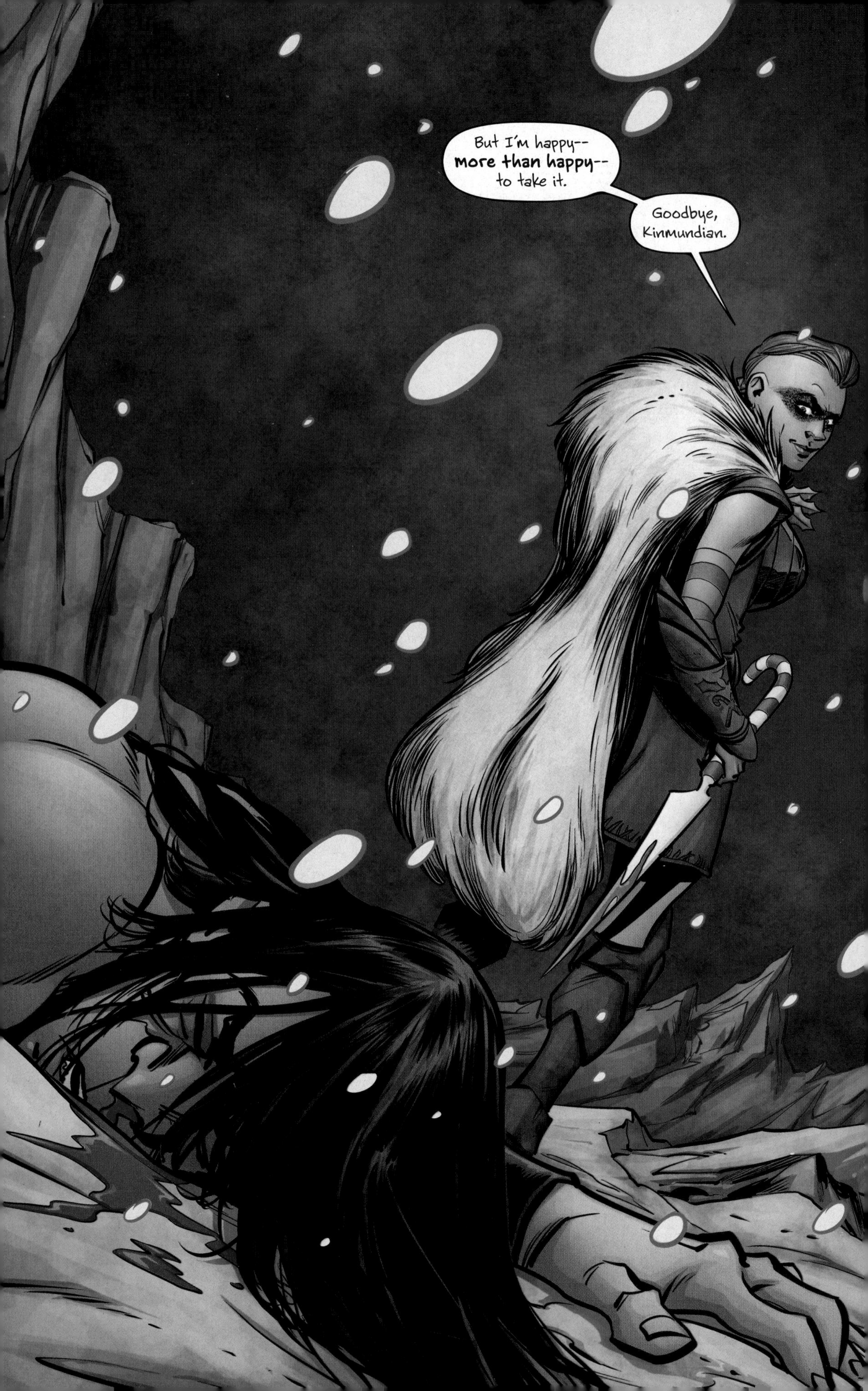

But I'm happy--
more than happy--
to take it.
Goodbye,
Kinmundian.

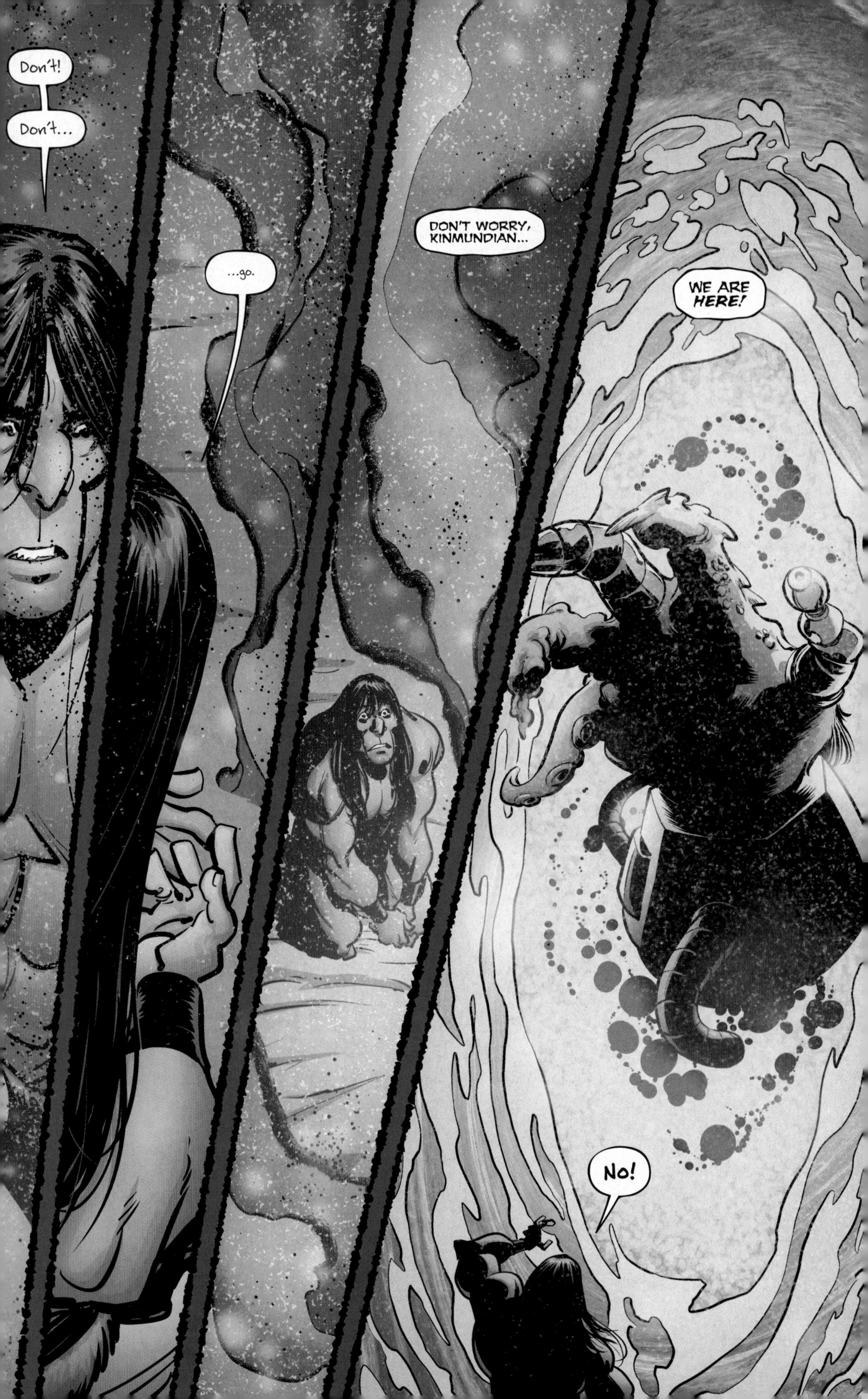
Don't!
Don't...
...go.
DON'T WORRY, KINMUNDIAN...
WE ARE HERE!
No!

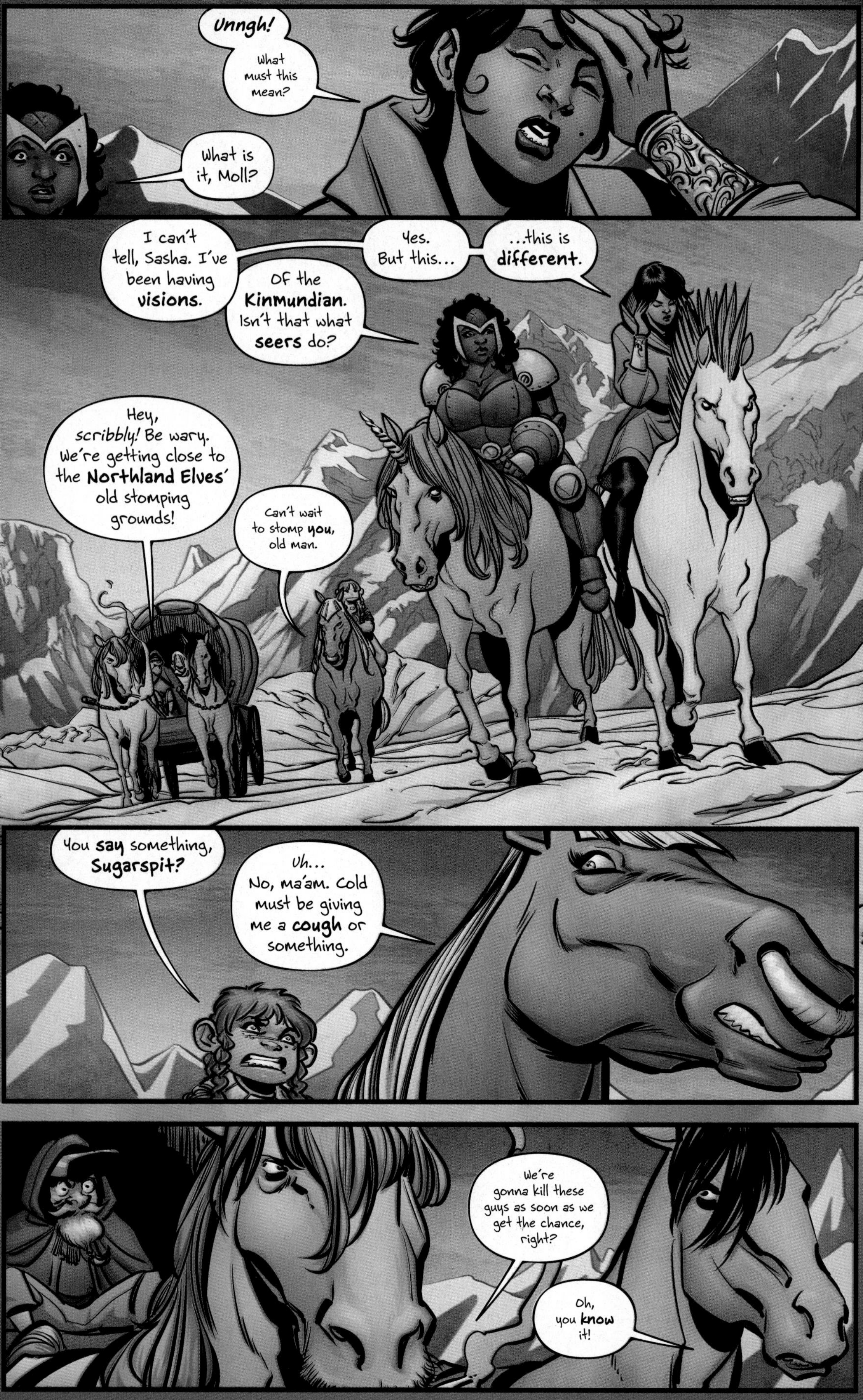
Unngh!
What must this mean?
What is it, Moll?
I can't tell, Sasha. I've been having visions.
Of the Kinmundian. Isn't that what seers do?
Yes. But this...
...this is different.
Hey, scribbly! Be wary. We're getting close to the Northland Elves' old stomping grounds!
Can't wait to stomp you, old man.
You say something, Sugarspit?
Uh... No, ma'am. Cold must be giving me a cough or something.
We're gonna kill these guys as soon as we get the chance, right?
Oh, you know it!

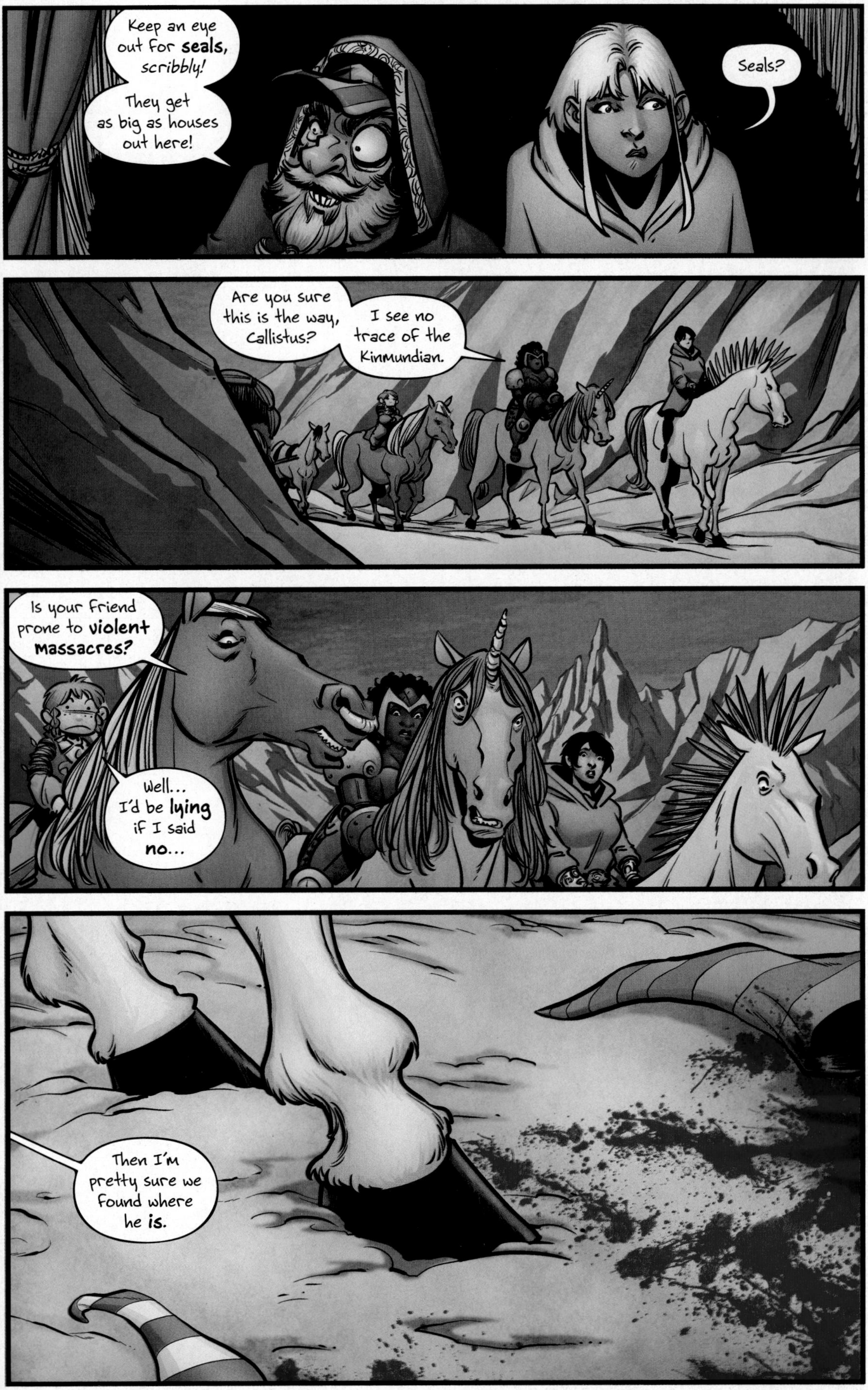
Keep an eye out for seals, scribbly!
They get as big as houses out here!
Seals?
Are you sure this is the way, Callistus?
I see no trace of the Kinmundian.
Is your friend prone to violent massacres?
Well... I'd be lying if I said no...
Then I'm pretty sure we found where he is.

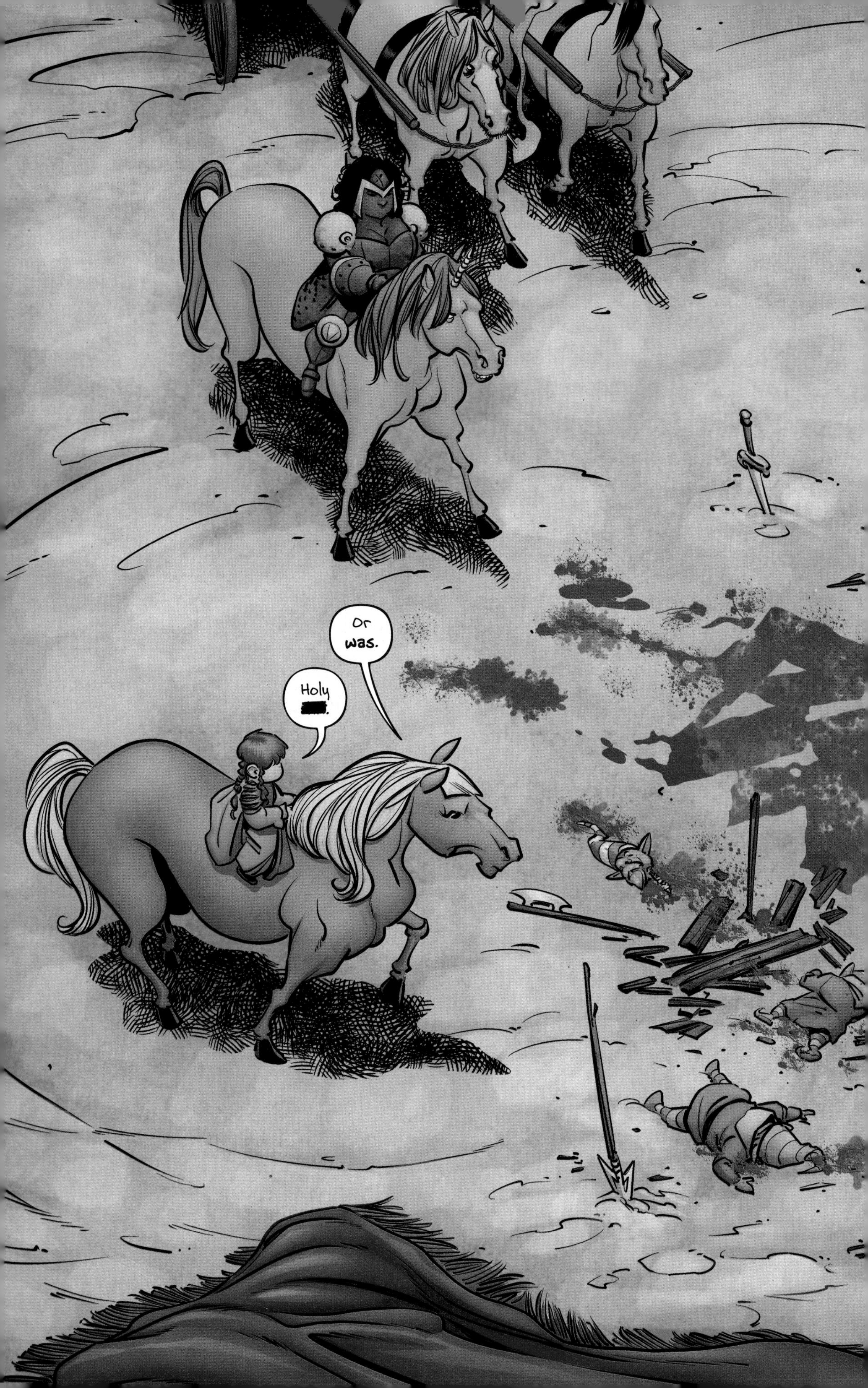
Or was.
Holy [redacted].

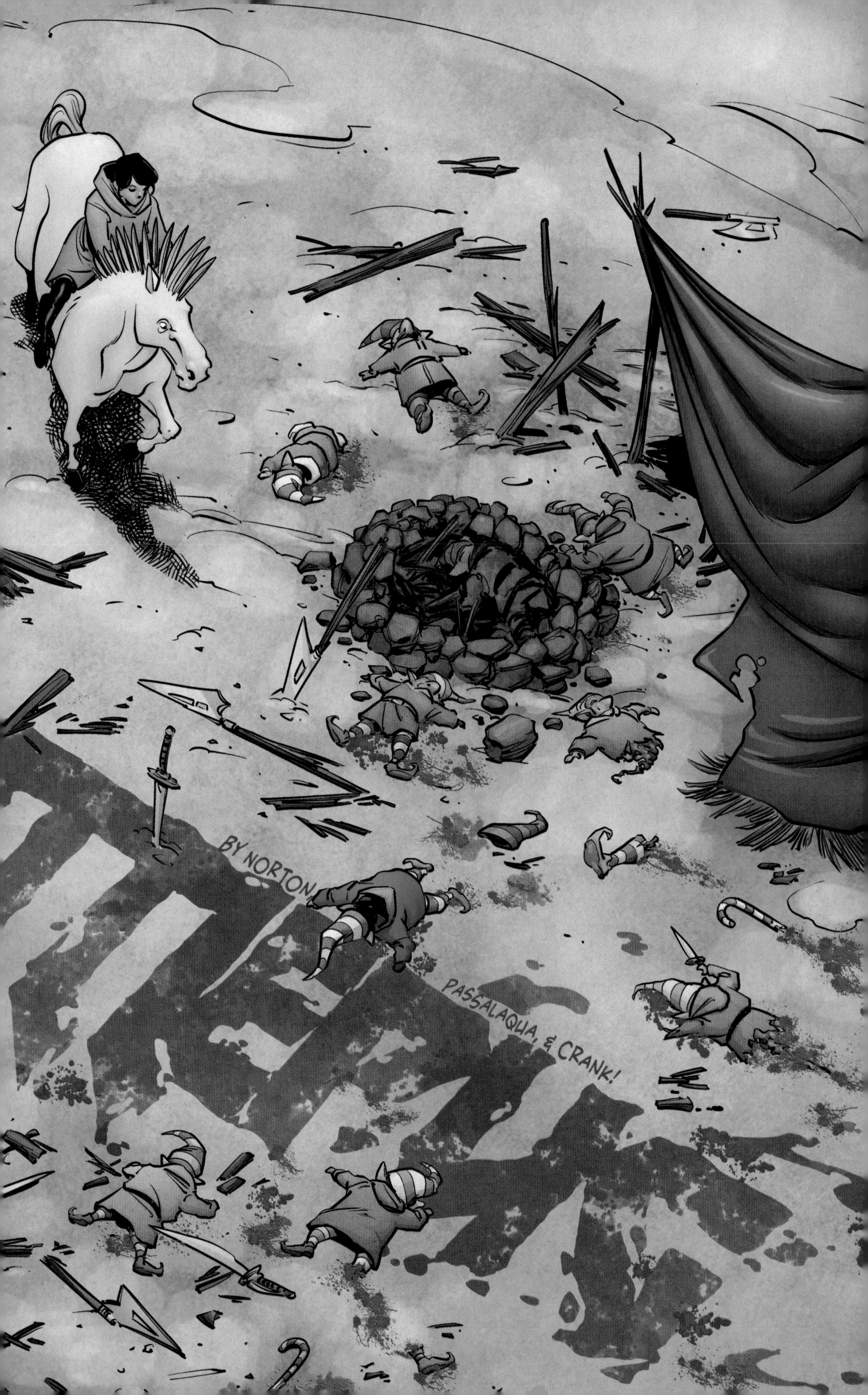
BY NORTON,
PASSALAQUA, & CRANK!

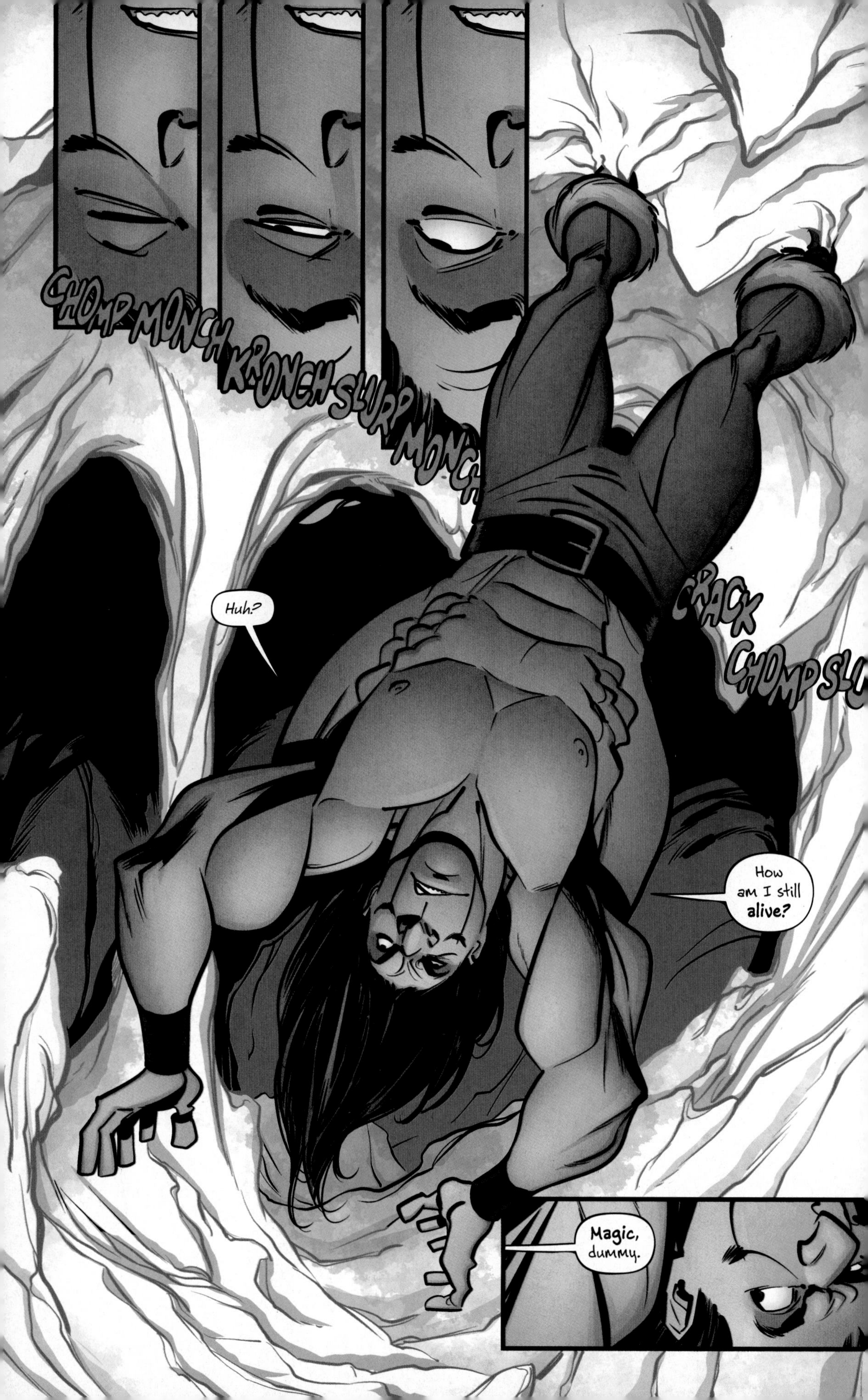
CHOMP MONCH KRONCH SLURP MONCH
Huh?
CRACK CHOMP SLU
How am I still alive?
Magic, dummy.

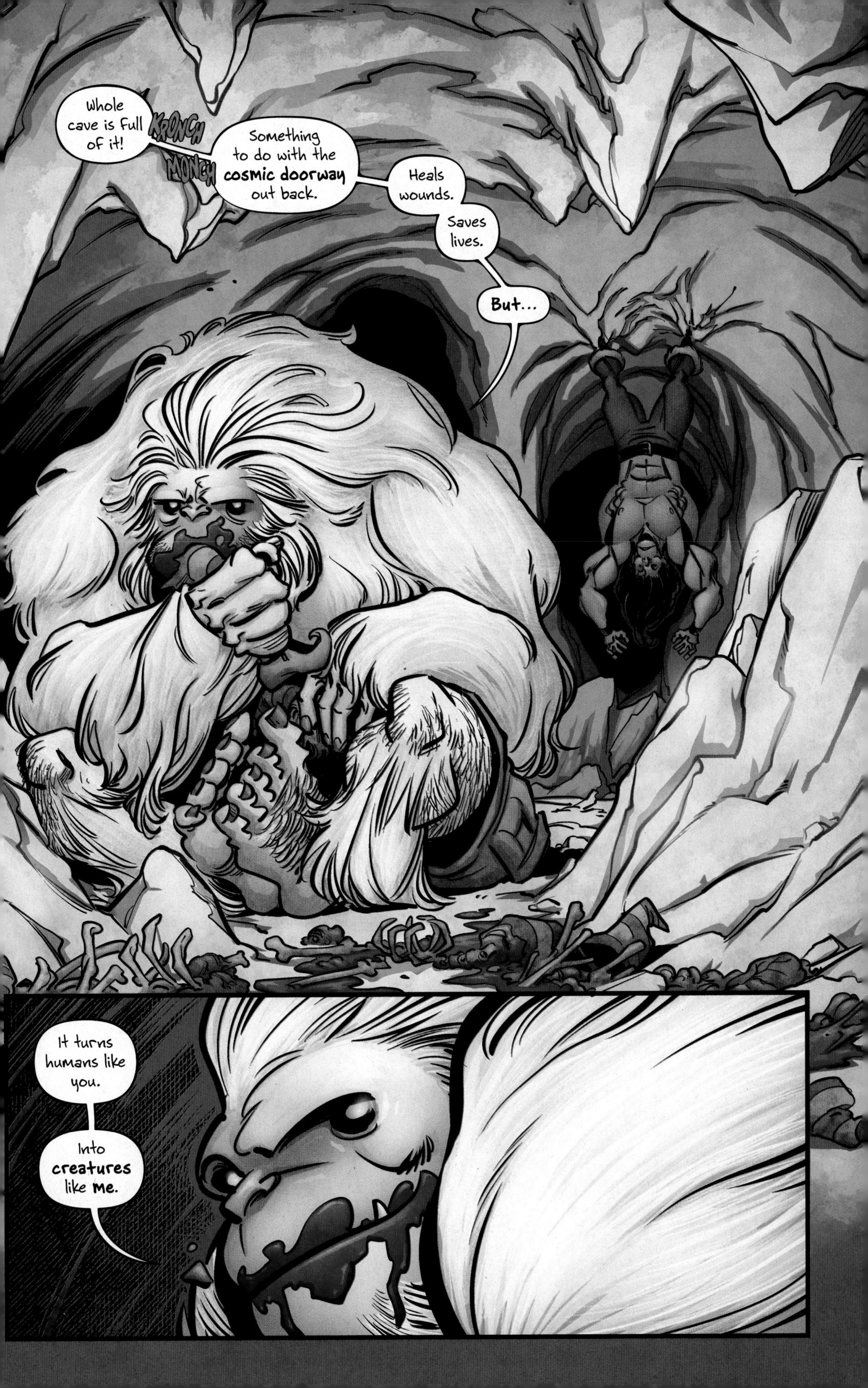
Whole cave is full of it!
KRONCH
MONCH
Something to do with the **cosmic doorway** out back.
Heals wounds.
Saves lives.
But...
It turns humans like you.
Into **creatures** like **me.**

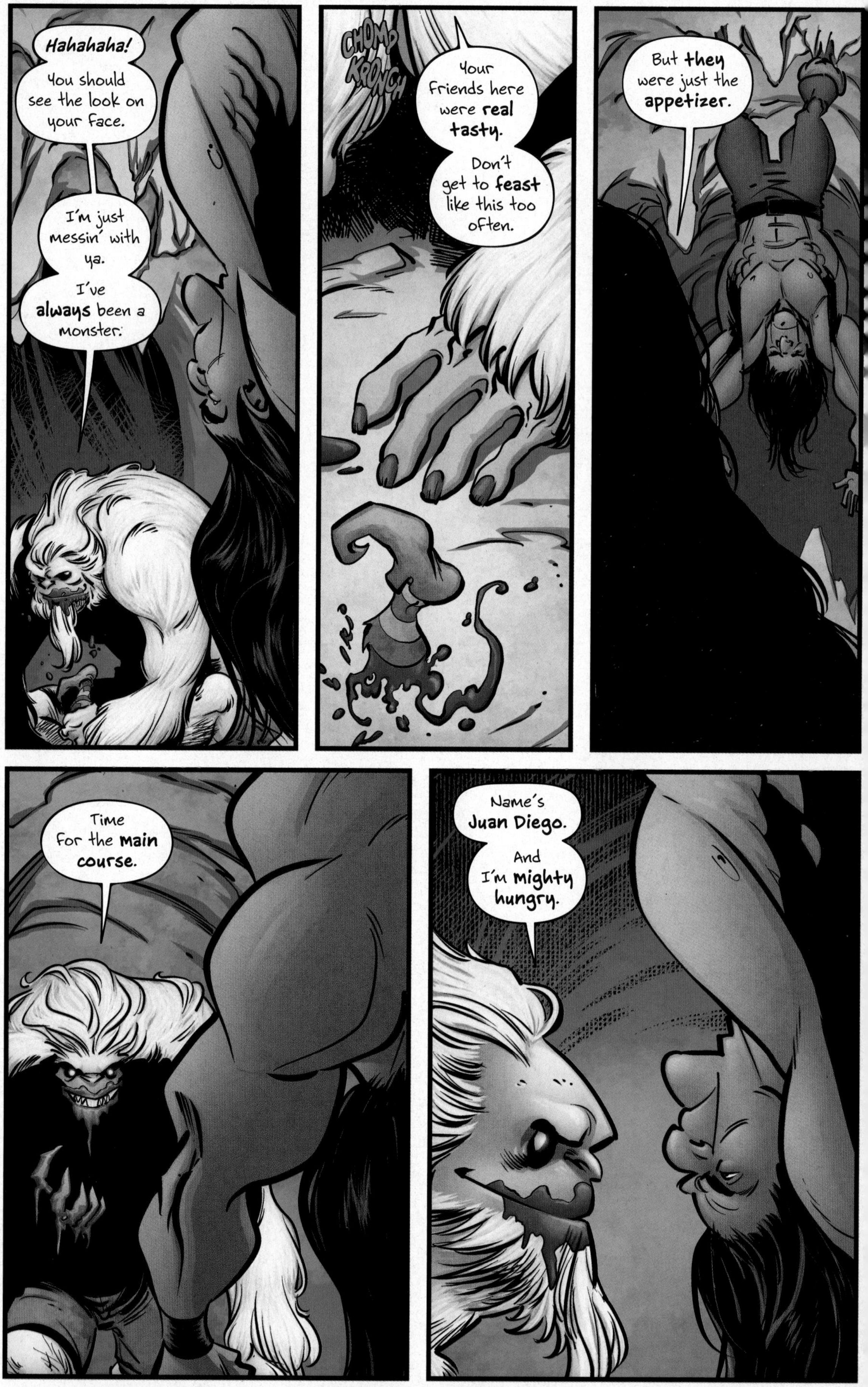
Hahahaha!
You should see the look on your face.
I'm just messin' with ya.
I've always been a monster.
CHOMP KRONCH
Your friends here were real tasty.
Don't get to feast like this too often.
But they were just the appetizer.
Time for the main course.
Name's Juan Diego.
And I'm mighty hungry.

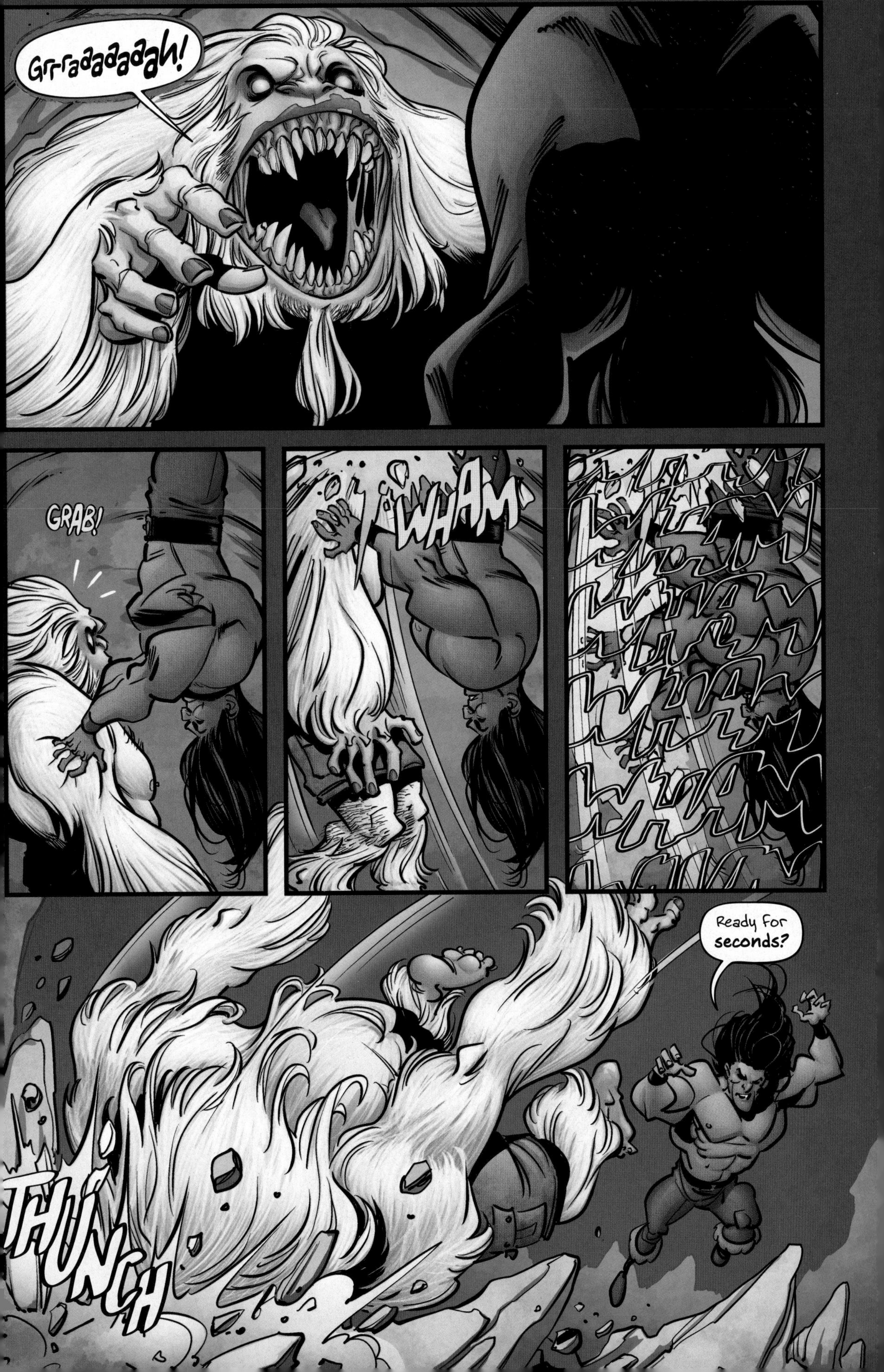
Grrraaaaaaah!
GRAB!
WHAM
THUNCH
Ready for seconds?

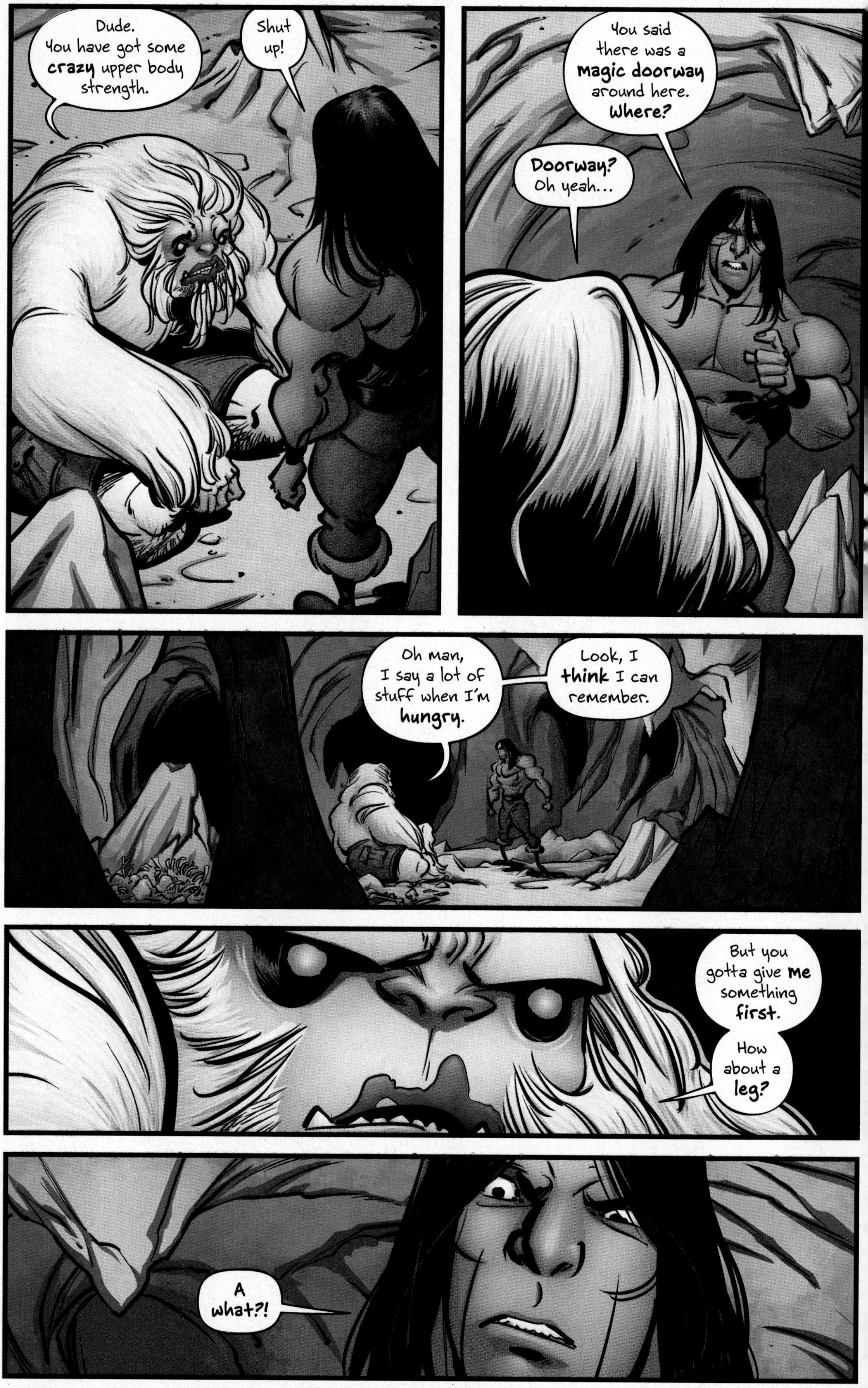
Dude. You have got some crazy upper body strength.
Shut up!
You said there was a magic doorway around here. Where?
Doorway? Oh yeah...
Oh man, I say a lot of stuff when I'm hungry.
Look, I think I can remember.
But you gotta give me something first.
How about a leg?
A what?!

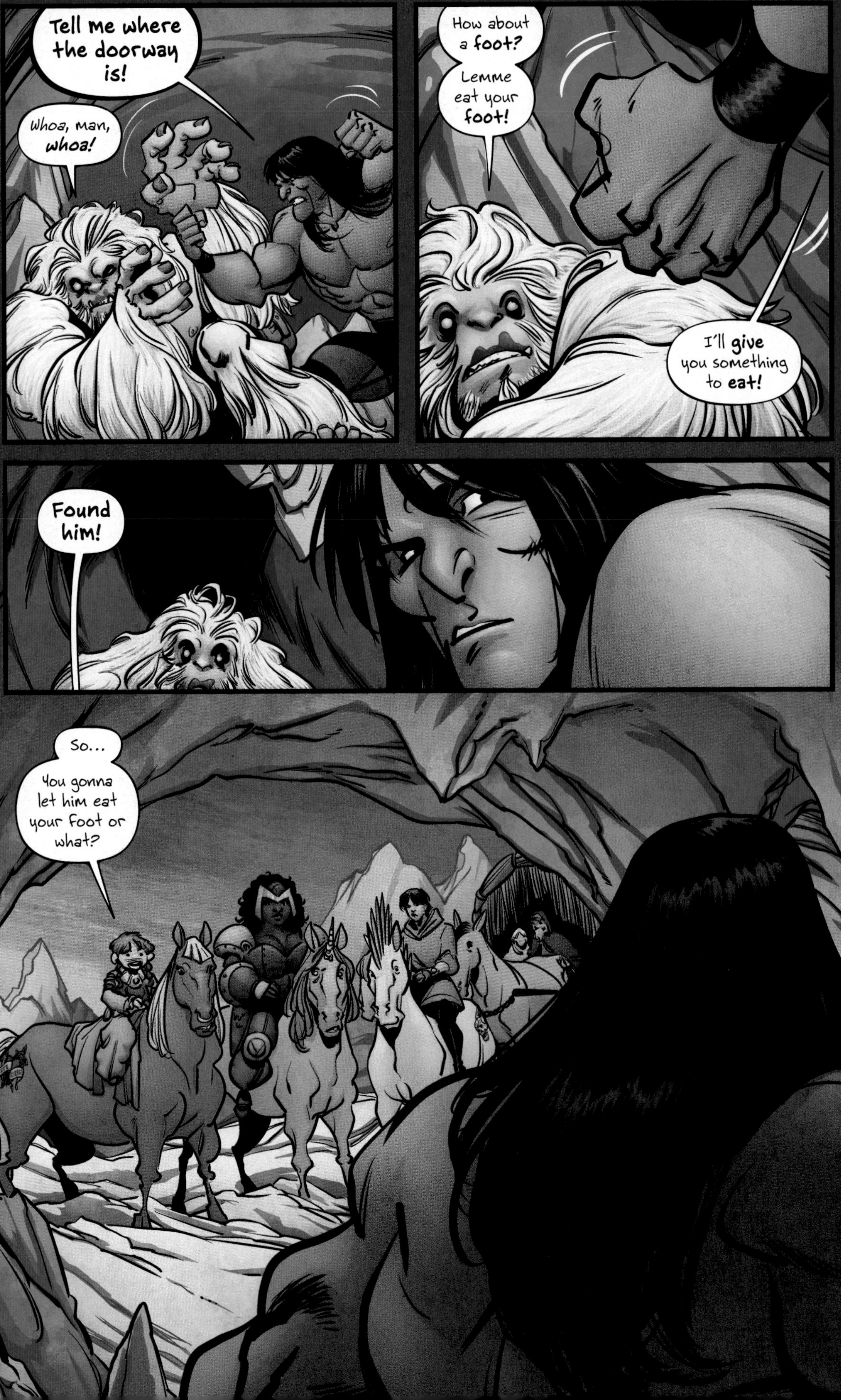
Tell me where the doorway is!
Whoa, man, whoa!
How about a foot?
Lemme eat your foot!
I'll give you something to eat!
Found him!
So...
You gonna let him eat your foot or what?

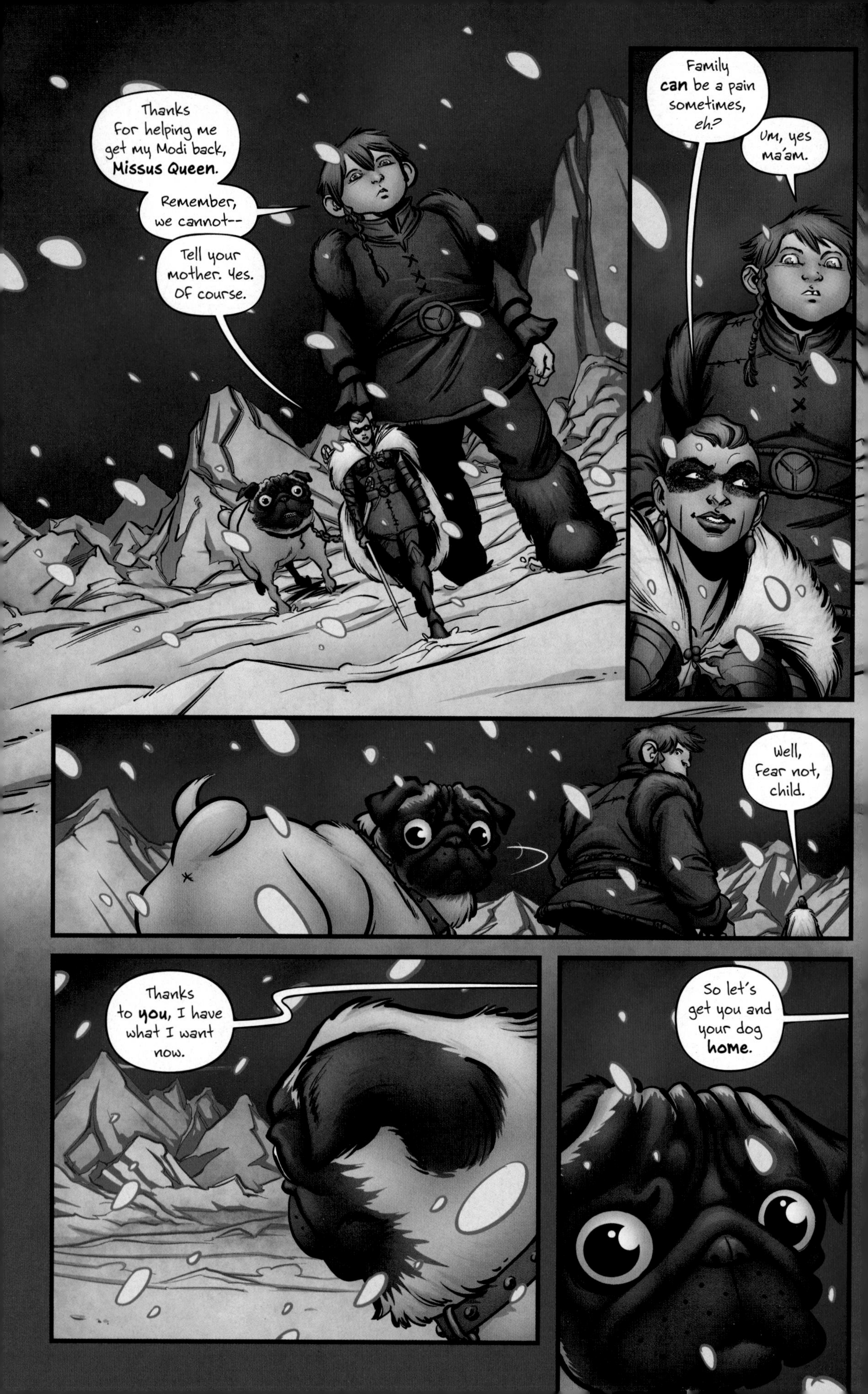
Thanks for helping me get my Modi back, **Missus Queen**.
Remember, we cannot--
Tell your mother. Yes. Of course.
Family **can** be a pain sometimes, eh?
Um, yes ma'am.
Well, fear not, child.
Thanks to **you**, I have what I want now.
So let's get you and your dog **home**.

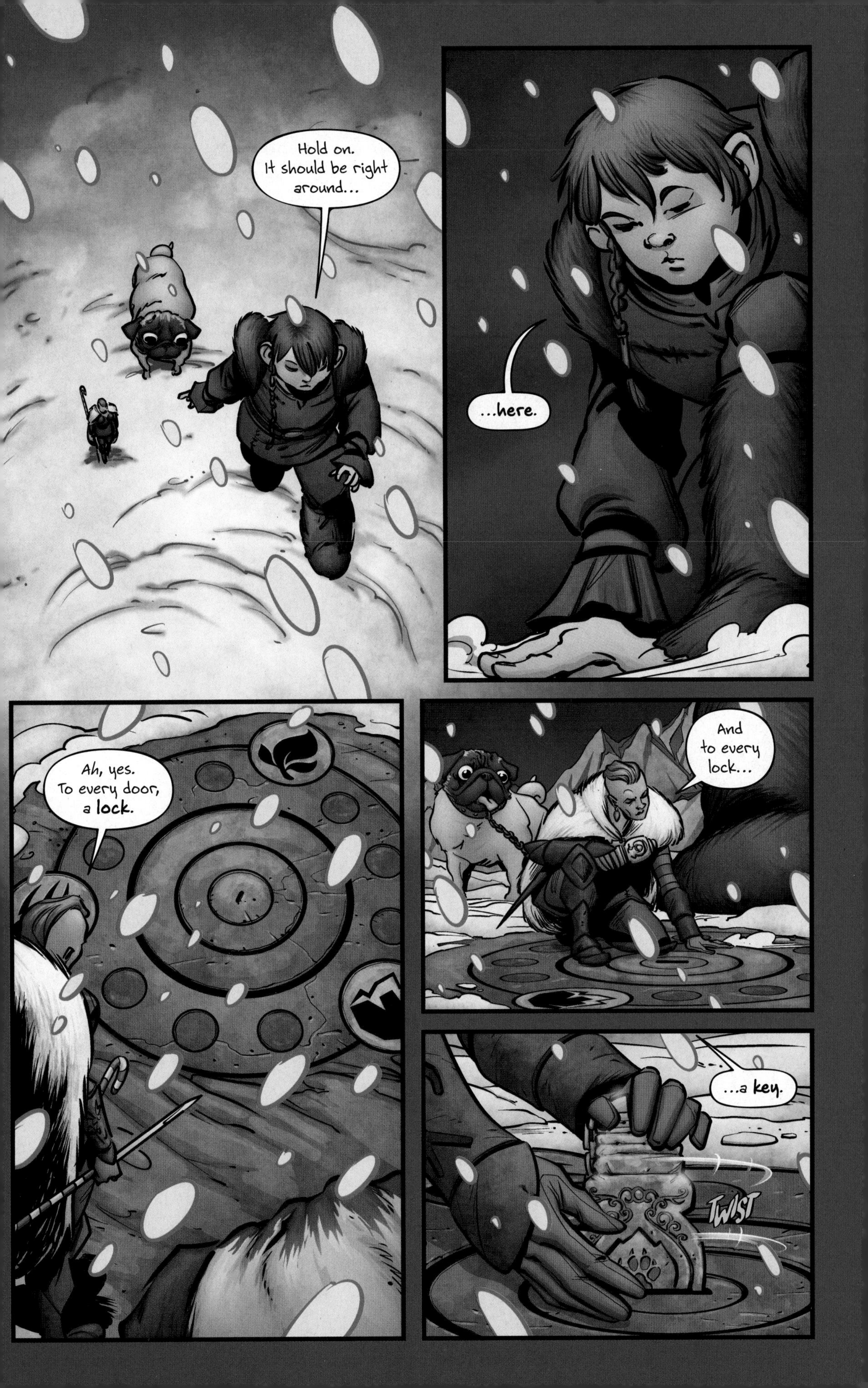
Hold on. It should be right around...
...here.
Ah, yes. To every door, a **lock**.
And to every lock...
...a **key**.
TWIST

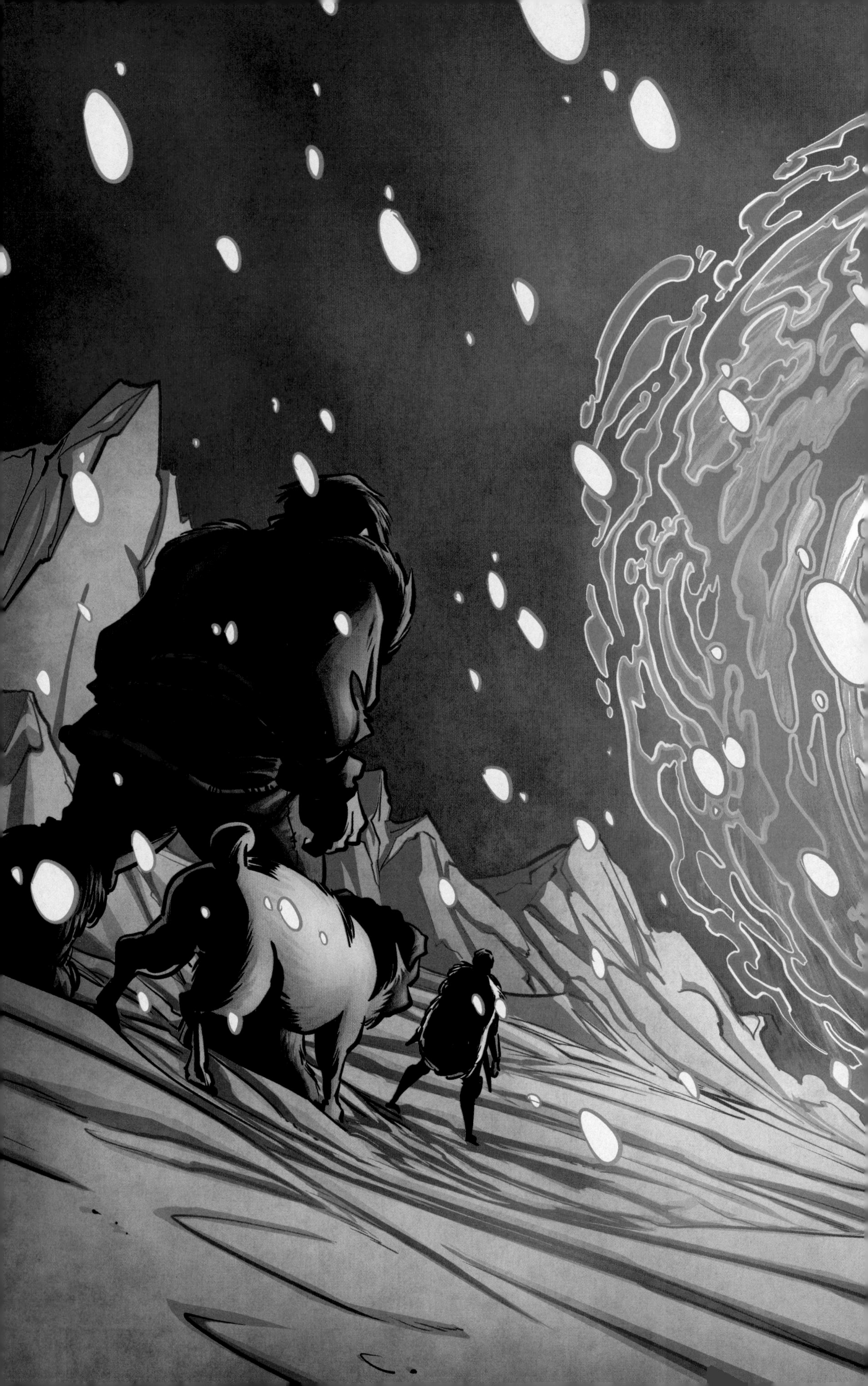

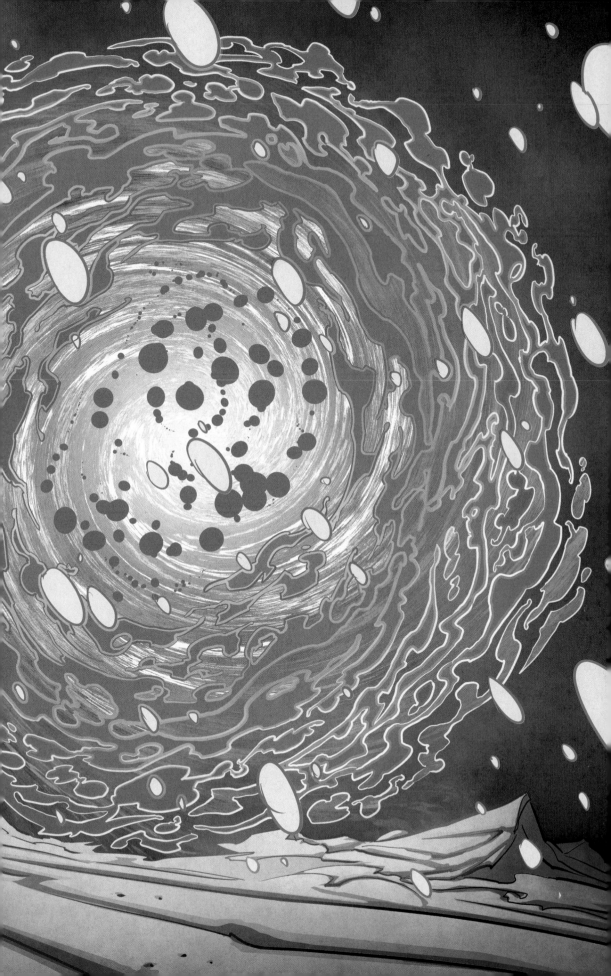

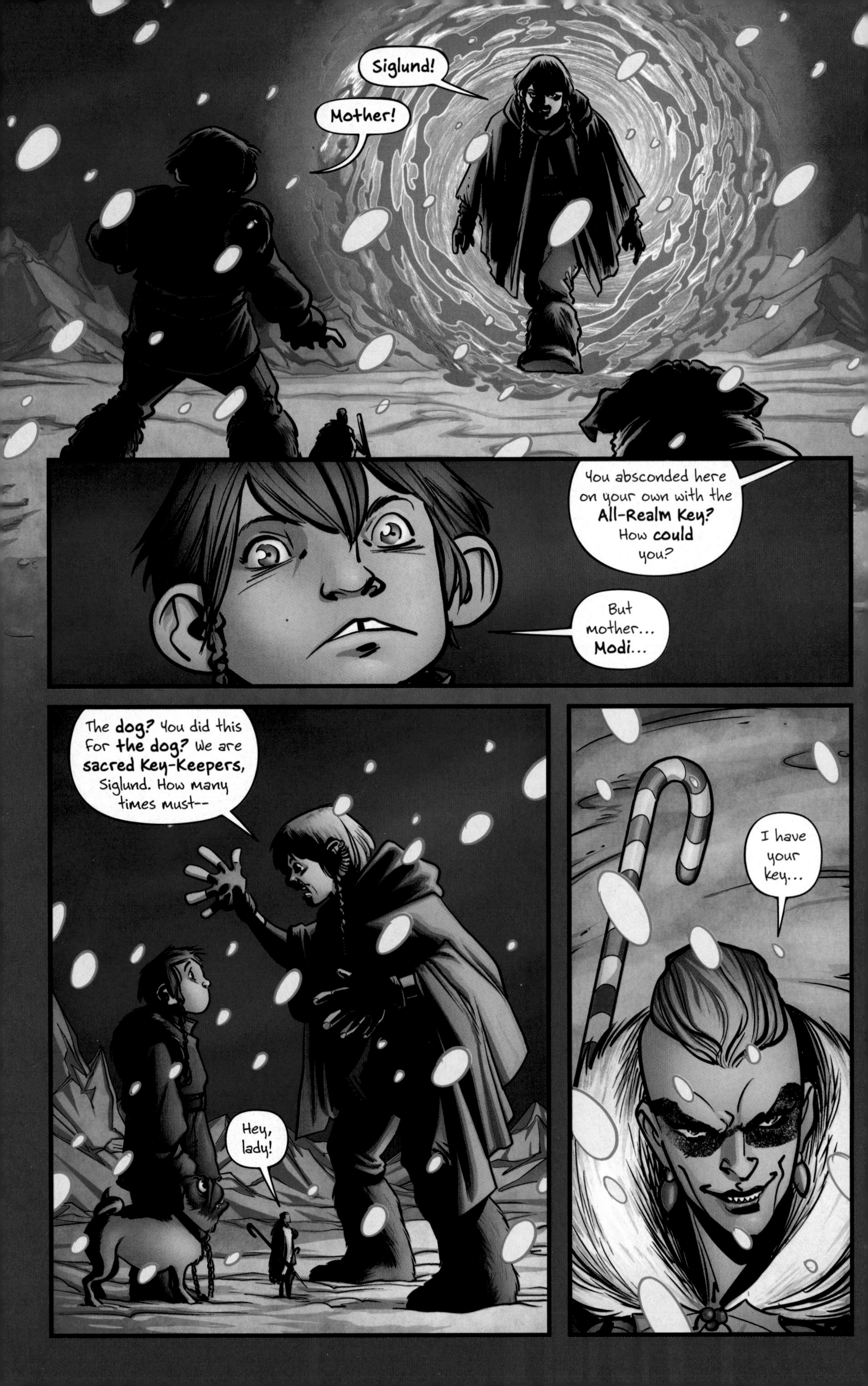
Siglund!
Mother!
You absconded here on your own with the All-Realm Key? How could you?
But mother... Modi...
The dog? You did this for the dog? We are sacred Key-Keepers, Siglund. How many times must--
Hey, lady!
I have your key...

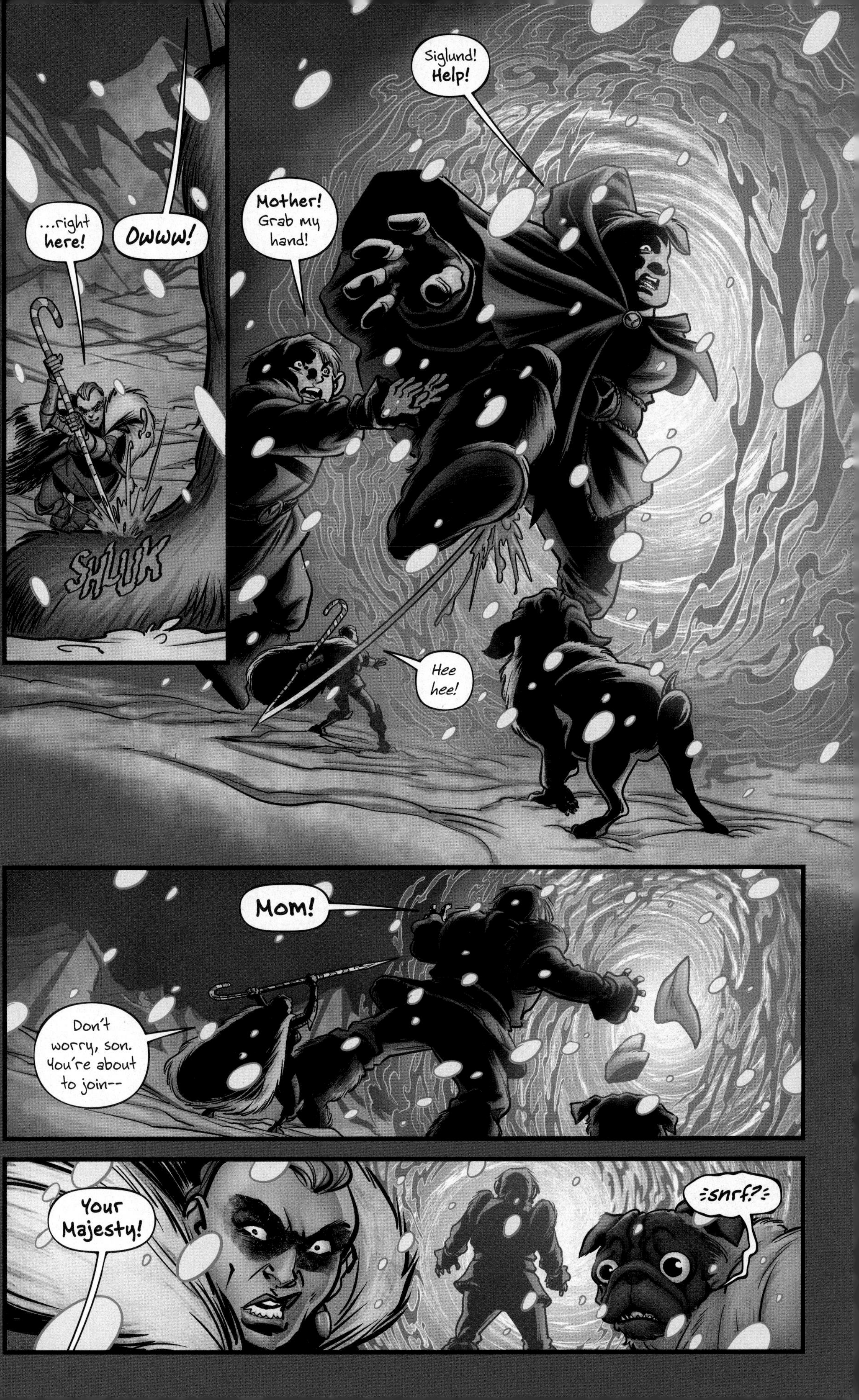
...right here!
Owww!
SHLUK
Siglund! Help!
Mother! Grab my hand!
Hee hee!
Mom!
Don't worry, son. You're about to join--
Your Majesty!
=snrf?=

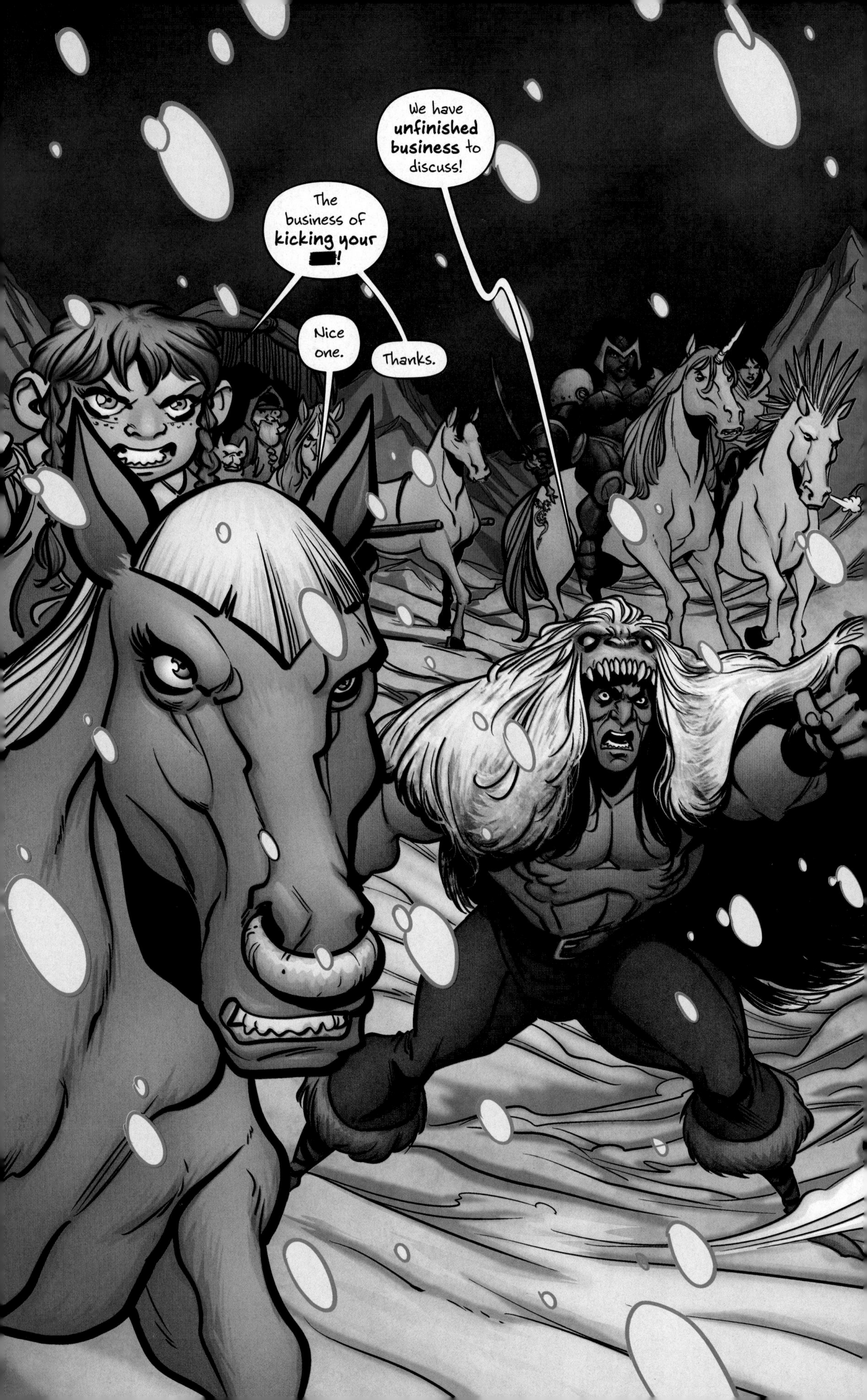
We have unfinished business to discuss!
The business of kicking your [redacted]!
Nice one.
Thanks.

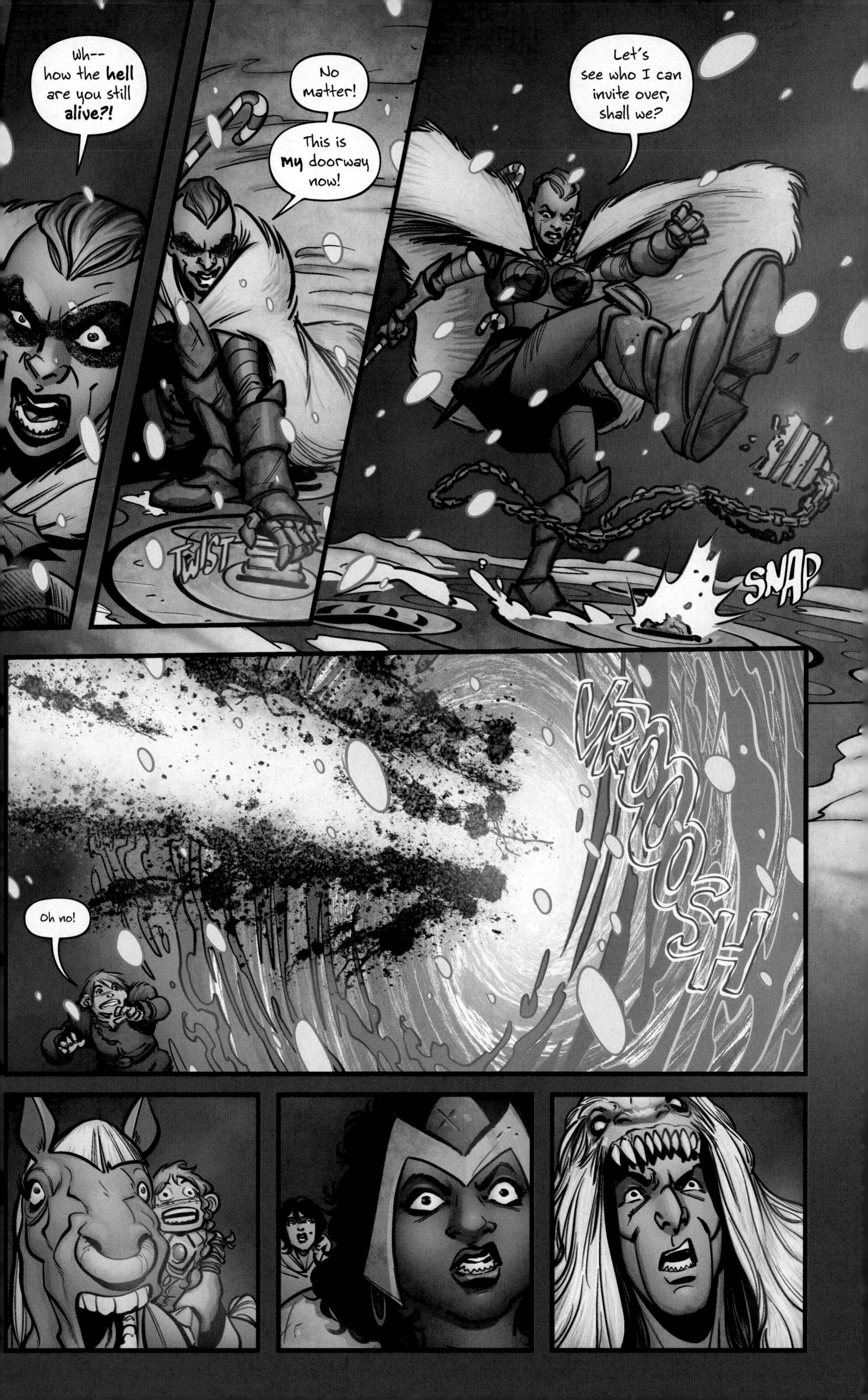
Wh-- how the **hell** are you still **alive?!**
No matter!
This is **my** doorway now!
TWIST
Let's see who I can invite over, shall we?
SNAP
VROOOOOSH
Oh no!

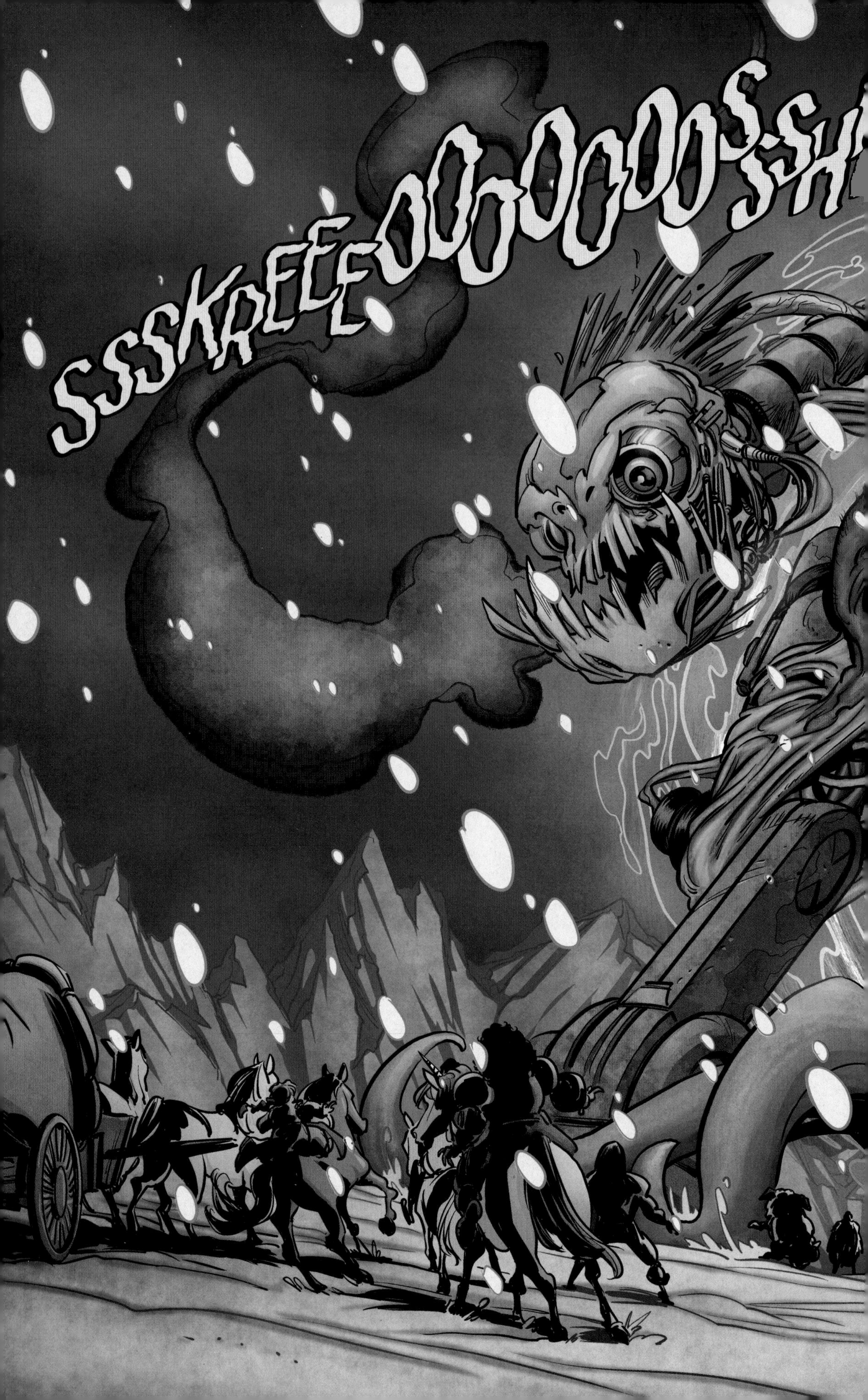
SSSKREEEOOOOOOOSSH

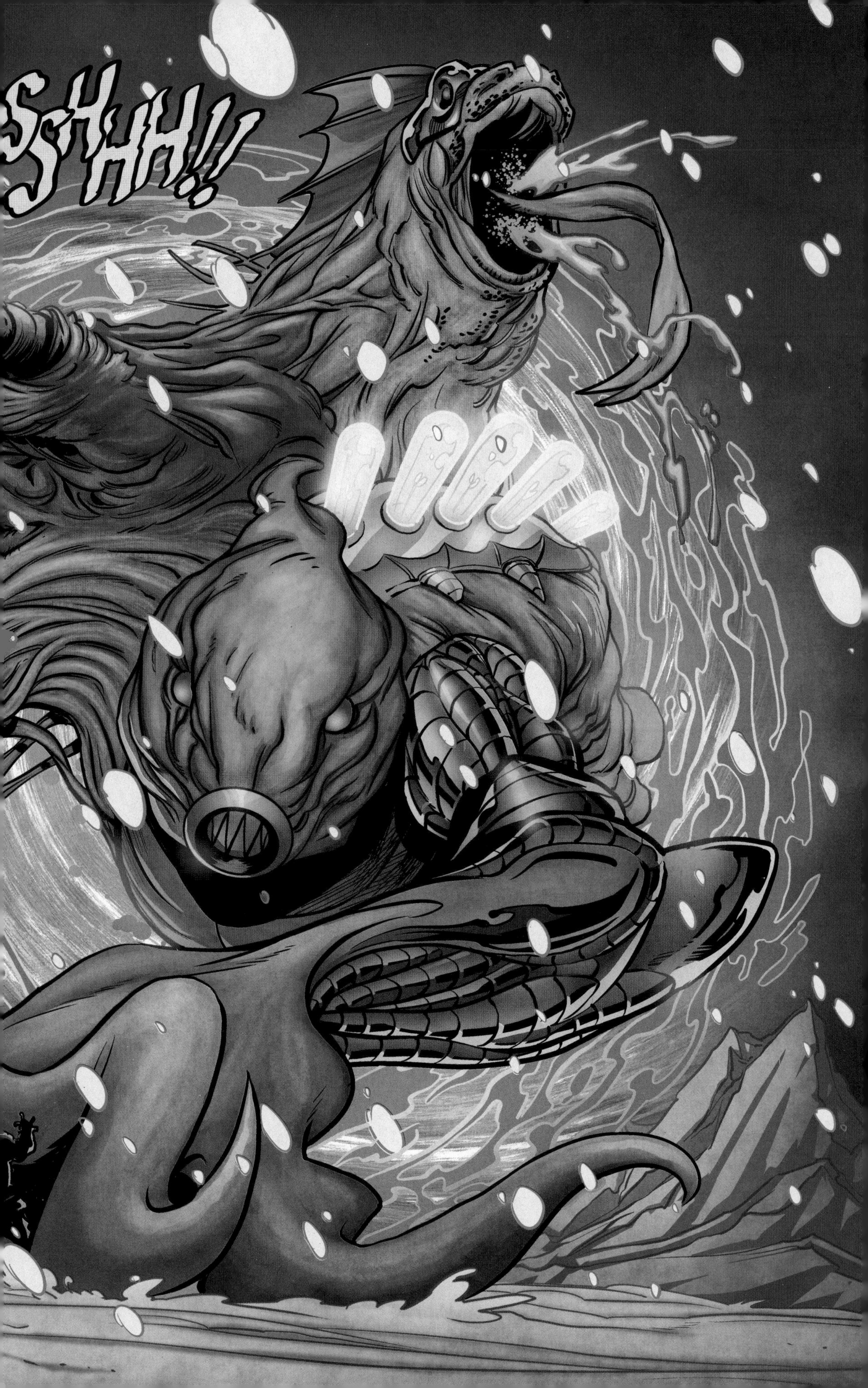
SHH!!

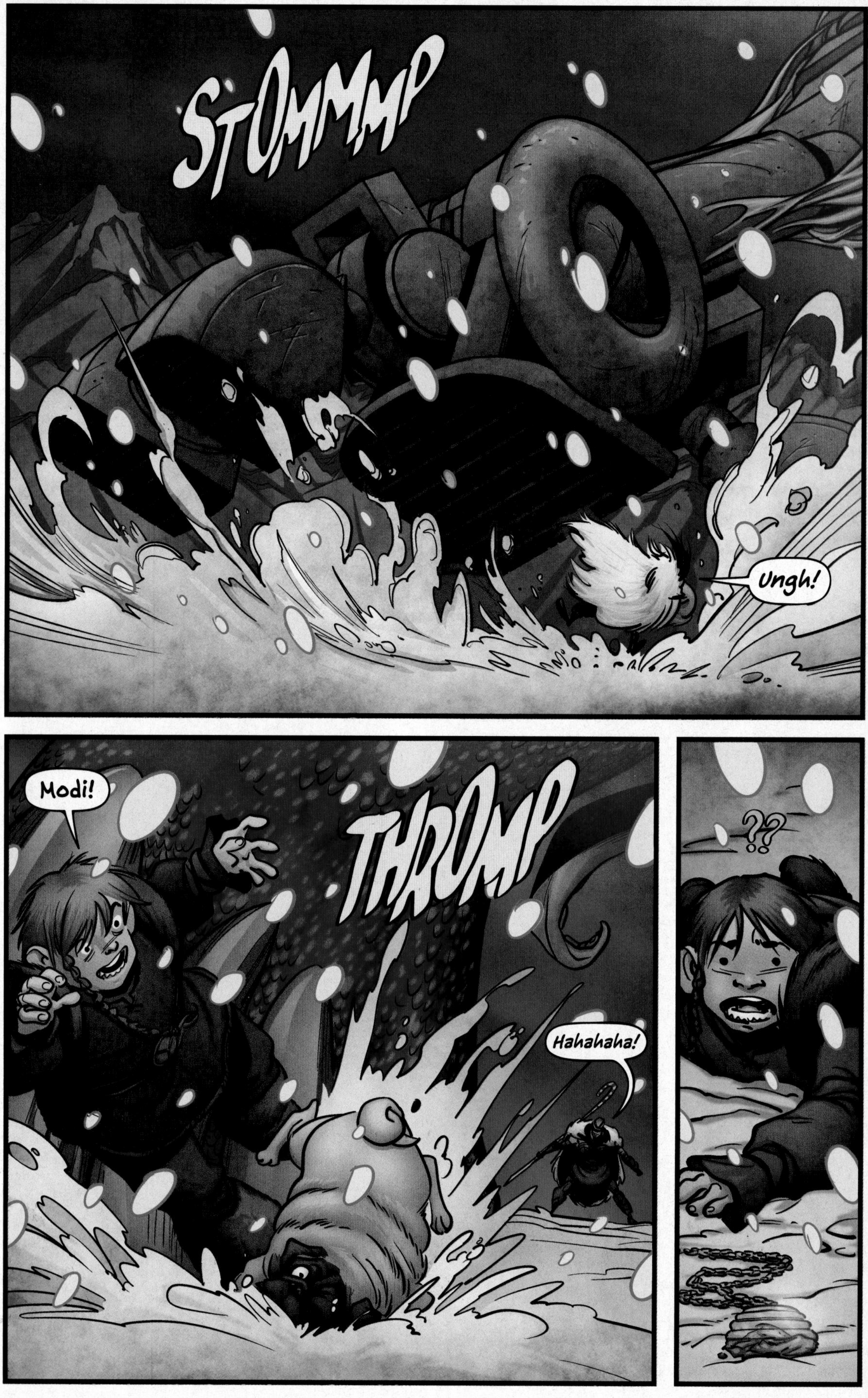
STOMMMP
Ungh!
Modi!
THROMP
Hahahaha!
??

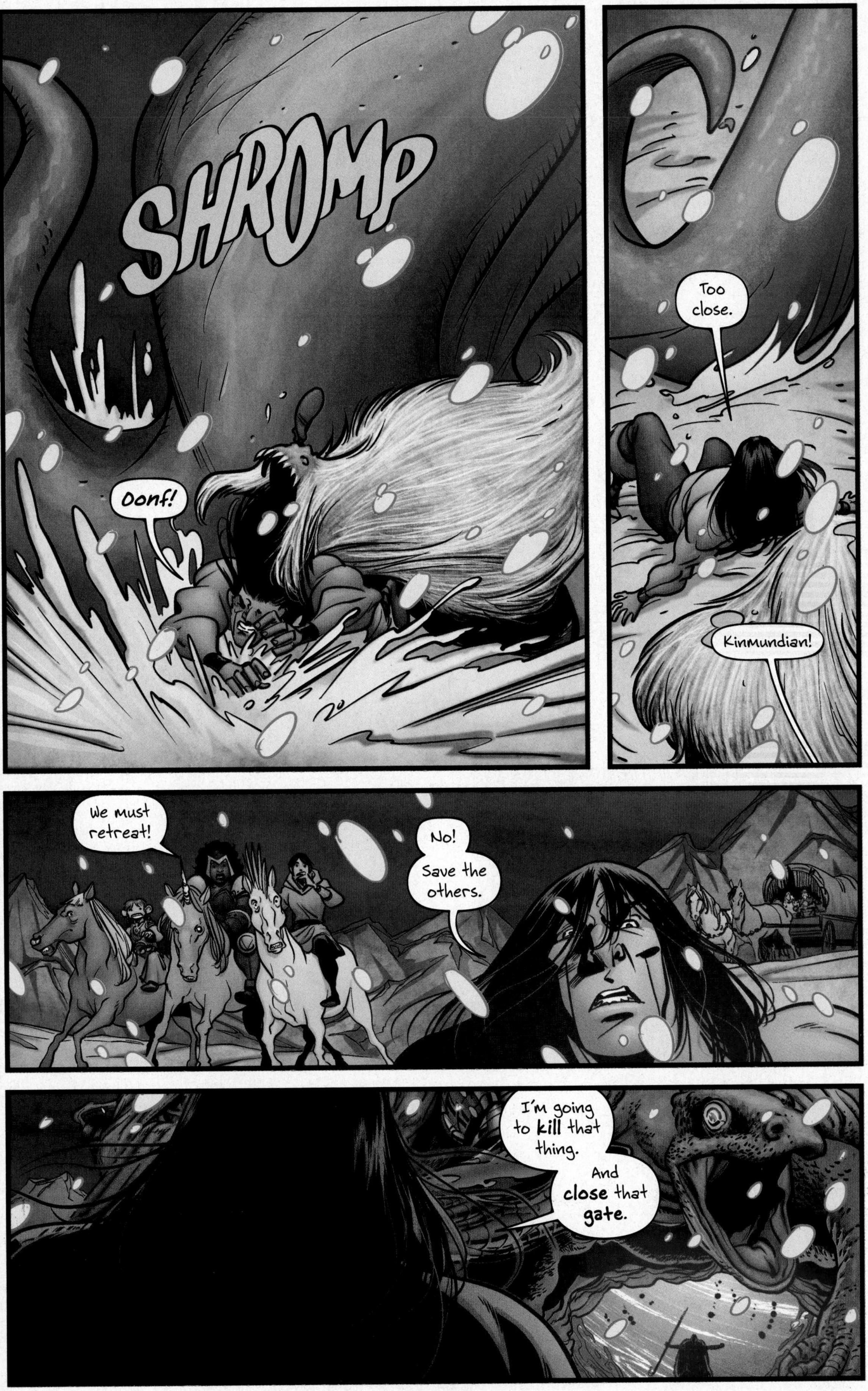
SHROMP
Oonf!
Too close.
Kinmundian!
We must retreat!
No! Save the others.
I'm going to kill that thing.
And close that gate.

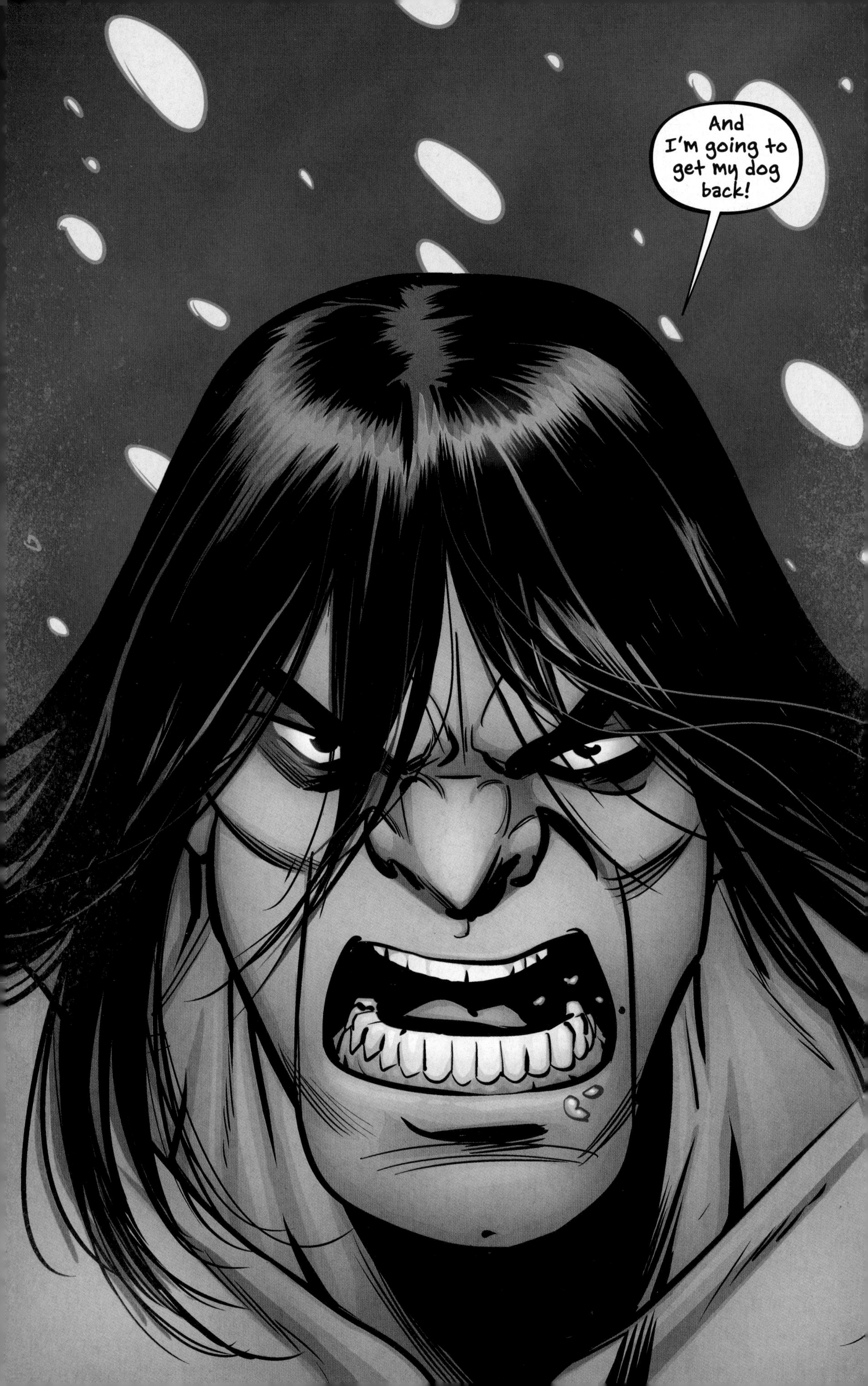
And I'm going to get my dog back!

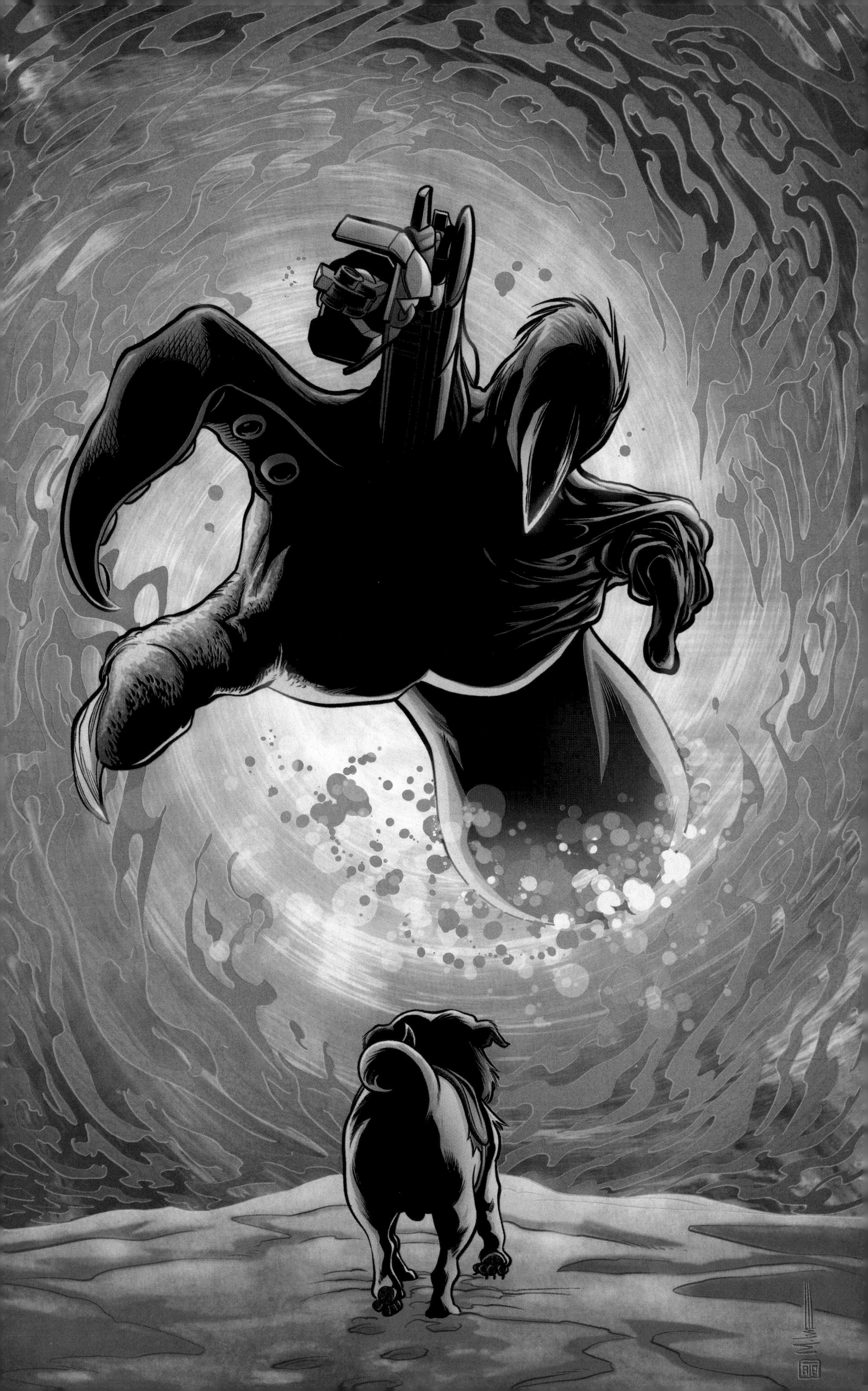

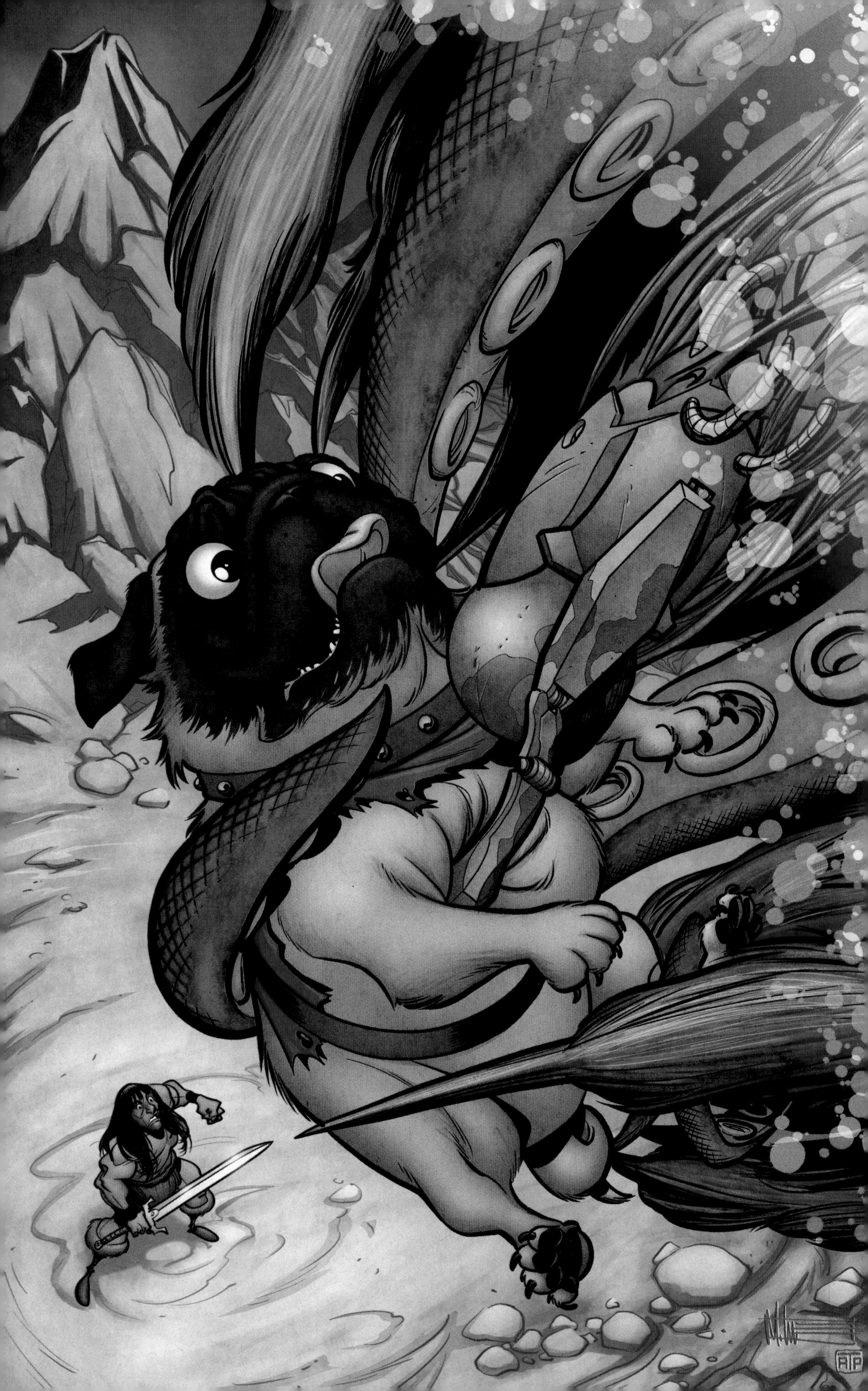

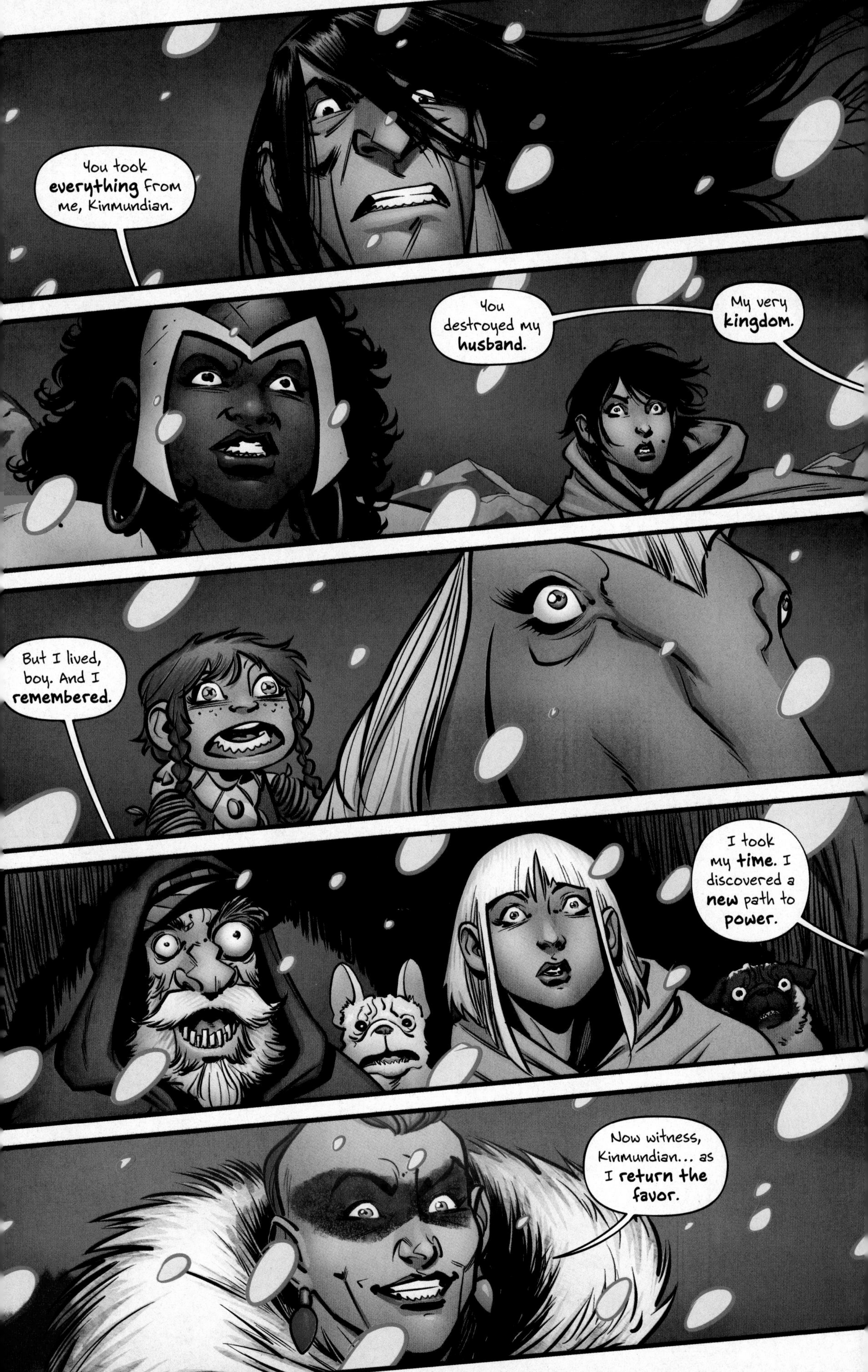
You took everything from me, Kinmundian.
You destroyed my husband.
My very kingdom.
But I lived, boy. And I remembered.
I took my time. I discovered a new path to power.
Now witness, Kinmundian... as I return the favor.

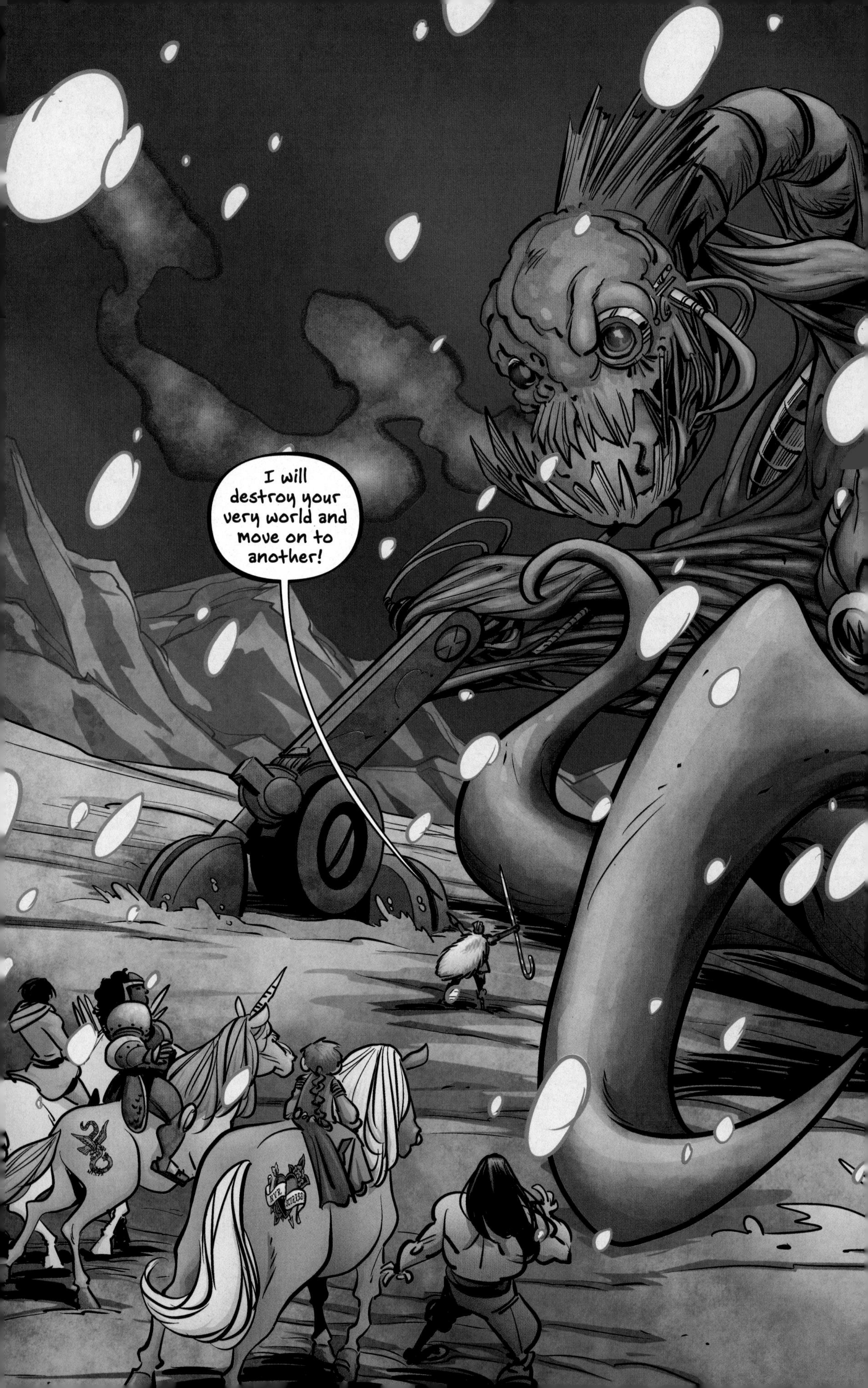
I will destroy your very world and move on to another!

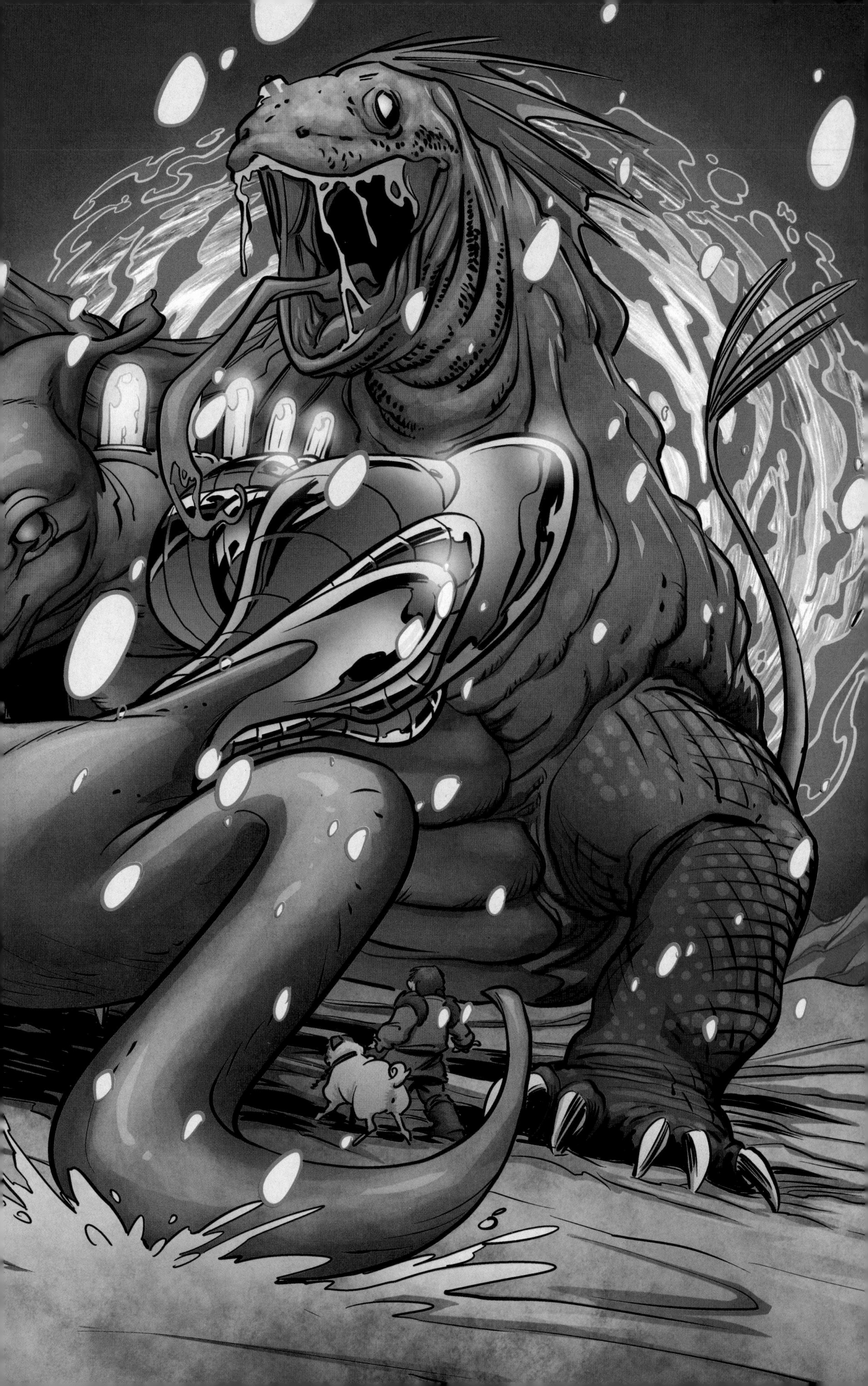

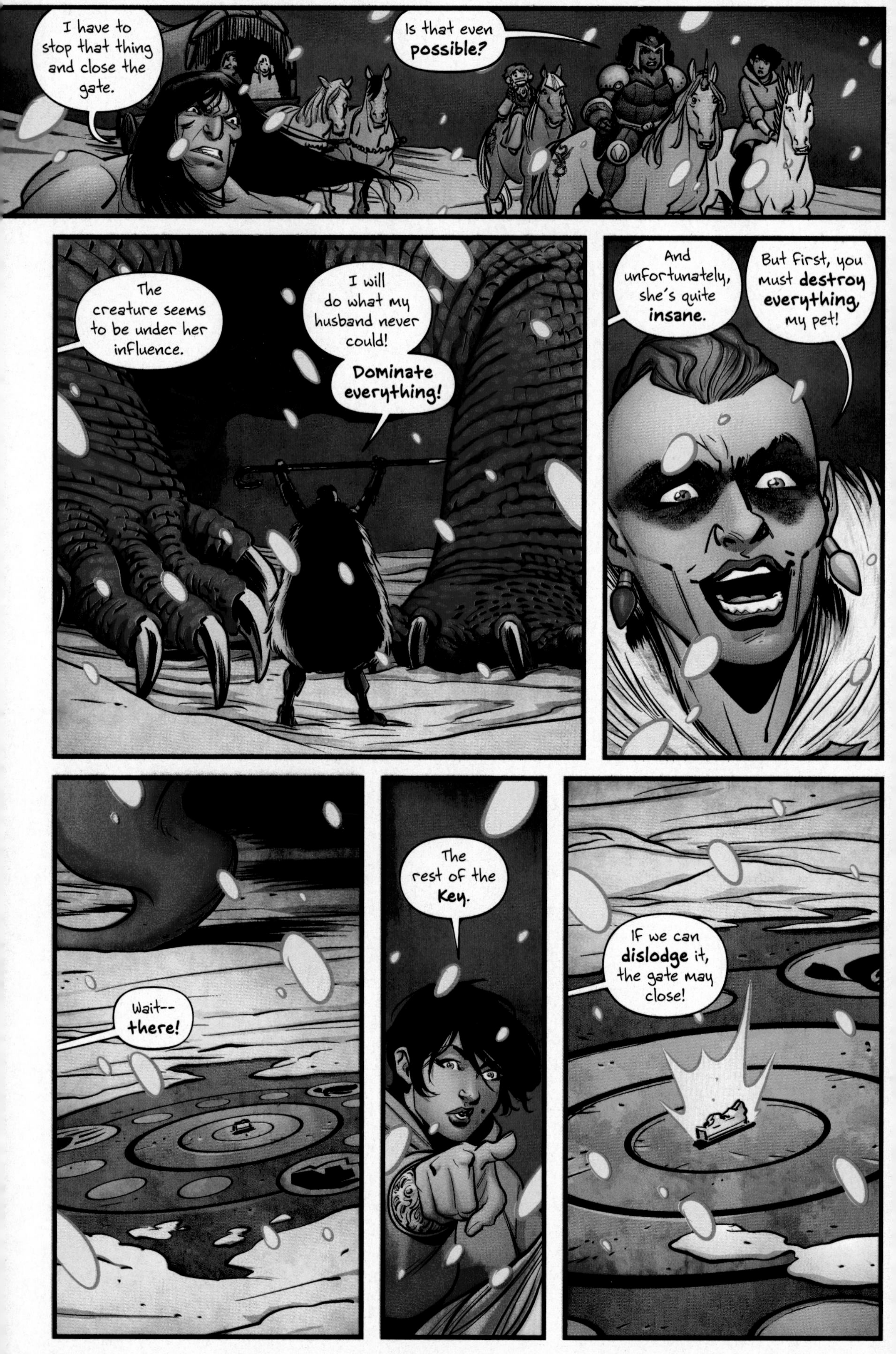
I have to stop that thing and close the gate.
Is that even **possible?**
The creature seems to be under her influence.
I will do what my husband never could!
Dominate everything!
And unfortunately, she's quite **insane.**
But first, you must **destroy everything,** my pet!
Wait-- **there!**
The rest of the **Key.**
If we can **dislodge** it, the gate may close!

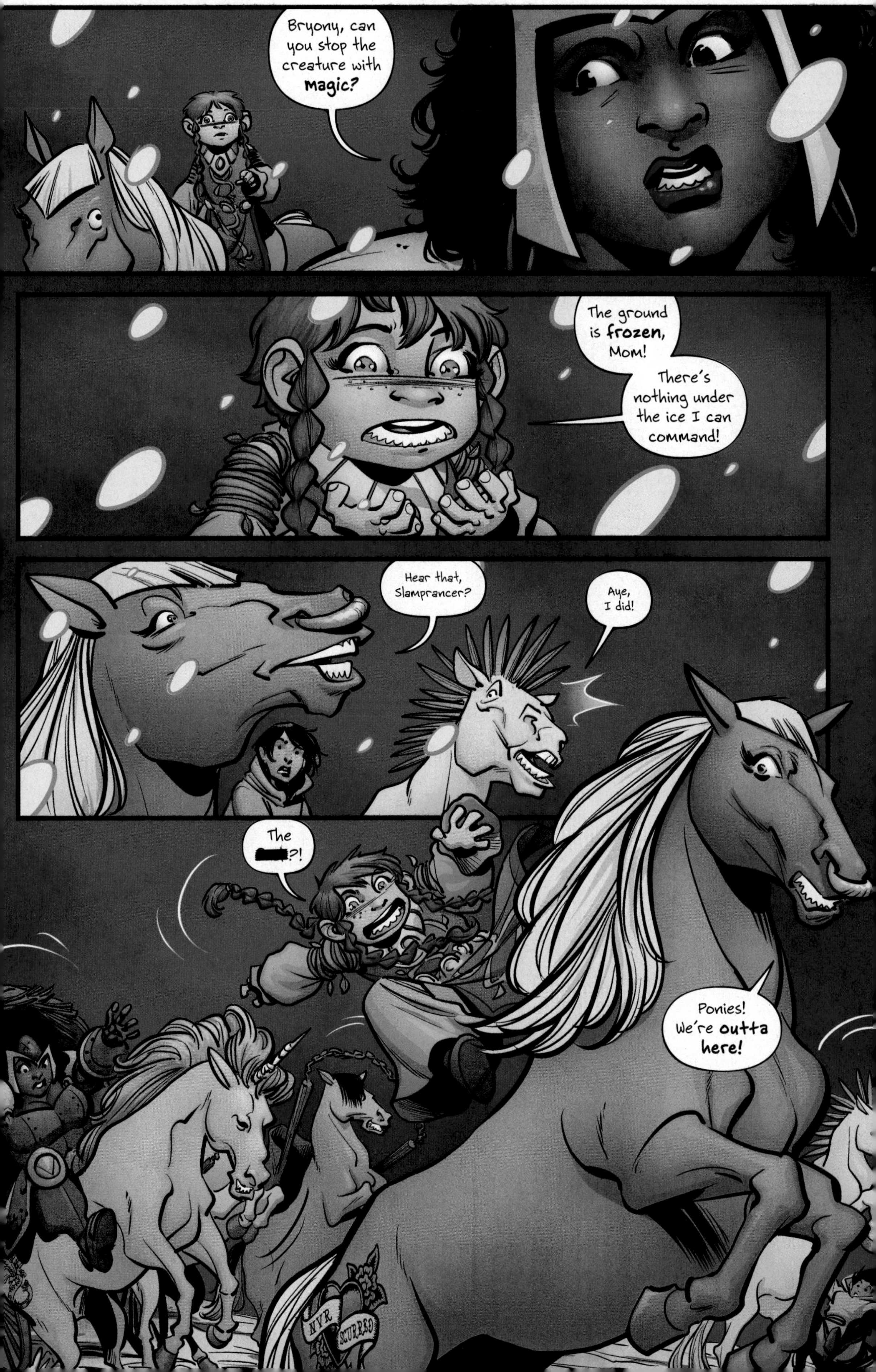
Bryony, can you stop the creature with **magic?**
The ground is **frozen,** Mom!
There's nothing under the ice I can command!
Hear that, Slamprancer?
Aye, I did!
The [redacted]?!
Ponies! We're **outta here!**
NVR SCURRED

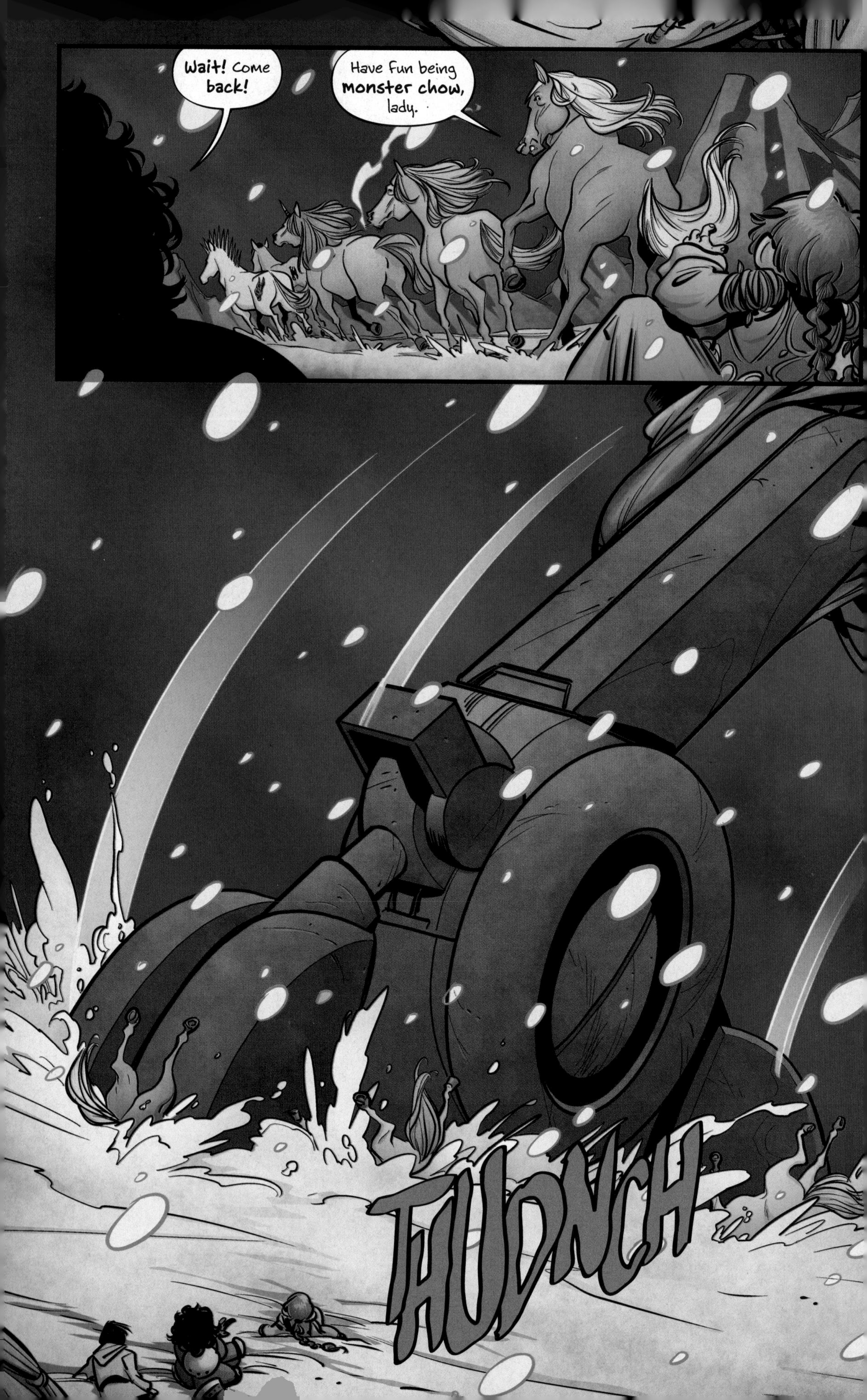

Wait! Come back!
Have fun being monster chow, lady.
THUDNCH

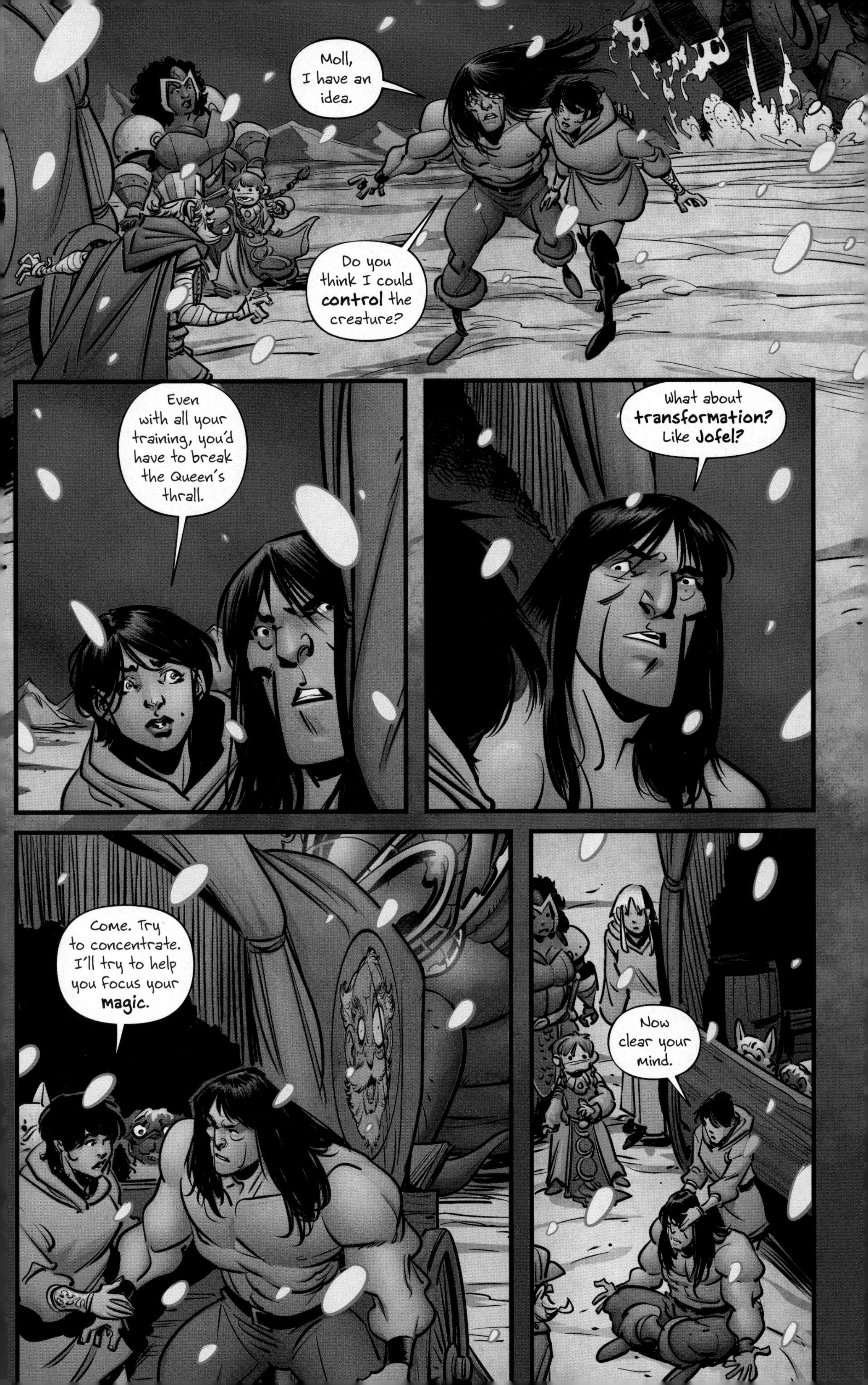
Moll, I have an idea.
Do you think I could **control** the creature?
Even with all your training, you'd have to break the Queen's thrall.
What about **transformation?** Like **Jofel?**
Come. Try to concentrate. I'll try to help you focus your **magic**.
Now clear your mind.

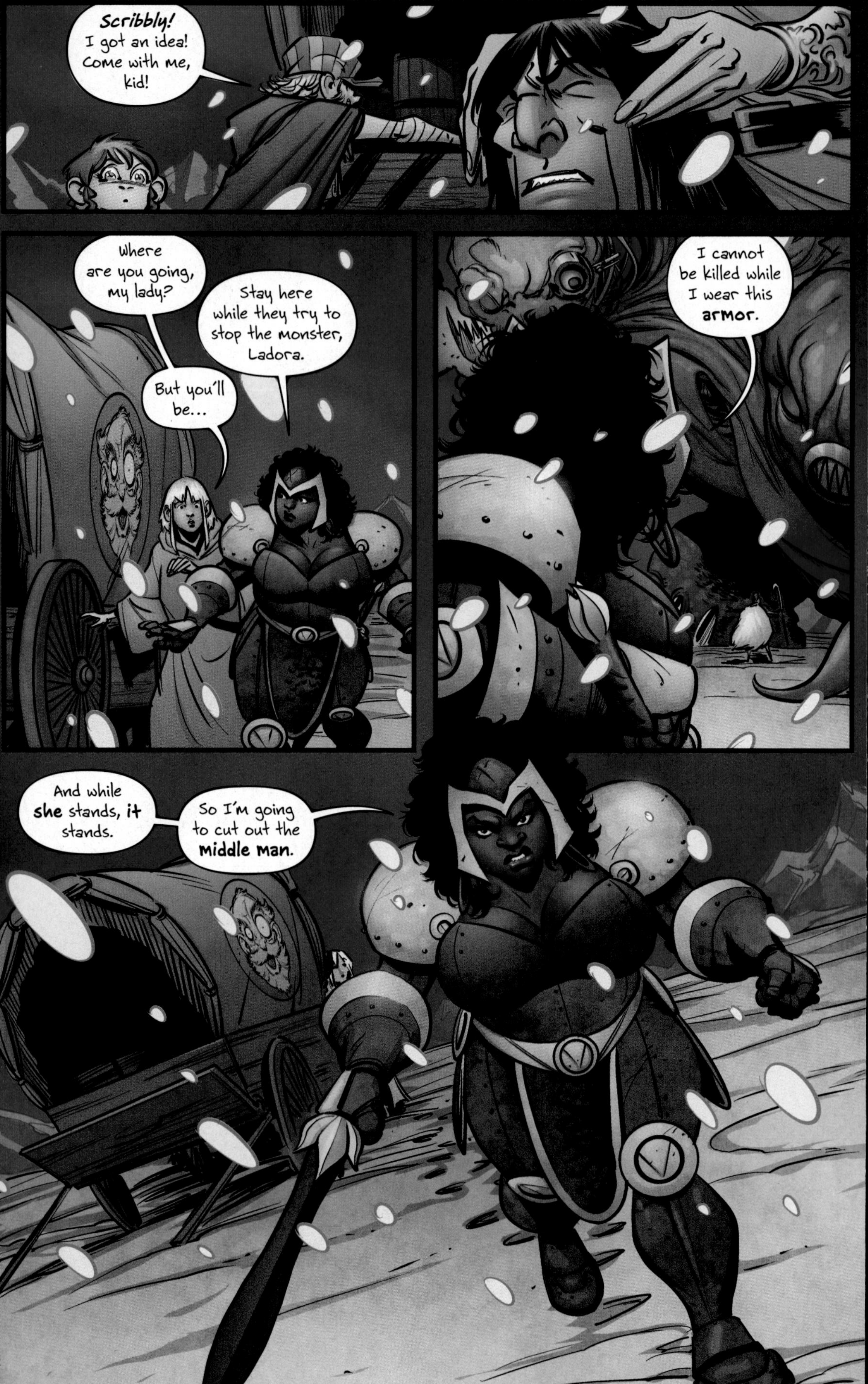
Scribbly! I got an idea! Come with me, kid!
Where are you going, my lady?
Stay here while they try to stop the monster, Ladora.
But you'll be...
I cannot be killed while I wear this armor.
And while she stands, it stands.
So I'm going to cut out the middle man.

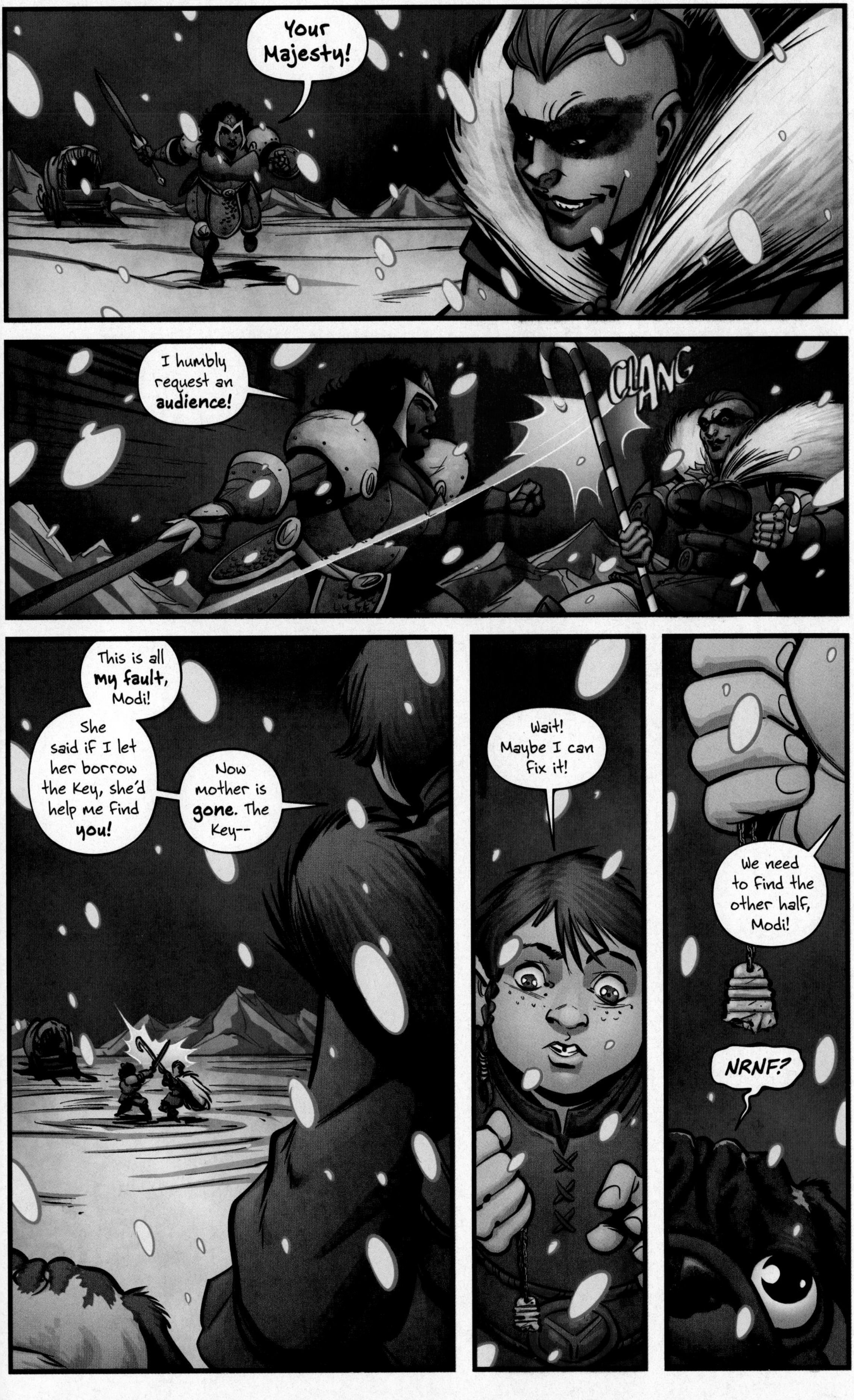
Your Majesty!
I humbly request an audience!
CLANG
This is all my fault, Modi!
She said if I let her borrow the Key, she'd help me find you!
Now mother is gone. The Key--
Wait! Maybe I can fix it!
We need to find the other half, Modi!
NRNF?

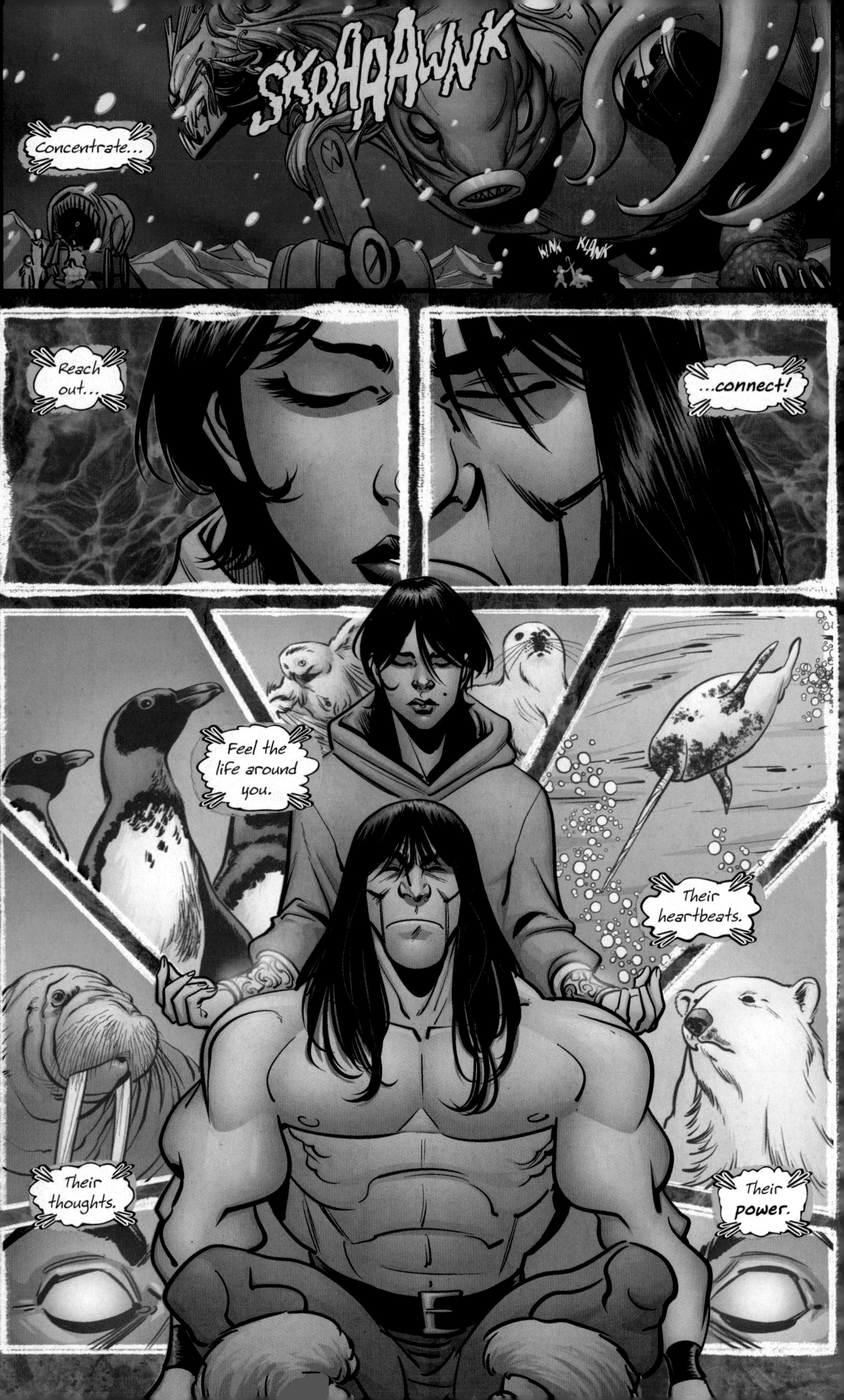
SKRAAAWNK
Concentrate...
KLINK KLANK
Reach out...
...connect!
Feel the life around you.
Their heartbeats.
Their thoughts.
Their power.

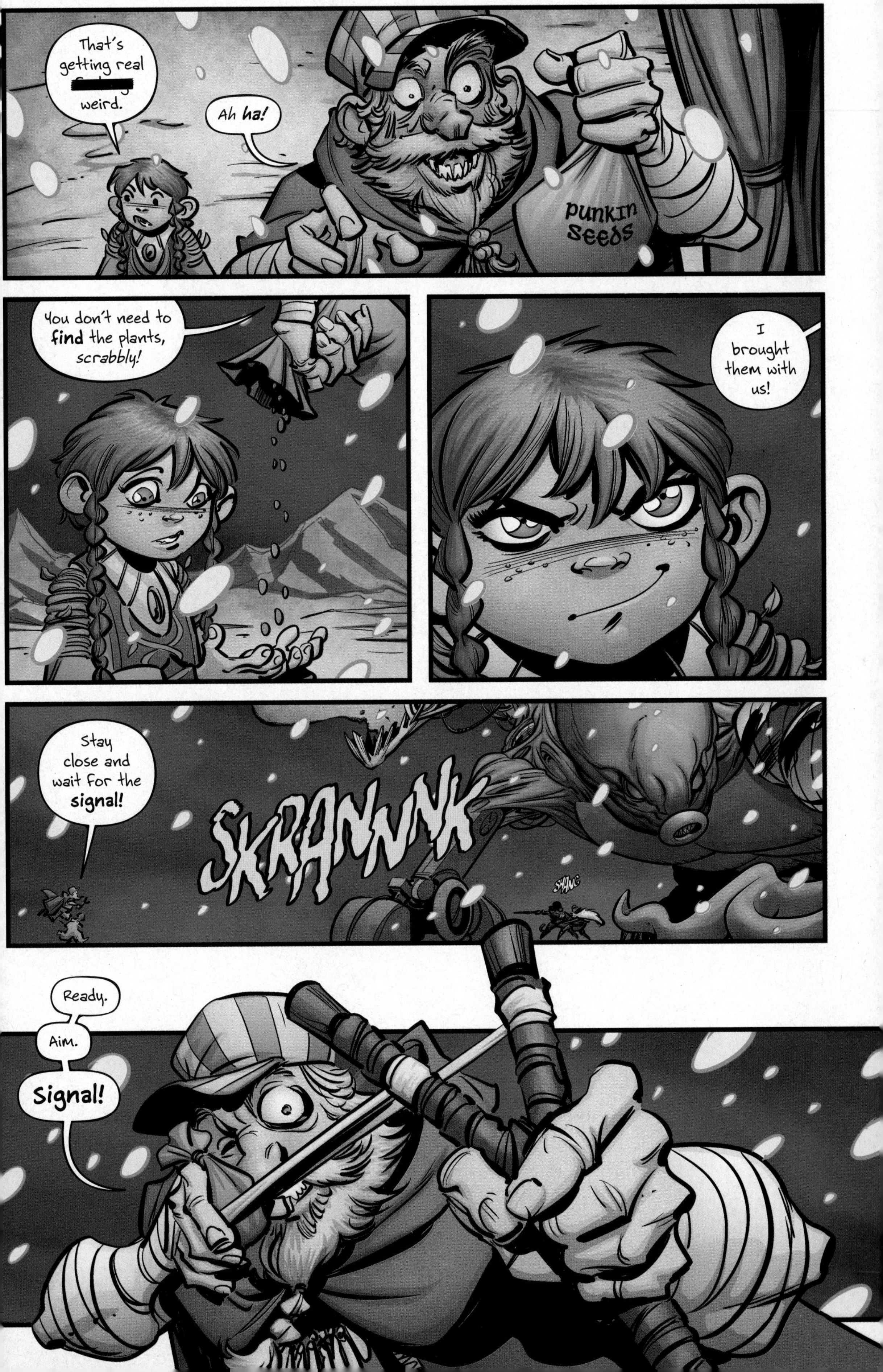
That's getting real [redacted] weird.
Ah ha!
PUNKIN SEEDS
You don't need to find the plants, scrabbly!
I brought them with us!
Stay close and wait for the signal!
SKRANNNK
Ready.
Aim.
Signal!

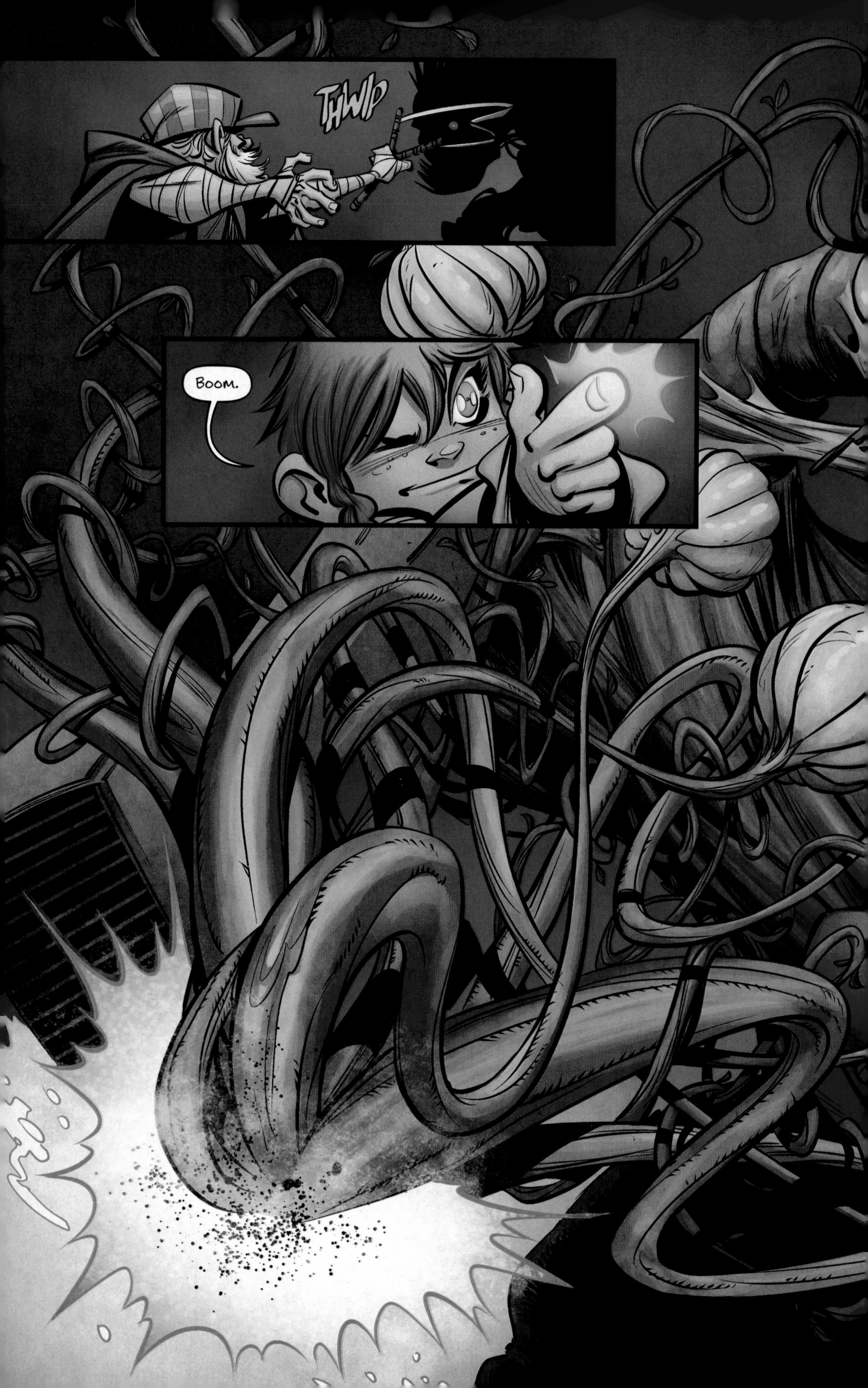
THWIP
Boom.

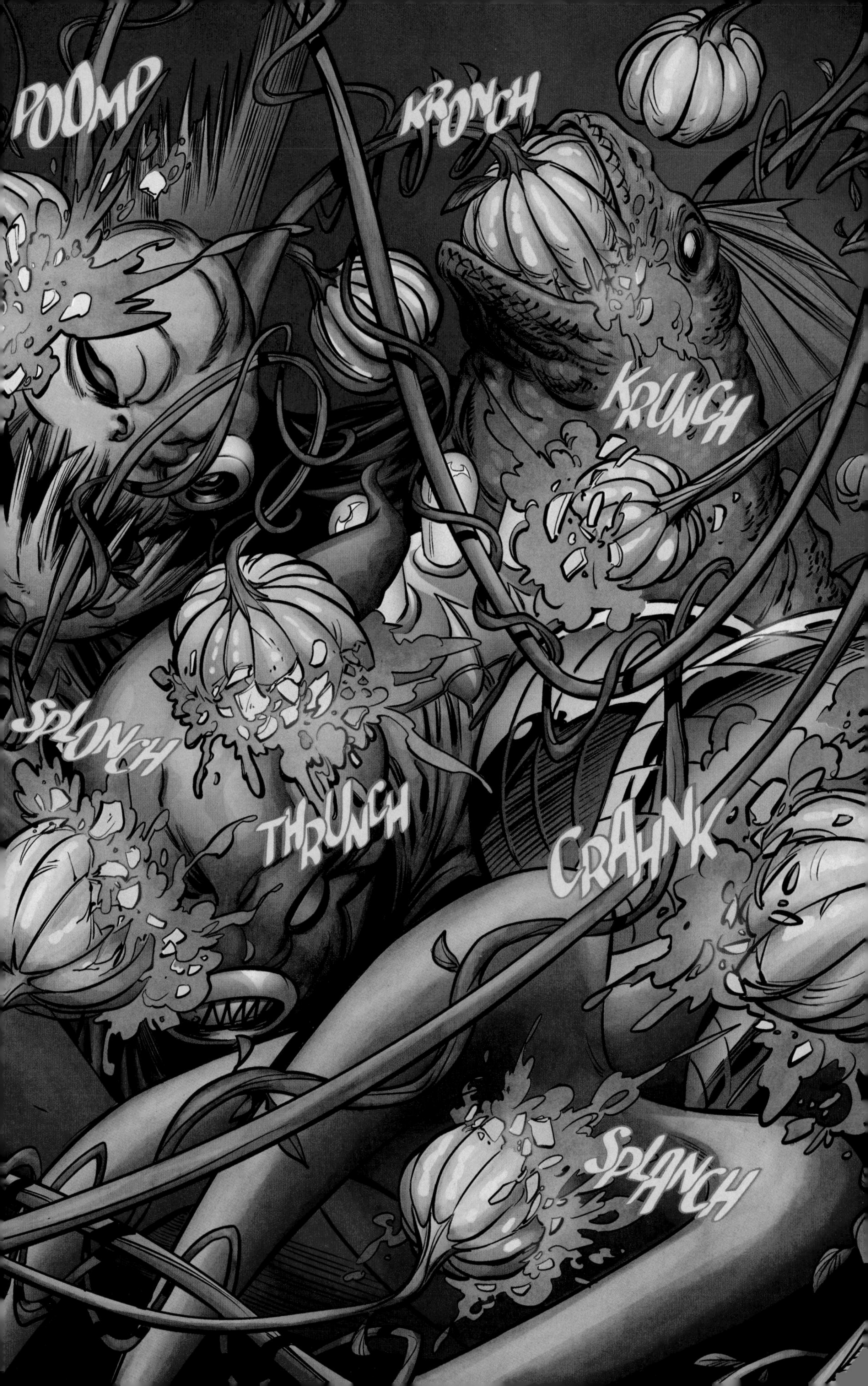
POOMP
KRONCH
KRUNCH
SPLONCH
THRUNCH
CRAHNK
SPLANCH

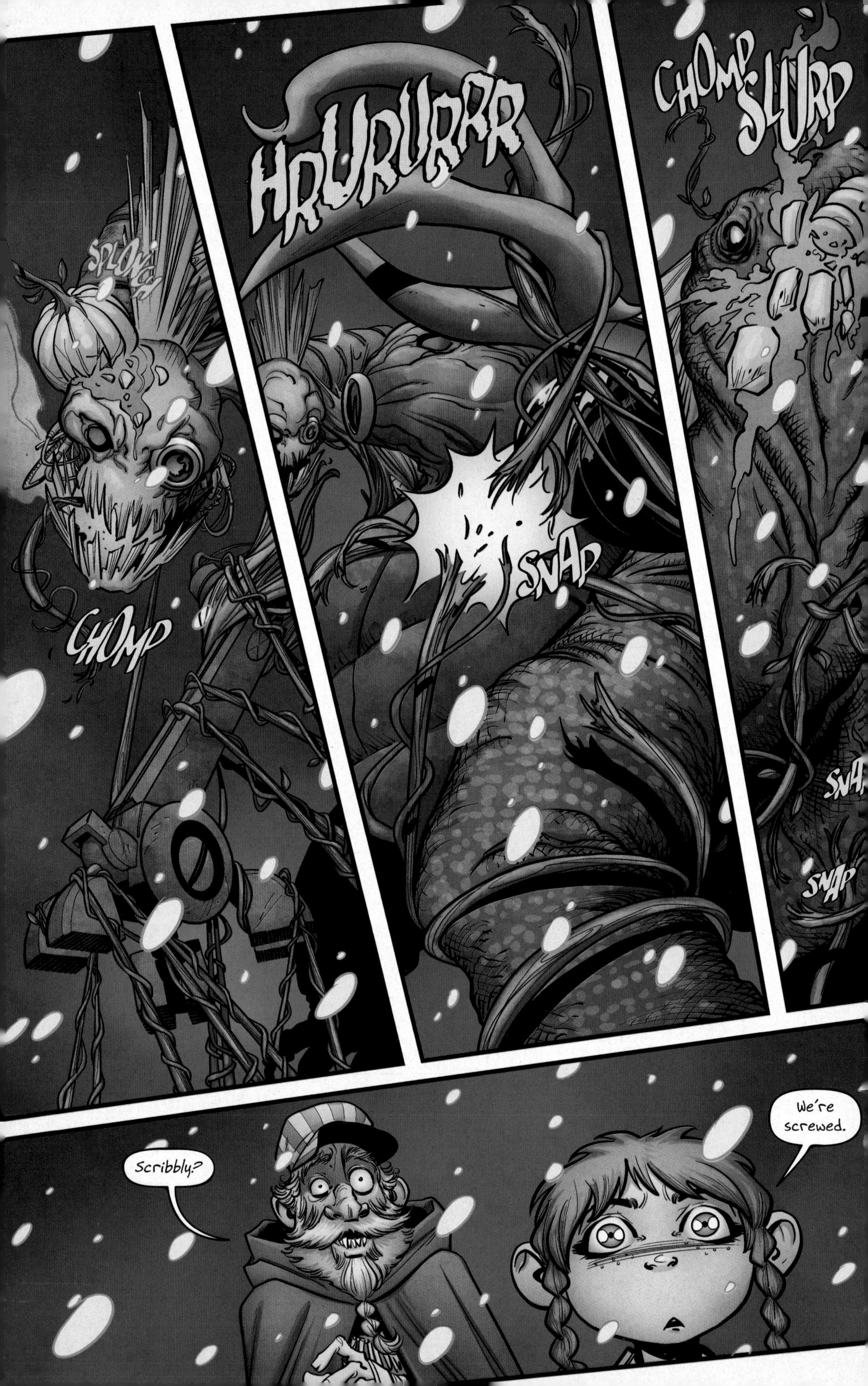
SPLONCH
CHOMP
HRURURRR
SNAP
CHOMP
SLURP
SNAP
SNAP
Scribbly?
We're screwed.

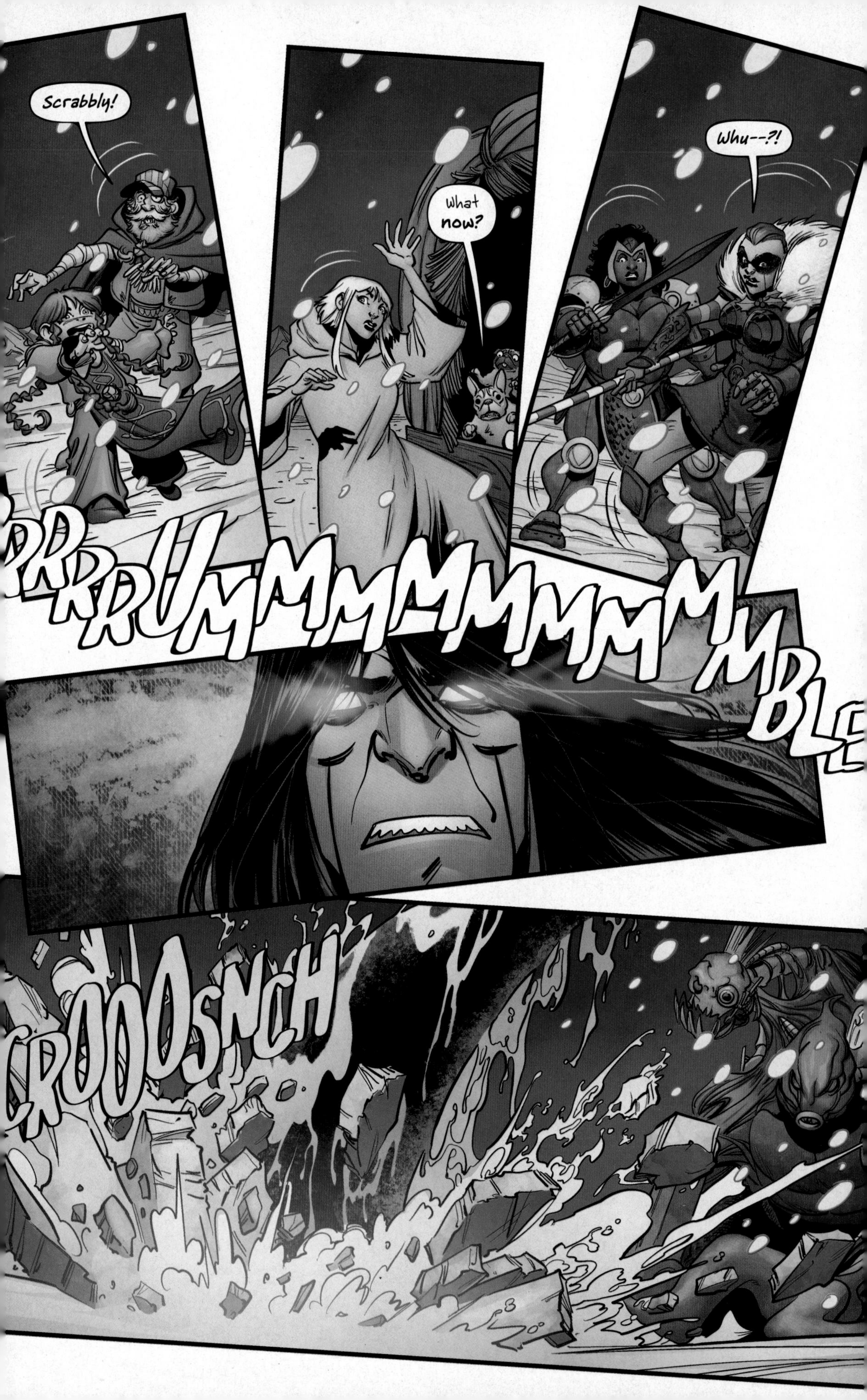
Scrabbly!
What now?
Whu--?!
RRRRRUMMMMMMMMMMMBLE
CROOOSNCH

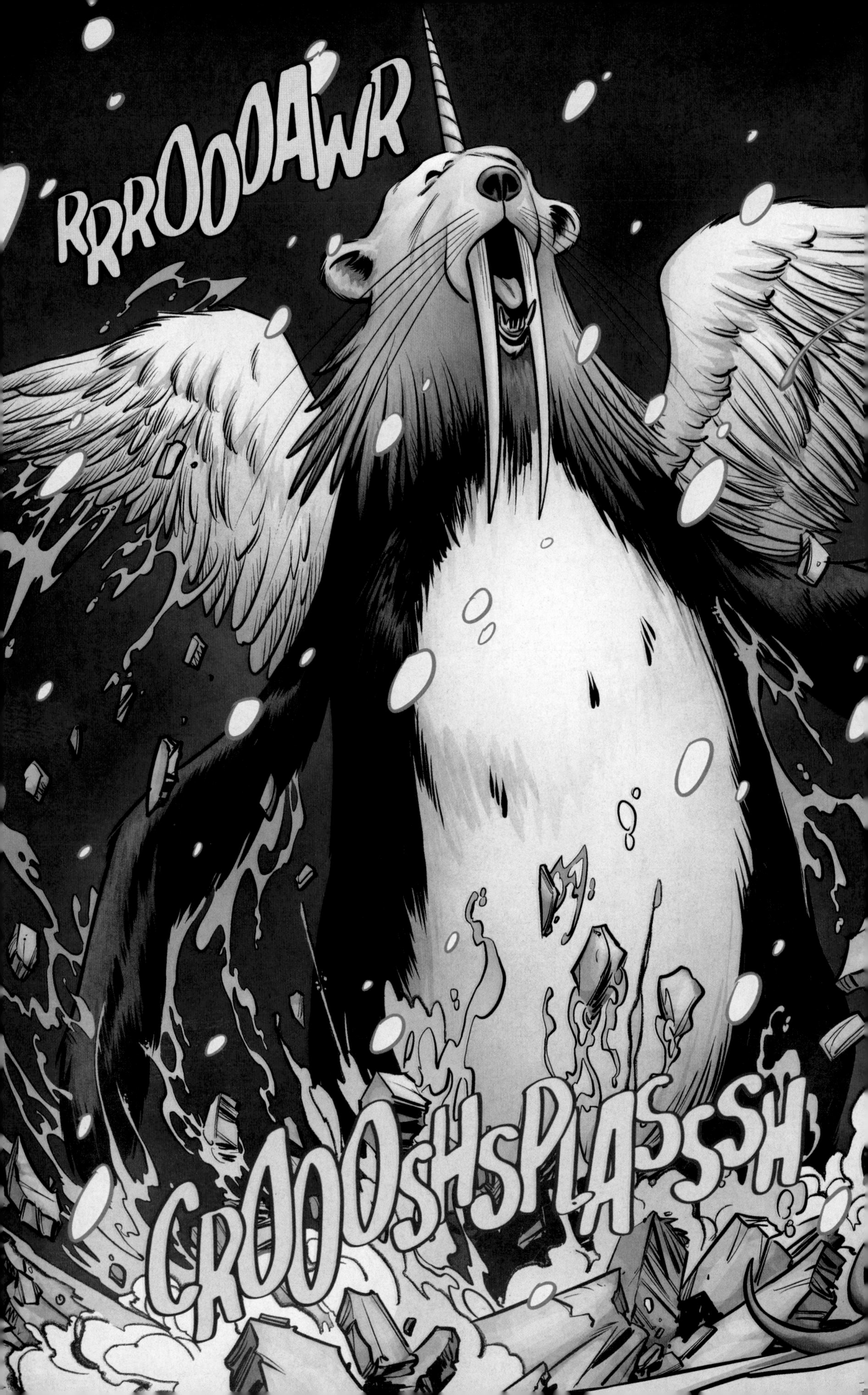
RRROOOAWR
CROOOOSHSPLASSSH

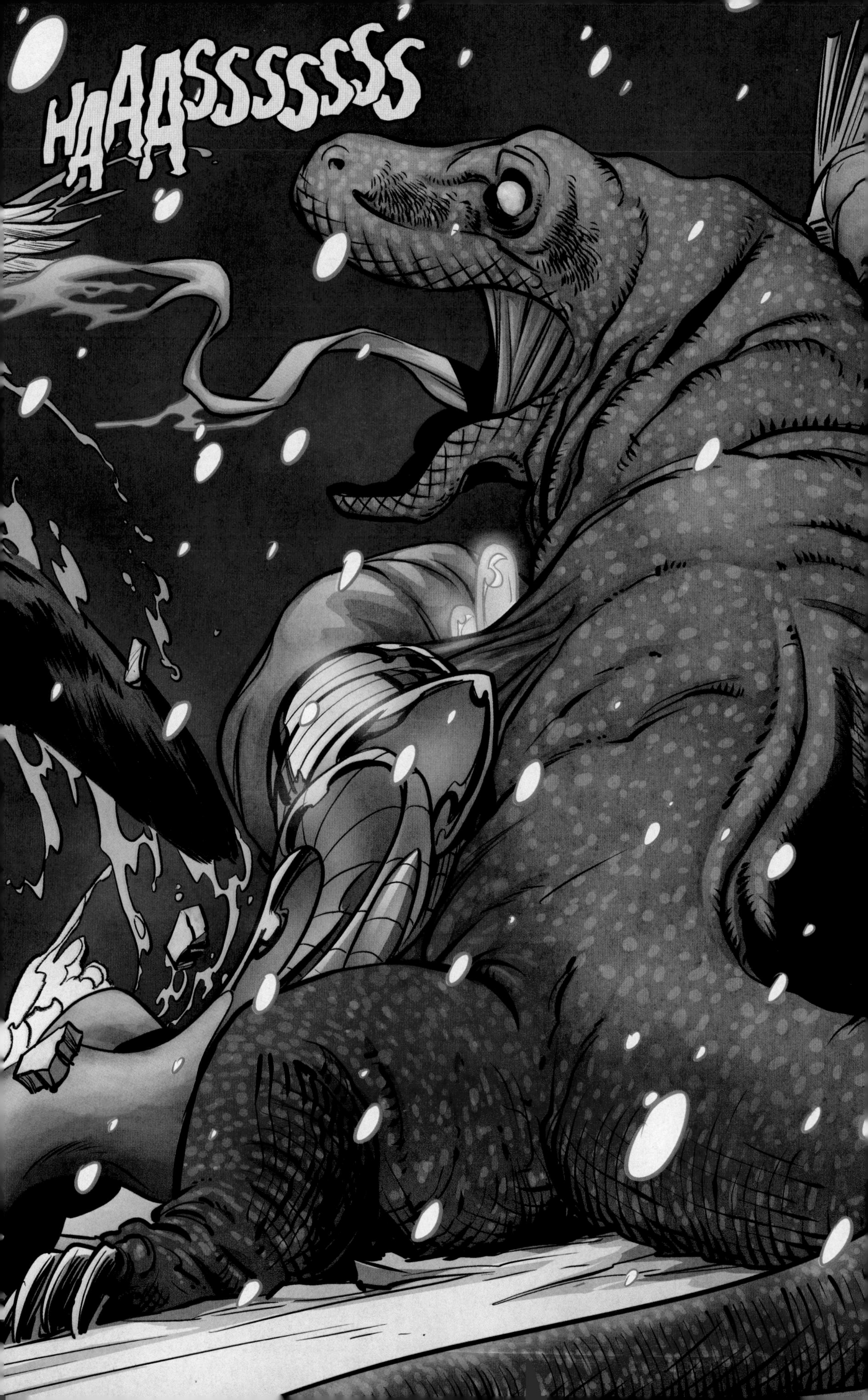
HAAASSSSSSS

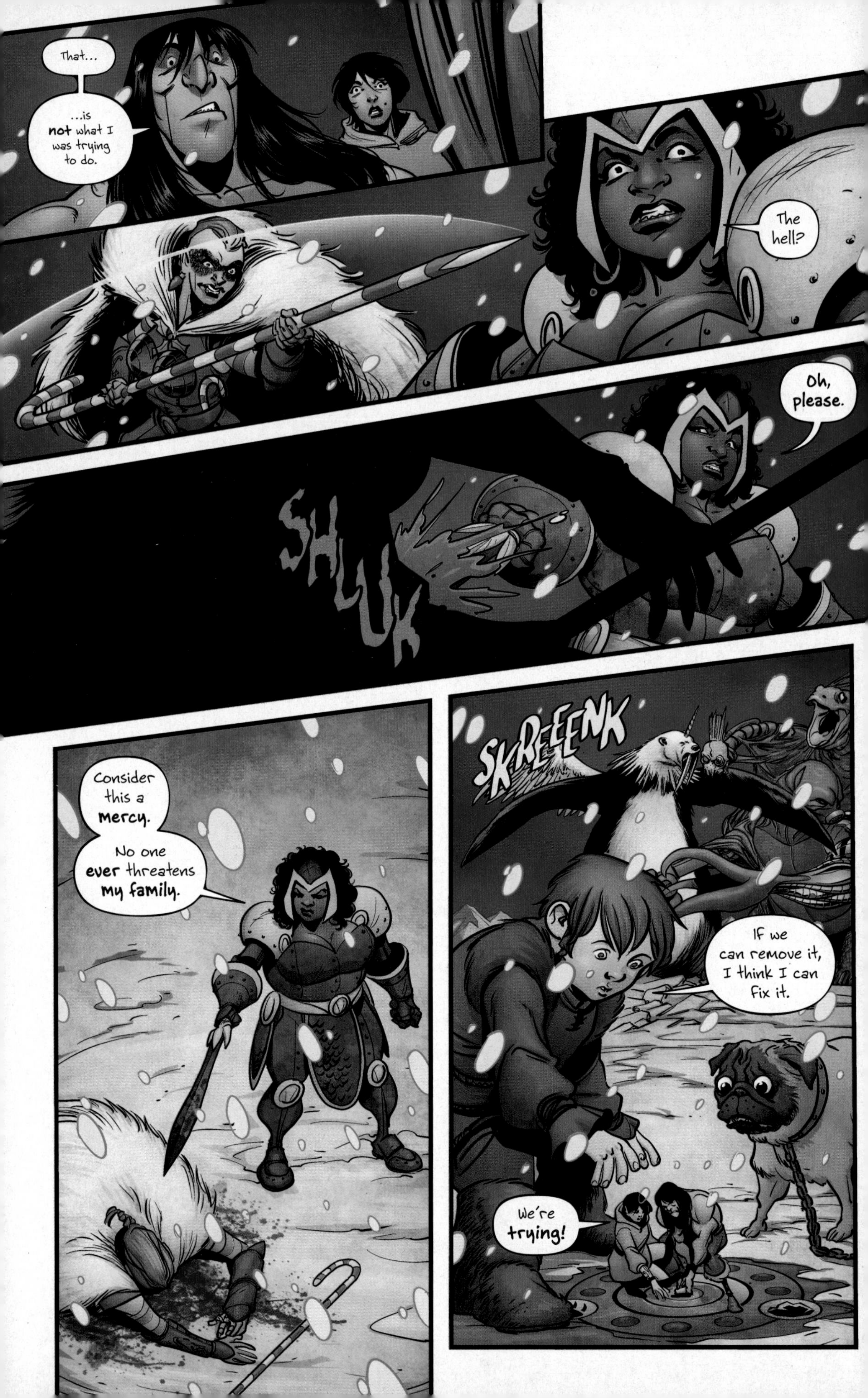
That...
...is **not** what I was trying to do.
The hell?
Oh, please.
SHLUK
Consider this a **mercy**.
No one **ever** threatens **my family**.
SKREEENK
If we can remove it, I think I can fix it.
We're **trying**!

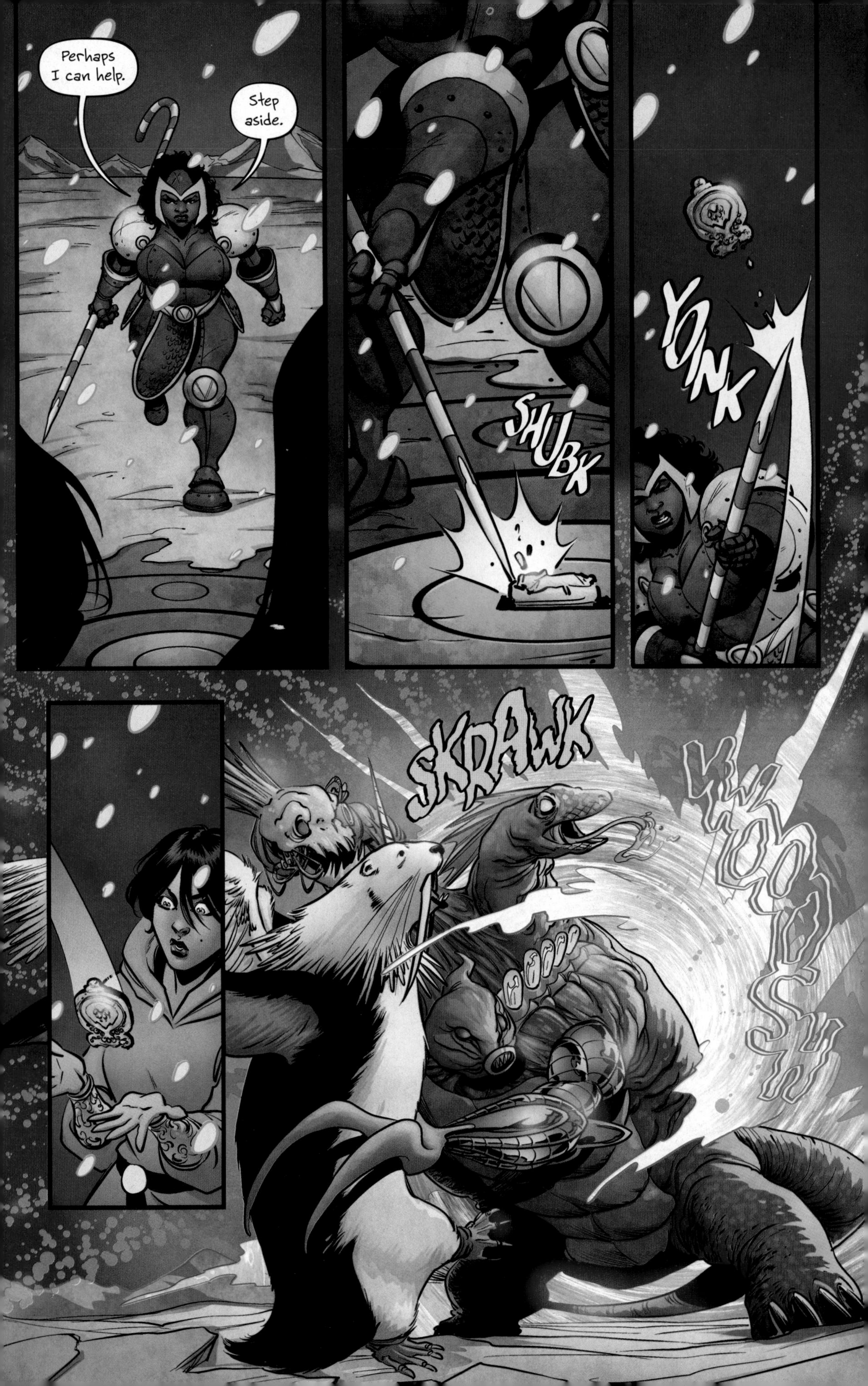
Perhaps I can help.
Step aside.
SHUBK
YONK
SKRAWK
VWOOOSH

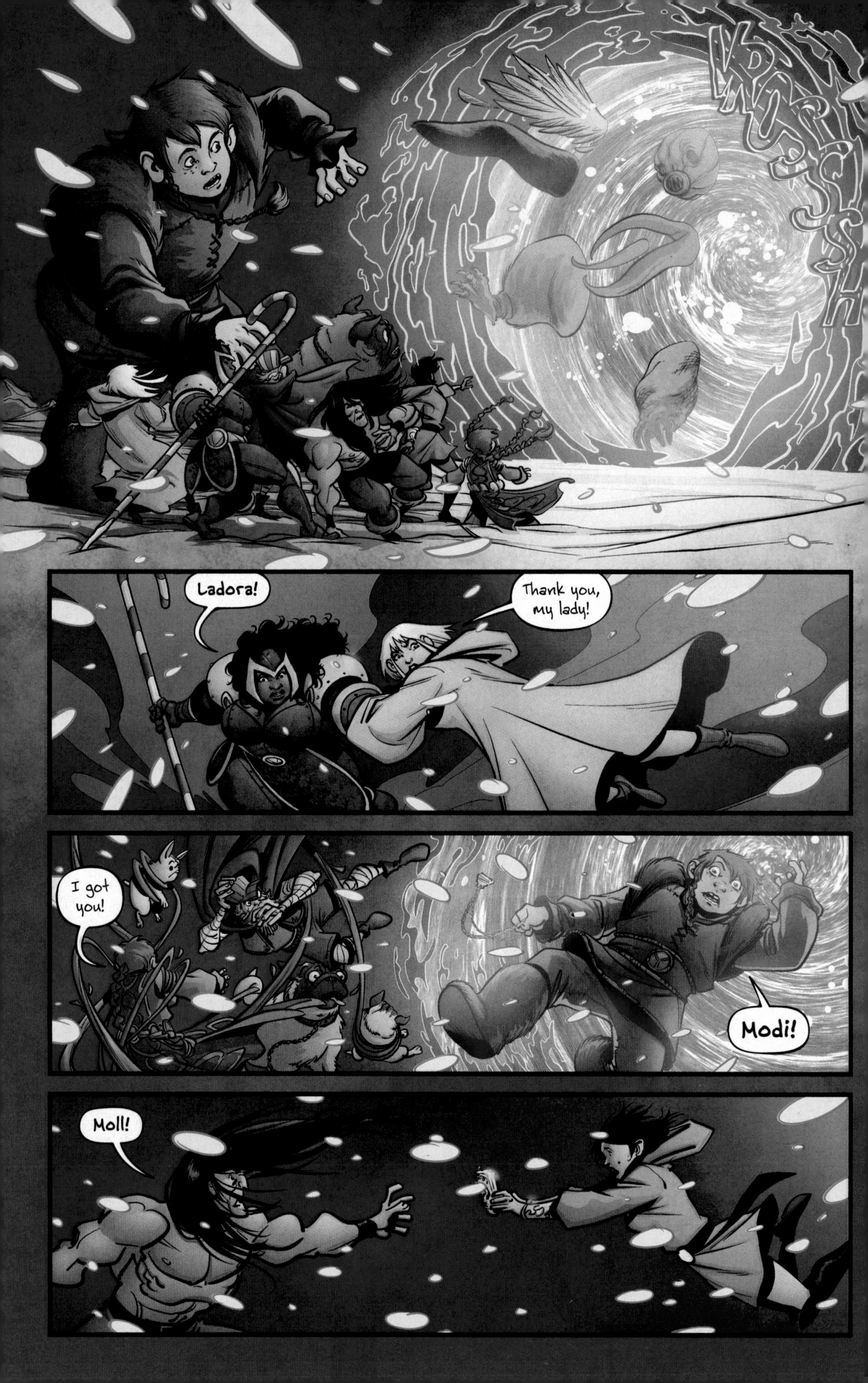
Ladora!
Thank you, my lady!
I got you!
Modi!
Moll!

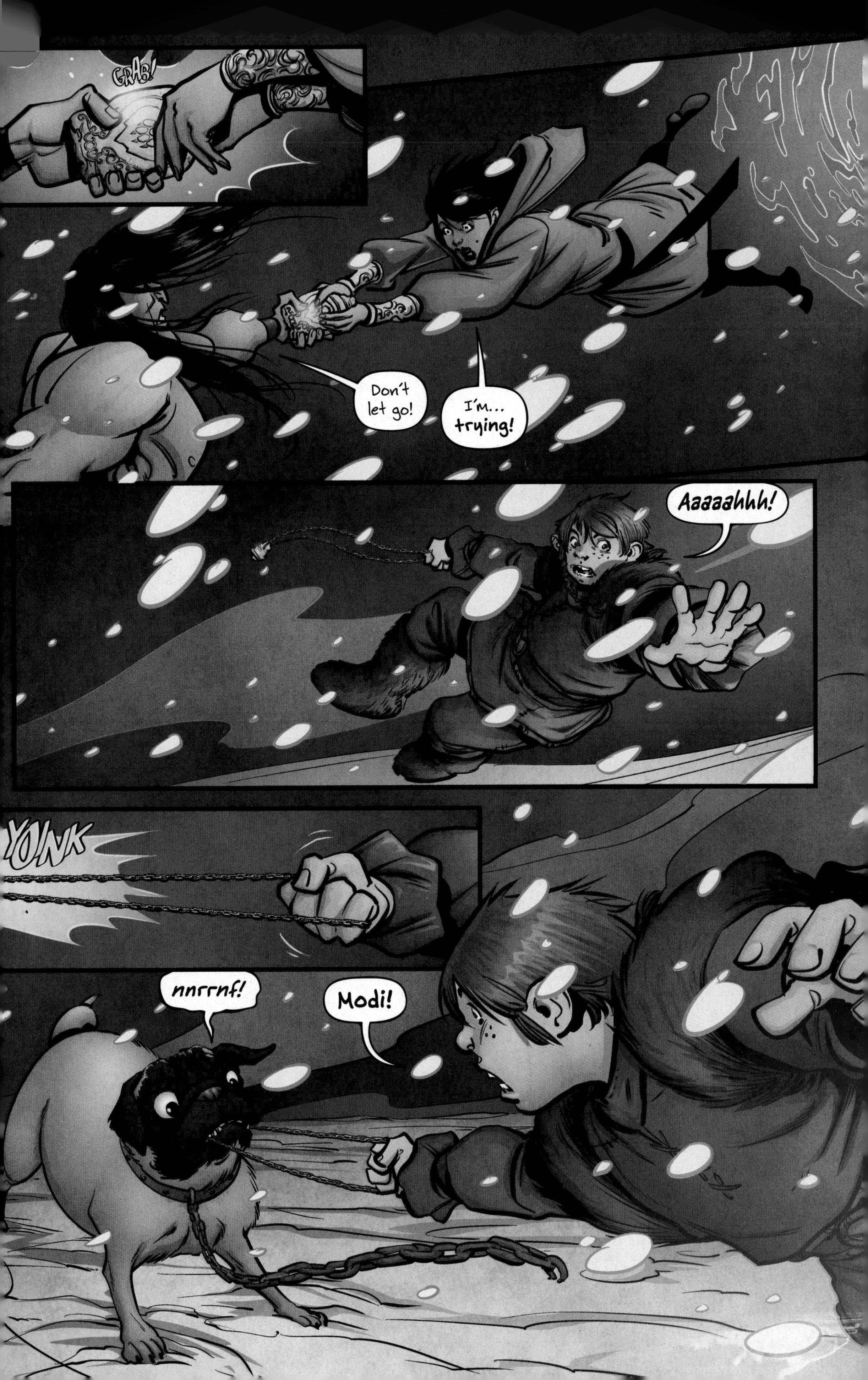
GRAB!
Don't let go!
I'm... trying!
Aaaaahhh!
YOINK
nnrrnf!
Modi!

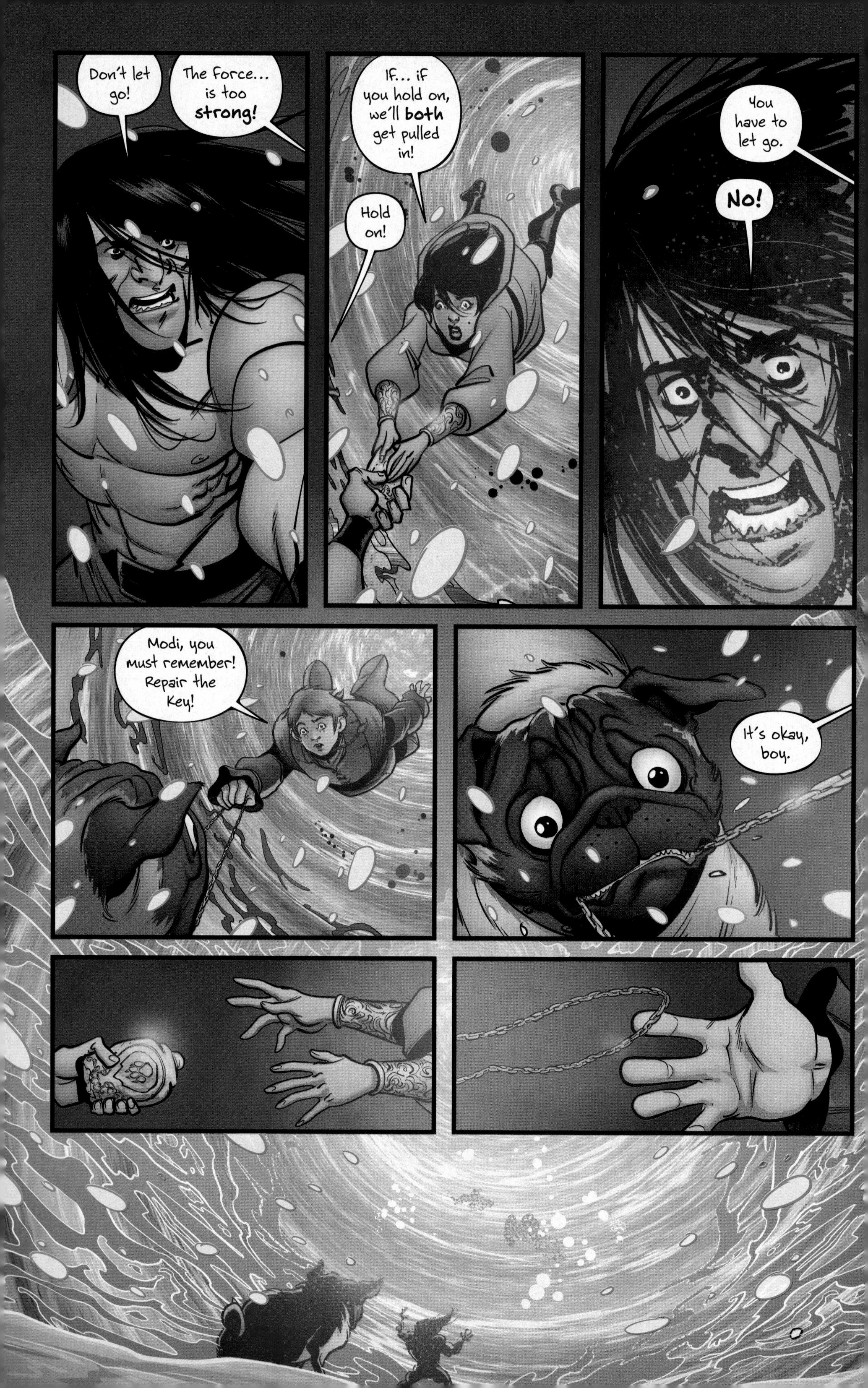
Don't let go!
The force... is too strong!
If... if you hold on, we'll both get pulled in!
Hold on!
You have to let go.
No!
Modi, you must remember! Repair the Key!
It's okay, boy.

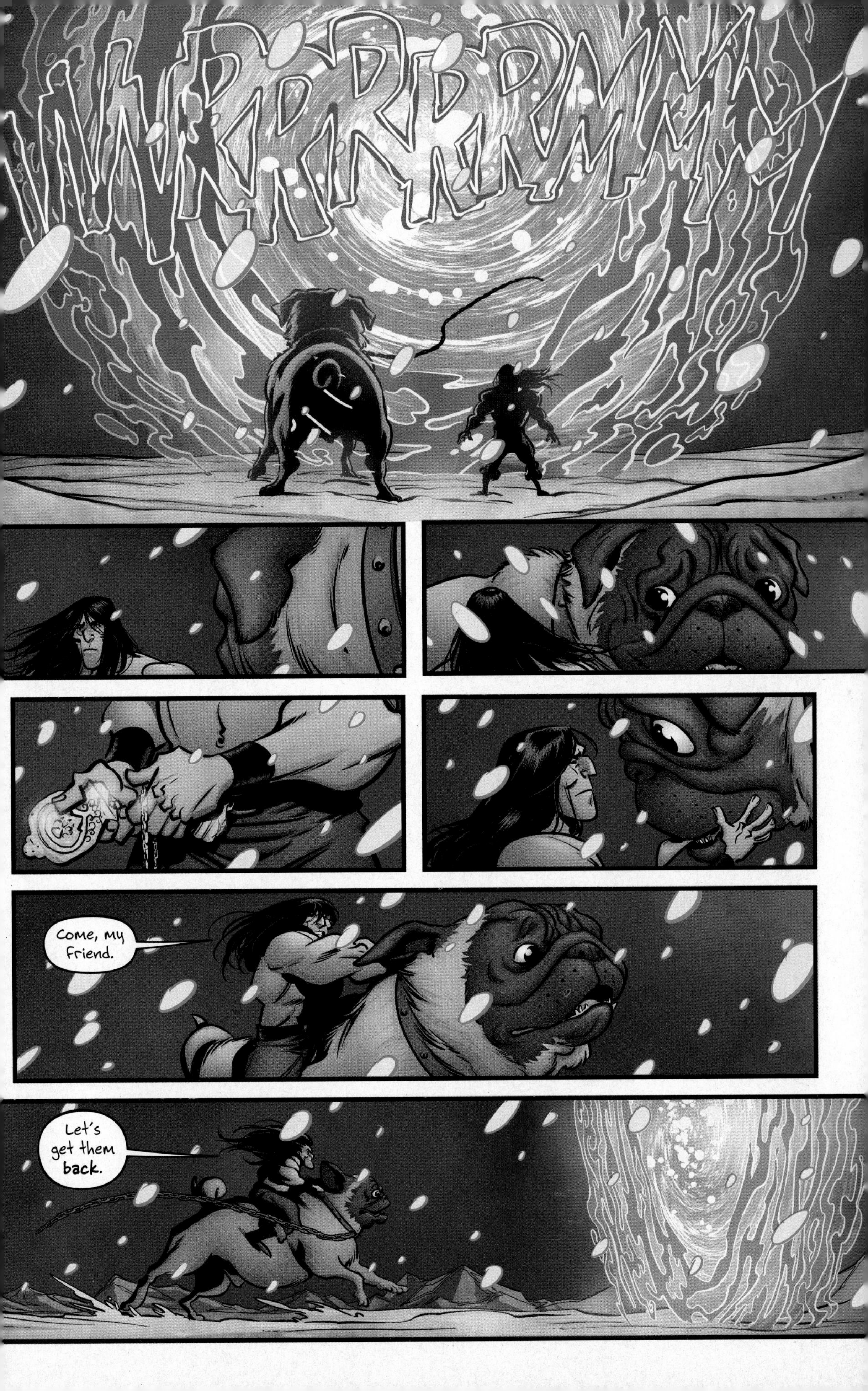
Come, my friend.
Let's get them back.

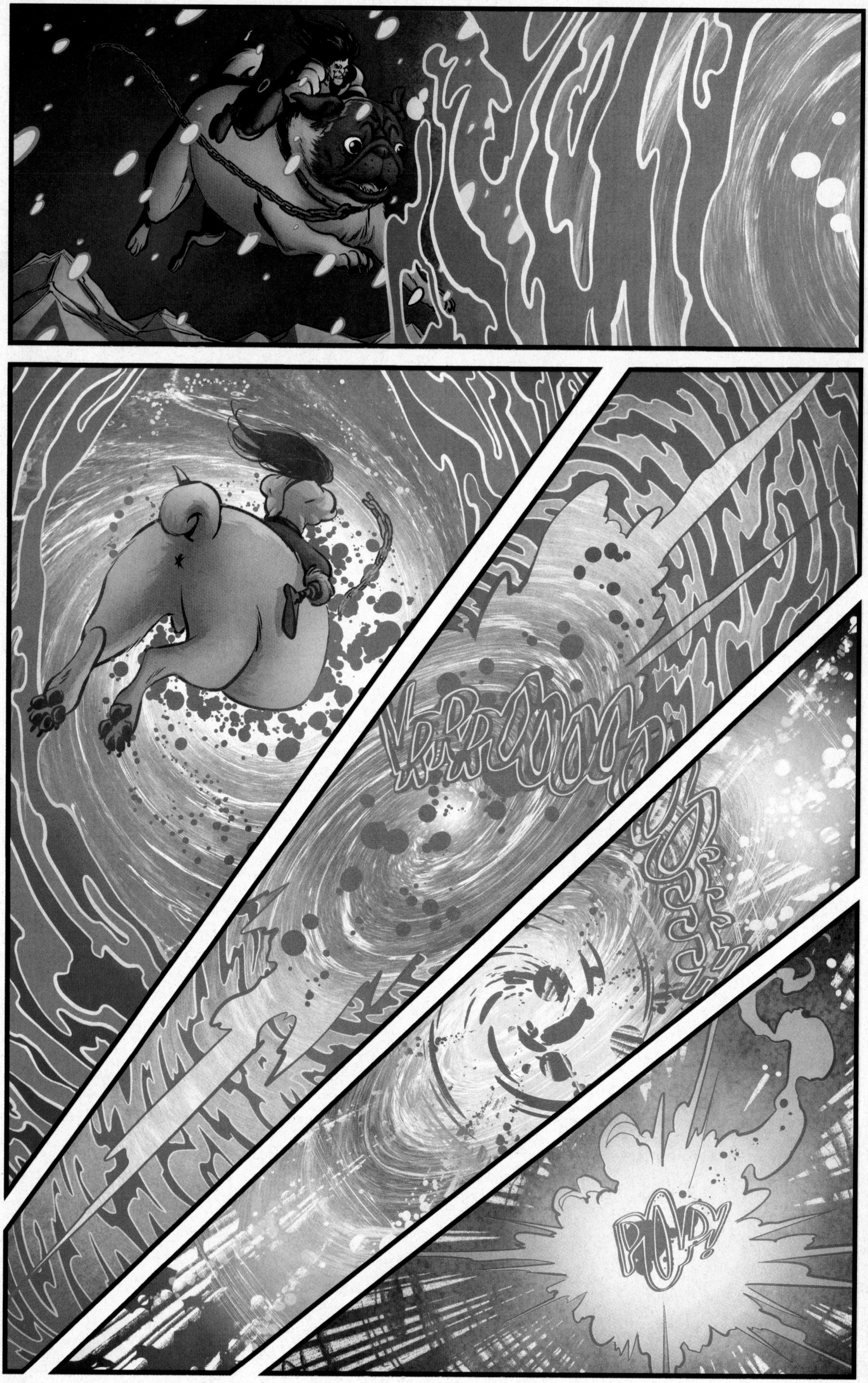
POP!

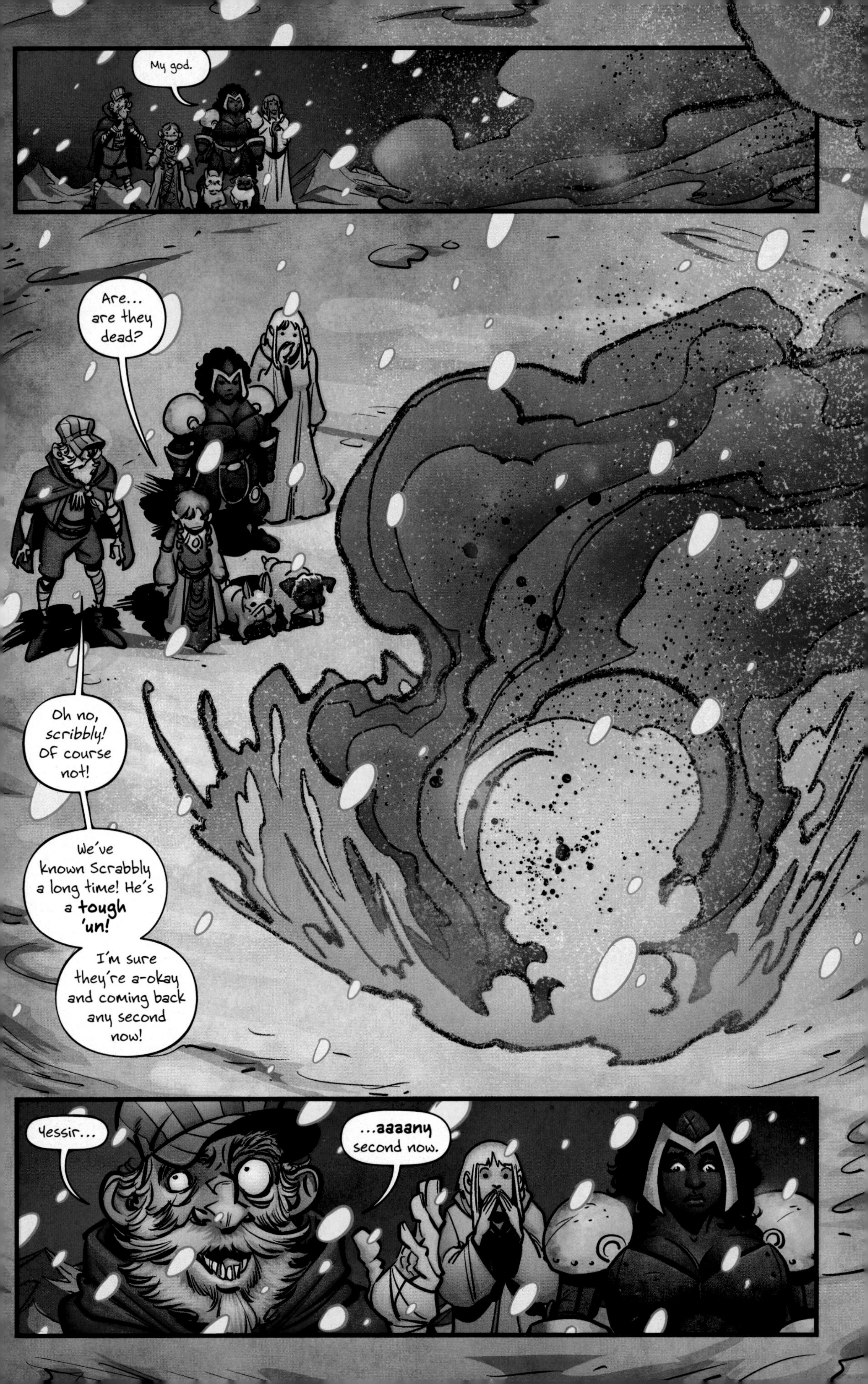
My god.
Are... are they dead?
Oh no, scribbly! Of course not!
We've known Scrabbly a long time! He's a **tough 'un!**
I'm sure they're a-okay and coming back any second now!
Yessir...
...**aaaany** second now.

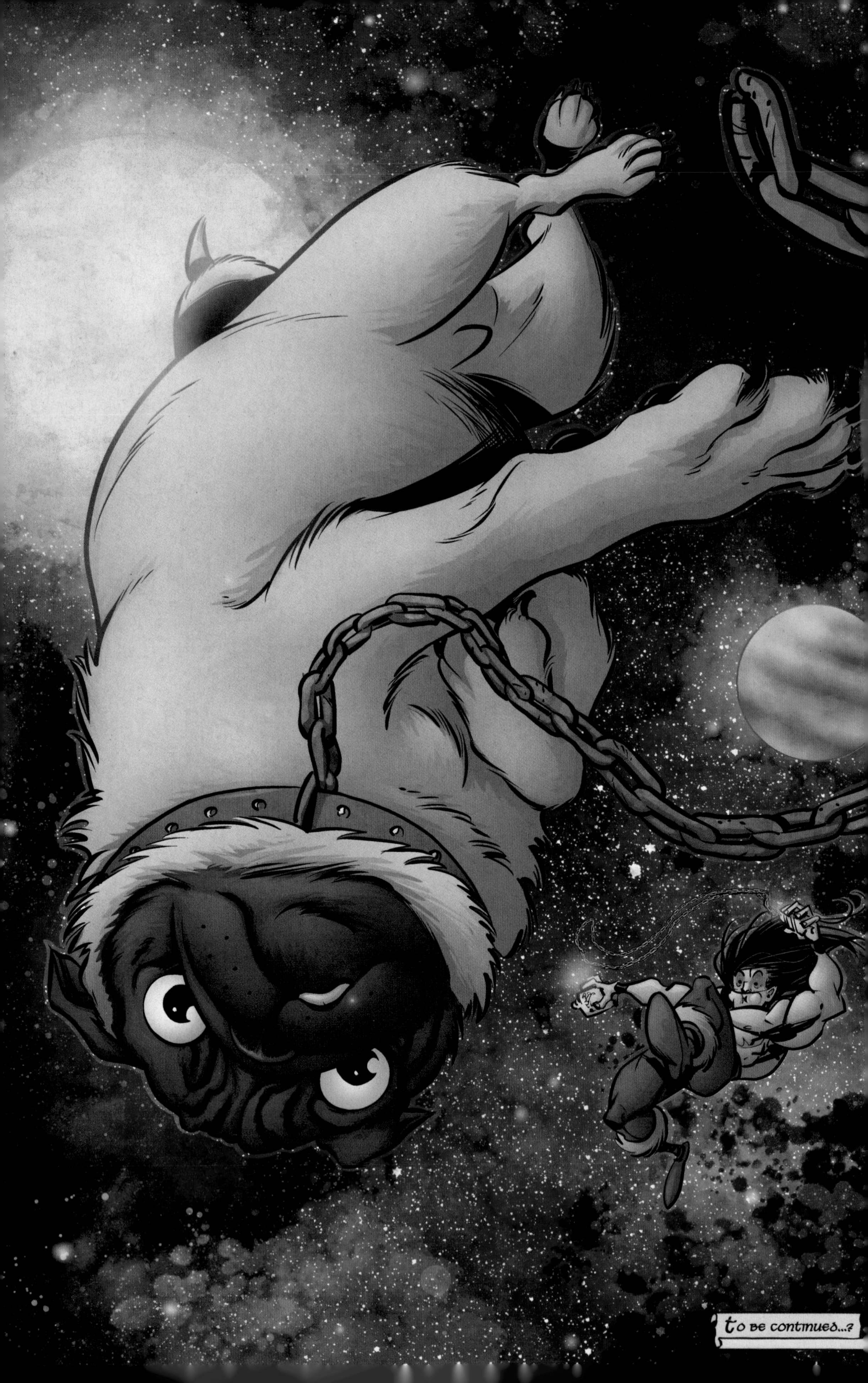
to be continued...?